ECONOMIC COMPULSION AND CHRISTIAN ETHICS

Markets can often be harsh in compelling people to make unpalatable economic choices any reasonable person would not take under normal conditions. Thus workers laid off in mid-career accept lower paid jobs that are beneath their professional experience for want of better alternatives. Economic migrants leave their families and cross borders (legally or illegally) in search of a livelihood, and countless Third World families rely on child labor to supplement meager household incomes. These are examples of economic compulsion, an all-too-frequent state of affairs in which people are driven to make choices under acute economic duress.

These economic ripple effects of market operations have been virtually ignored in ethical discourse because they are generally accepted to be the very mechanisms that shape the market's much-touted allocative efficiency. Albino Barrera argues that Christian thought on economic security offers an effective framework within which to address the consequences of economic compulsion.

PROFESSOR ALBINO BARRERA teaches in both theology and economics at Providence College. His most recent book is *Modern Catholic Social Documents and Political Economy*, published in 2001.

NEW STUDIES IN CHRISTIAN ETHICS

GENERAL EDITOR: Robin Gill

Christian ethics has increasingly assumed a central place within academic theology. At the same time the growing power and ambiguity of modern science and the rising dissatisfaction within the social sciences about claims to value-neutrality have prompted renewed interest in ethics within the secular academic world. There is, therefore, a need for studies in Christian ethics which, as well as being concerned with the relevance of Christian ethics to the present-day secular debate, are well informed about parallel discussions in recent philosophy, science or social science. New Studies in Christian Ethics aims to provide books that do this at the highest intellectual level and demonstrate that Christian ethics can make a distinctive contribution to this debate – either in moral substance or in terms of underlying moral justifications.

ECONOMIC COMPULSION AND CHRISTIAN ETHICS

ALBINO BARRERA

CAMBRIDGE
UNIVERSITY PRESS

CAMBRIDGE UNIVERSITY PRESS
Cambridge, New York, Melbourne, Madrid, Cape Town, Singapore, São Paulo

Cambridge University Press
The Edinburgh Building, Cambridge, CB2 2RU, UK

Published in the United States of America by Cambridge University Press, New York

www.cambridge.org
Information on this title: www.cambridge.org/9780521853415

First published 2005

Printed in the United Kingdom at the University Press, Cambridge

A catalogue record for this book is available from the British Library

Library of Congress Cataloguing in Publication data
Barrera, Albino
Economic compulsion and Christian ethics: attending to the market's unintended
consequences / Albino Barrera.
p. cm. – (New studies in Christian ethics)
Includes bibliographical references and index.
ISBN 0-521-85341-9
1. Economics – Religious aspects – Catholic Church. 2. Christian sociology – Catholic Church.
3. Christian ethics – Catholic authors. I. Title. II. Series.
BX1795.E27B36 2005
241'.64–dc22 2005046982

ISBN-13 978-0-521-85341 - 5 hardback
ISBN-10 0-521-85341 - 9 hardback

For my aunt Zeny, in thanksgiving for her example of Christian faith, simplicity, and service

Contents

General Editor's preface   *page* ix
Preface   xi

PART I   THE NATURE AND DYNAMICS OF
ECONOMIC COMPULSION

1   Markets and coercive pecuniary externalities   3

2   The regressive incidence of unintended burdens   43

PART II   SETTING THE MORAL BASELINE AND
SHAPING EXPECTATIONS

3   Economic security as God's twofold gift   77

4   Retrieving the biblical principle of restoration   111

PART III   CONTEMPORARY APPROPRIATION

5   Economic rights-obligations as diagnostic framework   141

6   Application: the case of agricultural protectionism   178

7   Summary and conclusions   213

References   227
Index   241

General Editor's preface

This book is the twenty-third in the series *New Studies in Christian Ethics*. There are many points of mutual concern between this important book and others within the series. Peter Sedgwick's *The Market Economy and Christian Ethics* takes a very similar inclusive approach to public theology in this area, from an Anglican position, as does David Fergusson's *Community, Liberalism and Christian Ethics*, from a Reformed position. Douglas Hicks's *Inequality and Christian Ethics* explores at length the issue of urban inequality that is one of the negative features of economic compulsion. And both David Hollenbach's *The Common Good and Christian Ethics* and the first monograph in the series, Kieran Cronin's *Rights and Christian Ethics*, set the whole discussion into a wider context of Catholic public theology.

Together these monographs admirably fulfill the two key aims of *New Studies in Christian Ethics* as a whole – namely, to promote studies in Christian ethics which engage centrally with the present secular moral debate at the highest possible intellectual level and, secondly, to encourage contributors to demonstrate that Christian ethics can make a distinctive contribution to this debate.

Albino Barrera's new book is particularly welcome because it involves an important subject, it is well and clearly written (you do not need to be an economist to understand it), it engages with the secular literature, it is theologically sophisticated and it reaches challenging conclusions. His focus is upon what his fellow economists term "pecuniary externalities" – especially upon economic hardships caused for individuals and impoverished groups because of changes induced unintentionally by fluctuations in the economy. He argues strongly that we need to take communal responsibility for such hardships – the effects of economic compulsion – and not simply leave them to "market forces." Christians have a particular moral imperative for addressing the concerns of vulnerable people negatively affected by economic compulsion and for challenging others in society to do so as well.

Qualified as both an economist and a theologian, Albino Barrera has written a creative book on economic compulsion, underpinned by Christian ethics (both Catholic and biblical), that should influence and challenge the religious and non-religious alike. What more can I say?

ROBIN GILL

Preface

Markets can often be harsh in compelling people to make unpalatable economic choices any reasonable person would not take under normal conditions. Thus, workers laid off in mid-career accept lower paying jobs that are beneath their professional experience and training for want of better alternatives. Economic migrants leave their families and cross borders (legally or illegally) in search of a livelihood. Over forty million United States residents forego health insurance in the face of unaffordable premiums. In response to unrelenting increases in drug prices, many elderly people on fixed incomes cut back on other essential expenditures like food and heat to purchase medication for their chronic ailments. Countless Third World families rely on child labor to supplement meager household incomes, and in the process, condemn their children to a lifetime of illiteracy and invincible poverty. Unable to keep up with rapidly escalating property taxes or rents, long-time residents of gentrified neighborhoods have had to move farther away from urban centers and put up with longer commutes to their workplace. These are examples of economic compulsion – an all-too-frequent state of affairs in which people are driven to make distasteful choices.

These cases share a common thread: They are about people who have been adversely affected by market price adjustments. They are about up-ended lives that have had to endure sudden and often devastating changes wrought by an extremely fluid economic environment. They reflect desperate and disagreeable market choices reasonable people would not make under ordinary circumstances. They are all painful dilemmas whereby vital interests are voluntarily, but reluctantly, relinquished in the face of acute material necessity. Such forbidding straits are often the damaging fallout of regular market operations. And, as seen in the examples cited, they occur in both wealthy and poor countries.

Market transactions have wide ripple effects and often inflict unintended consequences on unsuspecting third parties. Such externalities are

of two kinds: technological and pecuniary. Mainstream economic theory
and policy call for extra-market remedial measures to deal with technological externalities (such as pollution) because they impede economic
efficiency. In contrast, pecuniary externalities (such as losing one's job to
outsourcing) are deemed acceptable since these market-mediated adjustments are precisely the very mechanisms through which allocative efficiency is achieved.

Daniel Hausman argues eloquently against this asymmetric treatment
between technological and pecuniary externalities in mainstream economic
thought and policy.

Pecuniary externalities can totally transform people's lives. It is odd, if not
monstrous, to suppose that the power looms that destroyed virtually the whole of
the hand-weaver's capital (both human and otherwise) did those weavers morally
significant harm only insofar as the smoke they gave off smudged the hand-
woven cloth [technological externality]. Positive pecuniary externalities can
eliminate the greatest privations of the past and transform the human condition.
Negative pecuniary externalities can force people on pain of starvation to leave
their homes, occupations, families, countries, and cultures; indeed, they can
force people to starvation itself. Can one plausibly accept the view that human
actions with such overwhelming impact on the lives of other people raise no
questions of justice? (Hausman 1992: 104)

Pecuniary externalities are potent in their capacity to generate far-reaching
changes. Indeed, history is replete with evidence of how markets can be
transformative either for good or for ill.

Pecuniary externalities ought likewise to be a matter of policy concern
just like their technological variant, for at least two reasons. First, price
changes are a de facto market redistribution of burdens and benefits across
economic agents. Thus, even while many benefit, others may have to bear
a disproportionate share of the cost of moving the economy toward
greater allocative efficiency. The unfettered market is by its nature primarily geared toward letting prices allocate scarce resources to their most
valued uses; it is not concerned with the distributive ramifications of price
movements. Thus, questions of equity and fairness will go unattended
and unaddressed. Moreover, inadvertent market effects can be detrimental to the point of driving many to a state of economic compulsion as a
result of price and quantity adjustments. In other words, pecuniary
externalities can severely restrict the autonomy and hurt the welfare of
market participants in nontrivial ways. Second, unintended consequences
mediated through the marketplace ought to be examined closely because

they often inflict heavy costs on the very people who are least able to bear them, as we will find in chapter 2.

Given the extensive, abrupt, and even catastrophic collateral repercussions of market exchange, especially in the age of globalization, it is now all the more urgent for us to open a new front in ethical discourse: what to do about injurious pecuniary externalities and their resulting economic compulsion. Long before the industrial era, scholastic doctors had already grappled with the question of economic coercion (Langholm 1998). However, beyond expressing grave concern, medieval economic ethics did not address substantive issues of this phenomenon. For example, what constitutes economic compulsion? Are coerced economic choices morally significant? If they are, who should be held to account for such duress? Is there an obligation to rectify or even reverse such market outcomes? How do we separate routine from consequential pecuniary externalities? To what degree do we remedy economic compulsion and why? Who bears responsibility for such ameliorative action?

This book argues that Christian thought offers a rigorous, critical assessment of these questions. In particular, drawing from its theological and philosophical resources, Christian ethics provides (1) compelling arguments for a closer scrutiny of market-mediated third-party effects, (2) a conceptual framework for defining the threshold where negative pecuniary externalities turn into economic compulsion, and (3) an ethos within which such adverse unintended consequences ought to be redressed.

Part I examines the nature and dynamics of economic necessity. Chapter 1 defines the formal characteristics of what constitutes compulsion, using conceptual tools and language from the philosophical literature on coercion. I argue that Aristotle's notion of mixed action lends itself well to framing economic compulsion as a state of affairs in which market participants incur profound opportunity costs, that is, they have to give up vital interests to satisfy other unmet nontrivial claims that are even more pressing. Such a condition is precipitated by factors within the marketplace itself such as the limits it imposes on freedom of association, the inability of individual economic agents to change market processes on their own, bounded rationality, and the ubiquity of pecuniary externalities. Markets can be coercive in the negative unintended consequences they unleash by the nature of the attendant price adjustments of economic exchange.

Chapter 2 argues that economic distress often has a regressive incidence. The most ill equipped to deal with disruptive market ripple effects frequently end up having to bear more of them given their disadvantaged social and historical location. We find plentiful evidence of such a pattern in capital, labor, and product markets due to variations in individual capabilities, differences in the private cost of accessing social goods, and wide disparities in the communal valuation of personal endowments. Thus, it is all the more important to attend to the market's harmful consequences since it is the poor who often have to endure them.

Economic compulsion makes sense only in reference to a moral baseline of what is considered to be noncoercive, and part II surveys Christian contributions in setting just such a benchmark. Chapter 3 describes economic security as an unusual divine benefaction in that it embeds one gift within another: God not only provides for human material needs but also elicits human participation in effecting such bountiful providence. The economic precepts on debt-, slave-, and land-release in the Hebrew Scripture are fundamentally about ameliorating economic distress. The marginalized are restored to a position from which they can once again participate in the marketplace as free and equal members of society. Thus, economic security has three constitutive elements: (1) access to the requisite goods of life (2) through one's own efforts, to the extent possible, (3) within the confines of a nurturing community. This vision of the ideal economic order is adopted and repeatedly stressed throughout the Christian tradition, from the New Testament to the patristic writers to the scholastic doctors down to contemporary religious social thought. Economic compulsion is a privation of such a divinely proffered economic security.

The market's positive and negative side effects cannot and should not be separated from each other. If market exchange is truly about mutual advantages for all parties concerned, then the burden of bearing the concomitant liabilities of market operations ought to be borne by those who have reaped the most benefits. In other words, gains from the marketplace itself provide the means to compensate for its accompanying harms. Chapter 4 maintains that the Hebrew economic statutes provide excellent examples of such extra-market corrective-rehabilitative mechanisms and processes. The Chosen People's ethos of restoration merits retrieval and emulation in our own time as we wrestle with balancing both the good and the ills of global economic integration.

Christian ethics does not merely articulate the foundational warrants for why economic distress is morally significant, it also provides conceptual tools for implementing its insights. The two chapters of part III illustrate the value of Christian thought for contemporary economic ethics.

The Hebrew vision on the proper alleviation of harmful market outcomes in an ancient nomadic and agrarian economy needs to be adapted for our postindustrial age. Moreover, we have to learn how to deal with varying degrees of economic compulsion since all market exchanges are by their nature constrained choices; we have to be able to distinguish genuine needs from mere wants if economic compulsion is not to be tautological. Both of these requirements are met by rights language. Chapter 5 presents modern Catholic social thought's web of rights and obligations within its overarching common good tradition as an analytical backdrop for concretely defining the scope and severity of economic compulsion.

To demonstrate the utility of this study's proposed model, chapter 6 examines the detrimental subsidiary economic effects suffered by developing countries because of European, Japanese, and American agricultural protectionism. Farmers from both industrialized and poor countries have strong competing moral claims as they seek relief and shelter from a global market environment that threatens their long-standing agrarian way of life. The notion of economic security from Christian ethics and its contemporary expression in human rights-obligations provide practical guidelines both for adjudicating these clashing interests and for rectifying ruinous unintended consequences from international agricultural trade.

Written for scholars and students of economic ethics, religious social thought, poverty studies, sociology, and political economy, this book offers a fivefold contribution to the literature. First, it proposes a systemic account of economic distress by tracing its provenance to the nature of market exchange itself. Scholars believe that destitution is the outcome of social conflict, exploitation, or even personal choice (Blank 2003; Trimiew 1997: 137–52). Part I of this study argues that the unintended consequences of market transactions can occasion or exacerbate poverty.

Second, this study formalizes and traces the regressive impact of transaction costs and economic compulsion on the welfare of economic agents. Chapter 2 uses the household production model of consumer theory to account for how and why markets can be skewed in the distribution of their negative ripple effects. The marketplace is an effective price discriminator, charging unique prices for every market participant given the latter's human capital and sociohistorical location. To my knowledge, this argument has never been made before in economic scholarship or in social ethics.

Third, this research presents scriptural justification for why inimical secondary effects of the market ought to be rectified. Moreover, it examines and then calls for a retrieval of the Hebrew admonitions on mutual assistance and rehabilitation for injured third parties (chapters 3 and 4).

Fourth, most theological commentators deduce human rights from human dignity and God's claims. This study does the same but goes a step further by using human rights-obligations and economic security in setting the boundaries and the end of market operations respectively (part III).

Fifth, this book draws upon the network of duties and rights from contemporary Christian social ethics to propose a conceptual framework for analyzing pecuniary externalities (chapter 5). We can deal with economic compulsion only in the measure that we have the vocabulary and the necessary distinctions that allow for a nuanced application of abstract principles to the concrete particularities of the economy.

The market's adverse unintended consequences have received insufficient analytical attention and systematic ethical appraisal in the literature. This is a troubling deficiency in view of the profound suffering the most vulnerable often have to endure. For example, consider the story behind the cover of this book. Taken in 1936 in Nipomo, California for what was then the Resettlement Administration, this picture is from a series of photographs that have since become iconic images of the hard life of an earlier generation. In fact, the woman in these photos has come to be widely known as the "Migrant Mother." Dorothea Langes's account of how she came to take these photographs puts an unforgettable human face to the numbing helplessness of economic compulsion:

I saw and approached the hungry and desperate mother . . . She told me her age, that she was thirty-two. She said that they had been living on frozen vegetables from the surrounding fields, and birds that the children killed. She had just sold the tires from her car to buy food. There she sat in that lean-to tent with her children huddled around her . . . (*Popular Photography*, February 1960, p. 126)

Is there a communal obligation to reverse or at least mitigate the market's negative collateral effects? Should we have to face hard economic choices all on our own? These questions take on even greater significance in view of the increasing "marketization" of society in the postindustrial, globalized, knowledge-based economy.

Pecuniary externalities are unavoidable since they are intrinsic to economic life. They flow from the nature of market exchange itself and produce both benefits and harms. However, the market's negative unintended consequences deteriorate into a state of economic distress only if we, as individuals and as a community, permit them to proceed uncorrected. Consequently, unattended economic compulsion is in itself an indictment of our moral failure to be "each other's keeper." In advancing a better understanding of economic compulsion, I hope this work evokes a renewed personal and collective appreciation for the promise and the possibilities of partaking in God's initiative of providing for us through each other in the twofold divine gift of economic security.

Many have been generous during the writing and production of this book. Ernest Bartell, Dan Finn, Thomas Massaro, and John Lunn provided valuable comments, corrections, and ideas for improvement. I incorporated as many of their suggestions as space and time permitted. Any errors that remain are solely my responsibility. Carol Moran furnished excellent proofreading assistance. It has been a delight to work with Kate Brett of Cambridge University Press and Robin Gill, series editor, who have been most supportive, efficient, and professional in bringing the project to fruition. I cannot thank Joanne Hill enough for her exceptional copy-editing. To these good and kind mentors, colleagues, and friends, and for their wise counsel and encouragement, I owe a deep debt of gratitude.

PART I

The nature and dynamics of economic compulsion

Markets and coercive pecuniary externalities

INTRODUCTION

In the view of mainstream economic thought, there can be no economic compulsion in an unfettered marketplace because consummated transactions are purely voluntary and evidence of mutual advantages gained. A unique strength of the market as a societal institution and as a mechanism for allocating scarce resources lies in the unparalleled degree of autonomy it affords economic agents. In the perfectly competitive markets of neo-classical economics, people are completely free to trade whatever, when-ever, however, wherever, and with whom they so desire.[1] Moreover, since economic actors are rational and pursue what is in their best interest, we can presume that they engage in market exchange only to the extent that they improve, or, at the very least, remain at, their pre-trade welfare. It makes no sense for rational agents to partake of a bargain that leaves them worse off; they trade up and not down. People participate in the market only as they see fit. Consequently, there is no room for such a notion as compelled market exchanges in mainstream economic thought. This position is not peculiar to neoclassical economists alone, as some philoso-phers are also skeptical of claims that economic circumstances, and by extension the market, can be coercive.[2]

The object of this chapter is to show why and how the market's harmful unintended consequences can compel economic agents to make choices they would normally not take. To do so, however, it is first necessary to define the formal characteristics of what constitutes economic compulsion. Having done this, I will then examine particular elements in the nature and dynamics of the marketplace that occasion severely constrained economic exchanges.

---

1 For a brief exposition of the history and scope of neoclassical economic thought, see Landreth and Colander (1994: 210–317) or Blaug (1985: 294–613, 632–53).
2 For example, see Nozick (1974).

THE GRAMMAR AND NATURE OF COERCION

Determining whether a state of coercion exists or not is important for the ascription of responsibility. In much of the legal and philosophical literature, the concern ultimately revolves around the issue of whether the coerced have any obligations to fulfill the terms of contracts accepted under duress.[3] In contrast, this study deals with the questions of whether the coerced deserve special assistance from the community, and if so, who bears responsibility for relieving their plight and why. In both cases, however, there is a common need to establish first what constitutes coercion.

Much can be learned from the extensive philosophical literature on the subject. In what follows, I highlight only those works that are relevant and helpful for talking about whether market exchanges can be coercive. Aristotle's (1951) mixed action, Alan Wertheimer's (1987) moral baseline, David Zimmerman's (1981a and b) nonmoral account, and Joan McGregor's (1988–89) bargaining advantages all provide differing, albeit overlapping, theories of coercion that provide useful conceptual frameworks of analysis.

Mixed action

There is no mistaking that the economic conduct described in the earlier examples of distress cited in the preface were voluntary. People made decisions for themselves knowing full well the implications and the severe trade-offs that would follow in the wake of their actions. They could have just as easily walked away from their choices or chosen otherwise, but did not. Nevertheless, one cannot simply be narrowly focused on the moral agent to the exclusion of the coercive backdrop within which such agency was exercised. Aristotle's notion of the mixed act, situated between willing and unwilling action, is illuminative in this regard.[4]

Aristotle presents the case of the tempest-tossed ship whose crew jettisons cargo into the sea to save lives. Is this voluntary or involuntary action? Aristotle's distinctions are exceptionally helpful:

'Abstractly considered' (*haplôs*), no one would willingly throw his goods overboard, but any reasonable man would do so if it were a question of saving

---

3 See, for example, Wertheimer (1987).
4 My thanks to Nicholas Ingham for pointing this out and for reference to Wertheimer's (1987) work.

the lives of himself and his crew. Actions like these are of a mixed nature . . . for they are accepted as choiceworthy at the moment of performing them . . . [A]ction ought to be judged willing or unwilling with reference to whatever end was actually in view of a particular occasion of its performance . . . [S]uch actions, therefore, must be regarded as having been performed willingly; although from an abstract point of view they are doubtless against the agent's will, since no one would choose them for themselves. (Aristotle 1951: 201, Book III, i)

In the examples in the preface, economic agents were making mixed choices. Under normal circumstances, they would not have voluntarily solicited or engaged in the market exchanges that they did, as no reasonable person would ordinarily do so. In other words, the particular circumstances (especially the constraints) surrounding such choices hold the conceptual key to determining whether a completed market transaction is an instance of economic compulsion or of a welfare-improving exchange.

The moral baseline

Wertheimer (1987) distills common threads in the courts' adjudication of a wide variety of cases on the binding nature of obligations incurred under duress. Moving from law to philosophy, he synthesizes the rationale behind these legal rulings into a coherent theory of coercion. At the heart of his framework is the distinction between threats and offers; the former are coercive, the latter are not.[5] Observe the contrast in the two cases he examines:

The Stock Market Case. A realizes that B is about to lose a large sum in the stock market. A tells B that he will help B avoid the loss if and only if B gives him 15 percent of the amount he would have lost.
The Ambulance Case. A comes upon an auto wreck and an injured B on a desolate stretch of the road. A tells B that he will call an ambulance if and only if B gives him $100. (Wertheimer 1987: 214)[6]

A's proposal is coercive in the Ambulance Case, but not in the Stock Market Case. After all, there is an obligation in the former (to summon an ambulance), but not in the latter because A is not bound by any duty to help B avert an impending loss in the stock market. Thus, A's offer to call an ambulance in exchange for $100 is in effect a threat in the form of

---

5 Alternatively, one could present it as the difference between a coercion and an enticement. The former pertains to avoiding a harm, while the latter deals with reaching out toward a desired good (McGregor 1988–89: 49).
6 These cases were originally published in Gunderson (1979: 258).

"I will leave you here to die without medical assistance unless you compensate me for calling an ambulance." This is a coercive proposal. The Stock Market Case, on the other hand, is a genuine offer, a non-coercive proposal, because there are no ties or bonds that require A to alert and help B avoid financial ruin. A has a right to ask for remuneration in the Stock Market Case, but not in the Ambulance Case. Thus, one must weigh the web of obligations and rights binding the transactors, if any, before one can ascertain whether a condition of coercion exists or not.[7]

Another way of distinguishing the two cases is by using "better off–worse off" language in examining the consequences of A's proposals. In the Stock Market Case, B gains as a result of A's proposal since B would have lost a much larger sum of money than the 15 percent that B paid to A for the latter's assistance. In other words, in acceding to A's proposal, B is made better off by being able to keep 85 percent of what would have otherwise been lost. On the other hand, in the Ambulance Case, B will needlessly relinquish $100 in yielding to A's proposal. That B is alive (because of timely first aid) is an incalculable gain compared to the $100 fee. Nevertheless, B could have been saved just as well without having to shell out $100 had A been conscientious in doing what A should have been doing in the first place – summoning medical assistance with no strings attached. Thus, B is relatively worse off as a result of A's proposal because B could have and should have gotten an ambulance without having to disburse $100 in the *normal course of events*. Thus, A's proposition is not an offer but a coercive threat.

In both sets of criteria, the determination of whether a proposal is coercive or noncoercive is always in reference to a baseline.[8] In the first set of standards, the baseline is founded on the existence (or lack thereof) and strength of the network of mutual obligations and moral claims that bind the parties to each other. A had a right to ask for compensation in the Stock Market Case but not in the Ambulance Case because A was bound by a duty in the latter. The second approach (better off–worse off standard) is likewise dependent on a baseline. After all, statements on whether one is better off or worse off make sense only in reference to a benchmark.

Wertheimer's theory of coercion lends itself to another set of distinctions: an empirical or a moralized account of the baseline. For example, in

---

7 See also Nozick (1974: 262).
8 Note Wertheimer's (1987: 206) definition of the baseline: "B's baseline ordinarily includes the normal course of events *without* A's proposed intervention" (emphasis original).

the baseline governing the Ambulance Case, we can establish that A has an obligation to call an ambulance based on prevailing custom, law, or usage – an "empirical" account of what is considered normal within the community. Alternatively, such an obligation may be understood to be clearly part of what we owe each other as human beings. The latter requires further grounding in a moral theory.

A nonmoral account

Zimmerman (1981a and b) attempts a nonmoral account of what constitutes coercion by providing what he claims to be a simpler baseline. He presents the following case, which I have summarized:

A kidnaps Q, strands him on an island and offers Q a job to prevent him from starving. The only other employer on the island, B, also offers Q a job. The working conditions in both A's and B's factories are substantially worse than the jobs that were available to Q on the mainland. Are these job offers coercive or not? (Zimmerman 1981a: 133)

Zimmerman argues that only A's proposal is coercive as it is A who kidnapped Q, and in so doing, A is responsible for depriving Q of the much wider and better menu of choices available on the mainland. B's proposal, while just as exploitative[9] as A's, is not coercive because B is not in any way restricting the range of choices available to Q. In fact, B is expanding Q's choice set.

Wertheimer (1987: 244–51) argues that Zimmerman fails in his attempt to provide a truly nonmoral account of coercion because his proposed baseline is unavoidably founded on a moral theory also. He summarizes the formal characteristics of Zimmerman's nonmoral account of coercion.[10]

A state of coercion exists if and only if the following conditions are satisfied:

1 The coerced prefers the coercer's proposal (state Z) compared to his/her situation immediately prior to the proposal (state Y).
2 Nevertheless, the coerced would still have preferred an alternative state (state X) compared to the post-proposal situation (state Z).

---

9 We are not going to deal with the necessary conditions of what constitutes exploitation as this is properly the subject of another study. See, for example, Wertheimer (1996).
10 I have paraphrased Wertheimer's (1987: 245) formulation and have changed his references to "B" as "Q" for consistency with my preceding exposition.

3 Such preferred alternative state (state X) could have been readily and realistically provided as it is technologically and historically feasible to attain.

4 However, the coercer prevents the coerced from attaining this preferred feasible alternative state (state X) (Wertheimer 1987: 245).

Applied to Zimmerman's case, A's proposal to Q is coercive because:

1 Q prefers the horrible working conditions in A's factory (state Z) to starving on the beach (state Y).

2 However, Q would have much preferred to be working on the mainland (state X) rather than being stranded on an island and starving on the beach (state Y).

3 Q's being on the mainland (state X) is technologically and historically feasible.

4 A impedes Q from being on the mainland (state X) where Q would much rather be.

Based on these criteria, only A's proposal, and not B's, is coercive because it is only A, not B, who is hampering Q from attaining Q's preference for a job on the mainland. Condition 4 does not apply to B; thus, B's proposal is a genuine offer, albeit an exploitative one, that leaves Q better off than starving on the beach.

A truly nonmoral account of coercion would indeed be valuable as it avoids making normative commitments. Unfortunately, Wertheimer (1987: 247) points out that condition 4 is itself founded on a moral judgment. To make the statement that "A *prevents* Q from being on the mainland where Q would much rather be" is to describe an act of omission, at the very least, on the part of A (such as failing to undo the initial kidnapping by bringing Q back to the mainland). The terms *prevents* and *impedes* are not value neutral as they point to an a priori set of actions that one believes ought to be effected. In other words, there is a larger moral backdrop undergirding the prevention condition in number 4. Thus, Zimmerman's (1981a and b) nonmoral account fails; his baseline can be ultimately reduced to Wertheimer's (1987) better off–worse off or rights–obligations yardstick.

The bargaining position

McGregor (1988–89) is critical of what she calls the normalcy-criterion approach (such as Wertheimer's and Zimmerman's) to defining coercion in the philosophical literature. The use of a baseline as a reference for whether the coerced is better off or worse off in the post-proposal period is flawed because the legitimacy or propriety of that baseline is never questioned to begin with.

So much hinges on the normalcy baseline, it is startling that no one who employs the baseline or normal course of events argument questions whether *any* baseline is sufficiently justifiable to serve these purposes. This is especially troubling since there are . . . significant problems that can be raised for the normalcy baseline approach . . . [T]he proposed baselines themselves are not normatively neutral – each has a history . . . One would think . . . that the moral assessment of an action should include not only whether or not it advances one's position relative to a moral baseline, but some assessment of the appropriateness (morality) of the baseline itself. (McGregor 1988–89: 27 [emphasis original])

For example, people who are destitute can hardly get any worse, and by the normalcy criterion, most proposals they get, no matter how coercive or exploitative, would have to be viewed as offers rather than as intimidating threats because they make the poor better off given the dismal baseline from which they start in their pre-proposal state. Consequently, McGregor offers an alternative set of formal characteristics for what constitutes coercion based on relative bargaining strengths.

The neoclassical position (that a completed market exchange is prima facie evidence of mutual advantages for all transactors) is indeed correct in a perfectly competitive market.[11] After all, there are many buyers and sellers in such a setting, thereby leaving everyone – consumers, businesses, buyers, and sellers – as price-takers. Moreover, complete information is readily available to all. This means that no one has a "threat advantage" over anyone else to the point of being able to shape and impose single-handedly the terms of the exchange, just like a monopolist. There are simply too many other available offers; economic agents could simply walk away from bad deals and easily find and consummate a better trade elsewhere. Thus, everybody is in the same boat in the sense of being a price-taker, that is, having to accept prices as they are set by the market. More important, all agents are assumed to be desirous of improving their own welfare, and they are able to fend for themselves vis-à-vis other market participants. McGregor (1988–89: 24, 29) argues that it is only under these conditions of perfect competition – in which everyone is on a common, level bargaining field – that the normalcy criterion (better off/ worse off relative to a baseline) makes sense. A deterioration in an

---

11 Key assumptions underlying perfectly competitive markets include perfect mobility, perfect information, homogeneous commodities, and numerous buyers and sellers.

economic agent's post-trade welfare would indeed be evidence of coercion as no rational person would voluntarily trade down in a perfectly competitive market. Unfortunately, markets never satisfy the aforesaid conditions. Perfect competition is a heuristic device that is not at all replicated in practice; the norm is imperfectly competitive markets.

All other market structures besides perfect competition allow for some measure of control over economic outcomes and processes. The uneven distribution of such power becomes the proximate occasion for economic coercion. People enjoy different bargaining strengths, and they will exploit them to secure advantages for themselves in the marketplace. In a zero-sum setting, such gains can only come at the expense of their trading partners. Thus, for McGregor (1988–89: 34–35), a state of economic coercion must necessarily satisfy the following conditions:

1 The parties' relative bargaining strengths are "radically disparate" (24). The coercer has a clear and credible capacity either to inflict distress or to prevent harm from befalling the coerced.
2 The coercer is intent on taking advantage of such power and profiting from it.

The first is the condition of dependency, and the second is that of intentionality. As she notes:

A necessary condition for coercion is that the stronger party *takes advantage* of having the weaker party dependent on him to avoid the occurrence of evil. Recall that to take advantage of one's superior position the stronger party knows of his superior bargaining position and intentionally capitalizes on his advantages to causally effect his subsequent gain from the weaker party.

(McGregor 1988–89: 35 [original emphasis])

The coerced has only two choices: accepting the coercer's proposal or enduring the suffering that would ensue from failure to accept the coercer's proposition. The coerced has been cornered into an impossible situation and does not have any real meaningful choice. Just like the captain in Aristotle's example of the sinking ship, the coerced in such an unequal bargaining position is compelled to choose the lesser evil. There are no other feasible, reasonable, alternative courses of action. "[I]t is the presence of superior bargaining power in imperfect competition that is the key to understanding coercion in exchanges – not gain and loss relative to a baseline" (25).

Clearly, McGregor's method still uses a better off–worse off criterion. After all, the coerced is weighing and choosing which is the lesser of two evils – the coercer's proposal or the consequent harm that comes with rejecting it. However, unlike Wertheimer's and Zimmerman's methods, such a better off–worse off appraisal relative to the pre-proposal baseline is not the only formal characteristic that makes coercion what it is. Rather, it is also important to consider the circumstances that led to such an unsatisfactory choice set for the coerced. Thus, McGregor vividly contrasts her approach with the normalcy criterion in the following cases:

Case 1: Ms. Pecunious is approached by a gunman who says: If you refuse to have sexual relations with me I will shoot your baby.
Case 2: Ms. Impecunious has a baby who will die without an operation. Alas she has no money and no way of getting any. She is approached by a lecherous millionaire who puts the following proposal to her: If you agree to become my mistress, I will pay for the operation on your baby. (McGregor 1988–89: 24)[12]

Using the standard normalcy criterion in the philosophical literature, only the first case is coercive. Ms. Pecunious in case 1 is clearly going to be worse off compared to what should have been the normal course of events without the gunman's proposal. On the other hand, Ms. Impecunious in case 2 is clearly going to be better off compared to her initial position (not having the means to pay for her baby's surgery). Thus, despite being grossly exploitative, the lecherous millionaire's proposal is nonetheless merely an offer, rather than a coercive threat, since it opens possibilities that would have otherwise not been available to the distraught mother.

The alternative normalcy criterion of examining the rights and obligations undergirding these two cases leads to the same conclusion. Recall in the earlier illustrations how the Ambulance Case involves coercion while the Stock Market scenario does not because there is a duty to call an ambulance in the first instance, but no obligation at all to help avert an imminent financial loss in the latter. Similarly, the gunman is coercive in the first case because far from having the right to threaten Ms. Pecunious's baby with bodily harm, the gunman is in fact bound by the requirements of public order and common decency to desist from doing so. On the other hand, the lecherous millionaire is not bound by any obligation to pay for the badly needed surgery for Ms. Impecunious's baby. Just as in the Stock Market Case, the lecherous millionaire's proposition to Ms. Impecunious is no different from A's proposal to help B avert stock market losses in exchange for a portion of the funds saved. Both are offers that prevent an impending harm if the normal state of affairs were allowed to proceed unchanged.

12 This example is originally from Feinberg (1986).

By McGregor's reckoning, this descriptive difference in these two states of affairs is "indefensible" (24) and only serves to highlight the inadequacy of focusing purely on where the proposal stands relative to a baseline whose antecedents are neither questioned nor examined at all. Both cases are coercive in McGregor's view. After all, both cases are marked by a disproportionately uneven bargaining position; both the gunman and the lecherous millionaire are bent on pressing their advantage; and both leave the victims without any real meaningful choice of refusing the proposal without having to suffer an even greater harm.

THE FORMAL CHARACTERISTICS OF ECONOMIC COMPULSION

Two conceptual hurdles must be addressed before we can proceed with our analysis. First, which is the proper term to use in describing the plight of people who suffer from the adverse unintended consequences of market transactions: *coercion* or *compulsion*? Second, in order to make any discourse on economic compulsion or coercion meaningful, it is necessary to distinguish trivial from consequential effects in the marketplace.

Coercion versus compulsion

The philosophical language of coercion cannot be completely adopted without further qualification in specifying the formal characteristics of the economic compulsion that is of interest to us in this study. Economic circumstances do not "coerce" in the proper sense of the term; however, they can compel economic agents to make unappealing choices. There are significant differences between *coercion* and *compulsion* in describing how market conditions can force people to make decisions they would not have taken otherwise.

First, there is no perfect correspondence between *coercion* and *compulsion*. Recall Zimmerman's (1981a and b) baseline in the case of kidnapped Q. A's proposal is deemed coercive while B's proposition is considered to be an offer. After all, only A is responsible for leaving Q with such a poor set of choices. Examined from another point of view, however, we can properly describe Q as being compelled to accept a terrible job regardless of who offers the employment. Q is subjected to economic compulsion under both A's and B's proposals because Q would not have accepted these propositions under normal conditions and would have in fact preferred to do otherwise and be on the mainland working in the better jobs readily available over there. However, given his current situation (stranded on the island and starving), Q has no choice but to accept whatever employment there is. He is driven to do so for want of a better alternative. Thus, note how the terms *coercion* and *compulsion* are not identical (as in the case of B) even as they occasionally overlap (as in the case of A).

Second, coercion connotes blameworthiness; compulsion does not. In the analytical discourse on coercion, the key distinction lies in the difference between a threat and an offer in which the former is coercive while the latter is not. *Threat* and *offer* both require intentionality. In the full and proper usage of the term, a *threat* necessarily entails both forethought and intention and often implies an attendant blameworthiness in the background.[13] This volitional dimension is a necessary condition even in McGregor's theory of coercion based on bargaining disadvantages. In McGregor's framework, coercion arises only if the stronger party purposely capitalizes on the weakened position of the trading partner.

On the other hand, economic compulsion is not concerned with the intention animating the proposal, but with the restrictive options people face as a result of that proposition.[14] Moreover, in the majority of the cases of interest to us in this study, such exigent choices are precipitated not by ill intent or even by deliberate action on the part of other agents, but by the inadvertent consequences of very fluid market conditions.[15] Such adverse conditions may be brought about by chance and contingency in economic life and, thus, do not always or necessarily require normative judgment in assigning culpability. In other words, in its proper usage, the term *coercion* cannot deal with unintended market consequences while *compulsion* can readily accommodate them. Moreover, it would be very difficult to ascribe deliberate intent to the market per se even if it is viewed as the collective economic agency of the community. The most we can impute is a remote or mediated collective intent, and not a direct or immediate volition.

Third, since intentionality and a consideration of rights-obligations are important in ascertaining coercive situations, discourse that employs

---

13 Not all threats are blameworthy as in the case of threatening punishment to avert an evil.

14 Another way of distinguishing my notion of *economic compulsion* from the philosophical usage of *coercion* is to note Wertheimer's (1987: 202) observation, "Perhaps the key to coercion is not in the choice situation itself, but in the sorts of proposals that create B's choice conditions." Philosophers have centered their discourse on the latter, that is, on the nature of the propositions. In my case, I focus on the choice situation itself and its context, that is, on the background circumstances that shape the choices available to the person.

15 These are properly called *pecuniary externalities*, and we examine these in greater depth in the next section.

coercion must necessarily focus not only on the coerced but also on the coercer. Wertheimer (1987: 202–203) concludes that to establish coercion, one must deal not only with outcomes or processes but also with complications, to wit, the motives, intentions, and beliefs not only of the coercer but of the coerced as well. This is not even to mention the need to prove that the coercer's proposals are both clear and credible. The informational requirements are enormous.[16] This is also true of McGregor's (1988–89: 24) theory of coercion. On the other hand, the term *compulsion* requires only that we consider, at a minimum, the circumstances faced by the economic agent.

Finally, *coercion* entails a precise assignation of rights and obligations. Recall the earlier discussion on the Ambulance and the Stock Market Cases. In the former, A's proposal is coercive, a threat, because A has an obligation to summon an ambulance to begin with. In contrast, there is no duty in the latter; A may legitimately ask B for a fee in exchange for services rendered in helping B avert stock market losses. Thus, a clear specification of rights and obligations is essential in the proper use of the term *coercion*. Unfortunately, such an unequivocal delineation of rights and obligations in the marketplace is neither always easy nor straightforward.

John McMillan (2002: 90) believes that market participants are constrained (1) by the rules of the market and (2) by what they bring to the marketplace. Consider the key factors that shape the "circumstances" that economic agents face in the market. People maximize the satisfaction of their preferences by carefully apportioning their scarce resources in the purchase of the goods and services they require. Key to this exercise is the size of their purchasing power which in turn is contingent on (1) their income and (2) the market prices of goods and services. Household income is in turn a function of (1) the price at which people are able to sell their resources (including labor services) or output, (2) their work effort, and (3) their past investments in their human capital. The latter two determine both people's productivity and the quality of their production. Thus, economic agents who have devoted considerable effort, time, and resources to educating themselves and developing their skills most likely have more than enough purchasing power to procure their needs. What is important to note here is that *under normal conditions*, the economic circumstances in which people find themselves are the outcome

---

16 See Wertheimer (1987: 203, footnote 4) for a more precise, technical, and complete statement of all the necessary conditions for coercion.

of both market processes (which set the prices at which goods and services are bought and sold) and the economic agents' own discipline and work effort.[17] Thus, the market cannot be said to be completely responsible for shaping the opportunities of economic agents because the latter's purchasing power is partly a function of their own initiatives. Economic circumstances are not always purely exogenous shocks but most likely have endogenous underpinnings as well.

This presents intractable difficulties in assessing accountability because economic compulsion may in fact be the joint responsibility of the market and economic agents themselves. As we see in part II, the community bears an obligation to provide a safety net that ensures basic economic security for every member in its ranks. However, the gift of economic security itself also obliges these individual members to exert their personal effort in providing for themselves and others, to the extent possible. In appraising the possible sources of economic compulsion, it is not always easy to judge whether it is the market or the individual, or even both, who have failed to live up to their duties. For example, in the earlier cases cited in the preface, is it always the market that is responsible for compelling economic agents to make such unappealing choices? It may be entirely possible that people who experience difficulty finding a new line of work may have taken no initiative in the past in continuing their own training or education that would have constantly upgraded their skills. Should the market be blamed even in cases where people are not able to buy their medicine in their old age because they never made any effort to save in the past? Unless one can accurately track how well people have discharged both their past and present personal and communal obligations in the marketplace, it is difficult to use the normalcy criterion of rights-obligations in ascertaining whether the market is indeed coercive or not. In contrast, we can always use the language of "compulsion" without having to examine blameworthiness first. Regardless of whether or not the elderly or the unemployed had put in their own effort in the past, we can nonetheless state that given current market conditions, they are compelled to make unpalatable choices. This is different from the statement "The market coerces them to make such choices." *Economic circumstances*

---

17 One cannot overemphasize the importance of the qualifier "under normal conditions" in assigning partial responsibility to economic agents for the opportunities they face. People can often be trapped in the vicious cycle of poverty that leaves them unable to pursue initiatives either to improve their condition or to invest in their skills and education. Consider, for example, the plight of children who have been compelled to forego their schooling in order to work and supplement their families' paltry income.

cannot "coerce" in the full and proper sense of the term, but they can compel market participants.

Consequential unintended effects

It is important to specify clearly that only nontrivial interests are subject to economic compulsion. Economic decisions are by nature constrained choices. People seek to satisfy their preferences within their limited budgets. Given their unlimited wants, this means that economic agents can never be completely satisfied in their economic decisions. There will always be something they desire that is simply unattainable given their purchasing power and market prices. There will always be wants left unsatisfied. Economics, after all, is about weighing, trading off, and minimizing opportunity costs.[18] Thus, *the formal characteristics of economic compulsion cannot be based simply on the existence of opportunity costs, but on the nature and severity of such opportunity costs.*

For example, person A may have to forego a vacation in Europe because a much weakened US dollar relative to the euro simply makes such travel unaffordable. Even while entailing an unsatisfied want, this does not qualify as an instance of economic compulsion as it involves merely an unmet want rather than a pressing need. Neoclassical economics is unable to deal with the notion of economic compulsion because it does not distinguish needs from wants, given its goal of being a purely positive science of human choices.

Such a distinction is unavoidable if economic compulsion is not to be tautological. Otherwise, all economic decisions are compelled choices. Separating trivial from consequential market outcomes requires prior work on three related issues: (1) defining the content of the basket of essential human needs, (2) ranking these needs in a hierarchy of importance, and (3) differentiating the degree of urgency in the face of unmet or incompletely met needs. We will examine these in part III. Meanwhile, it is clear that any meaningful discourse on economic compulsion requires that we consider only nontrivial human claims that are put at risk. Joseph Raz describes the relation between economic necessity and economic compulsion well:

---

18 Opportunity costs are the foregone alternatives of one's choices. There would have been no need for economics to begin with if people were always able to procure whatever they desired.

Much of the writing on autonomy focuses on an agent's ability to form informed and effective judgements as a condition of autonomy . . . But there are two more aspects to autonomy as (part) authorship of one's life. One is relational: an autonomous person is not subjected to the will of another. *The other aspect of autonomy concerns the quality of the options open to agents: Their choices must not be dictated by personal needs* . . .

. . . *The autonomous agent is one who is not always struggling to maintain the minimum conditions of a worthwhile life. The more one's choices are dictated by personal needs, the less autonomous one becomes.* (Raz 1982: 112 [emphasis added])

Personal freedom is severely curtailed if one is completely preoccupied, indeed driven, by the ceaseless need to scrounge for the essential means for survival and basic health. Severe economic necessity is both a necessary and sufficient condition for economic compulsion. Thus, the destitute can be said to be in a state of chronic economic compulsion with little real autonomy.

Defining economic compulsion

Given the aforementioned differences between *coercion* and *compulsion*, this study employs Aristotle's notion of mixed action in assessing un-appealing choices in the marketplace. For the rest of the book, I define *economic compulsion as a condition in which market participants unavoidably incur profound opportunity costs. People give up nontrivial interests in order to satisfy, safeguard, or procure their other vital claims that are at even graver risk.* In other words, economic compulsion leads people to volun-tarily accept a significant deterioration in their welfare in order to avert what would have otherwise been an even more catastrophic decline in their well-being. Note that my use of the term *compulsion* is different from its medical usage in referring to addictions, eating disorders, or other dysfunctions. Unlike compulsive behaviors, economic *compulsion* is a voluntary act and focuses on the severe constraints faced rather than on the absence of volition on the part of the agent. Its distinctive characteris-tic is the absence of any "technologically and historically"[19] feasible and reasonable alternative to forestalling the even greater harms that would ensue in declining the current proposal, completely reprehensible as it may be. The choice set is essentially one of minimizing losses, much along the lines of the proverbial dilemma of having to acquiesce to the lesser of two evils. Economic compulsion is a state of affairs in which people are

---

19 See Zimmerman's (1981a) third condition.

driven to select unappealing choices that no reasonable person would make under normal conditions, just like the crew in Aristotle's example of the wind-tossed ship jettisoning its cargo.

Giving up vital interests in order to secure other even more significant claims clearly reflects an effort to prevent being made worse off. It is to avoid the more insidious of two privations. In this regard, we are able to use the philosophical literature's criterion of worse off–better off relative to a predetermined moral baseline in determining whether a proposal is an offer or a coercive threat. Such a comparison relative to a pre-established moral reference point is entirely consistent with and, in fact, reinforces my preceding argument on the need to distinguish needs from wants.

McGregor (1988–89: 27) is correct in highlighting the central import-ance of first establishing the morality of the baseline to be used. Obvi-ously, the choice of that standard is itself normative. The baseline approach of the philosophical literature can be adapted and retooled for this study by using it to separate trivial from consequential claims that are foregone in the face of economic compulsion. In fact, chapter 5 revolves around deriving and justifying this all-important reference point.

Finally, trading off essential interests is indicative of desperate choices. What makes economic compulsion a compelling subject of moral dis-course is the enormous pain, suffering, and hardship it inflicts on people. In fact, an alternative description of economic compulsion is "hard choices."

Sometimes one faces a choice situation in which rejecting a proposal means remaining in dire straits, but accepting the proposal is also unpalatable. Call this a *hard choice*. Hard choices are importantly different from other choices. They have a particularly severe constraining effect.
                                        (Wertheimer 1987: 233 [original emphasis])

Wertheimer (233) goes further in noting that the two dimensions of "(very) hard choices" are inversely proportional: The more restricted the choices available, the more acute is the personal experience. In fact, he suggests that we can go so far as to "plausibly use the family of coercion terms to describe hard choice situations." I agree with Wertheimer's position in using the terms *compulsion, hard choices, duress,* and *coercion* interchangeably. Nonetheless, readers are reminded that for the rest of the book, I use the terms *coercion* or *coercive* in the qualified sense I described earlier for the term *compulsion.* Moreover, this study is only about the economic compulsion that arises from chance and contingency or from negative pecuniary externalities, that is, market-generated shocks that require people to readjust their behavior at a cost to their welfare (adverse unintended consequences). We do not examine instances of economic coercion in which one party purposely capitalizes on and exploits the weakened state of a trading partner. These have already been treated extensively in the legal and philosophical literature.[20] Moreover, Langholm (1998) has already examined classical, scholastic, and modern economic thought on this type of economic coercion. Rather, this book is about the economic compulsion generated by the unintended consequences of market exchange.

THE CONSTITUTIVE ELEMENTS OF THE MARKETPLACE

As mentioned earlier, a much-vaunted strength of the market is the wide range of freedoms it affords its participants. The economic agents of neoclassical economics enjoy an expansive autonomy, from setting their own goals, to choosing the basket of needs and wants they fill, to deciding when and how they are to satisfy their preferences, and finally to selecting with whom they would like to collaborate. Given such extensive liberties, it may seem puzzling as to why and how market exchange can still give rise to economic duress. This section examines limits to this much-touted freedom even in the most optimistic scenario of perfectly competitive markets. In particular, I focus on four characteristics of the marketplace that together intersect to occasion economic compulsion.

Circumscribed freedom of association

Freedom of association is both a necessary and sufficient condition if the marketplace is to be free of coercion. Milton Friedman explains this claim well. In describing the economy, he notes: "[C]o-operation is strictly individual and voluntary *provided*: (a) that enterprises are private, so that the ultimate contracting parties are individuals and (b) that individuals are effectively free to enter or not to enter into any particular exchange, so that every transaction is strictly voluntary . . ." (Friedman 1962: 14–15 [original emphasis]).

---

20 Wertheimer (1987: 23–28) provides a quick sampling of cases of economic coercion in which contracts with unfavorable (and unjust) terms are consummated under duress.

Friedman further observes that this economic freedom will be maintained for as long as law and order prevents physical coercion. Moreover, in the absence of "neighborhood effects"[21] and monopolies, he touts the market's capacity to effect freedom of action in a most nonintrusive and efficient manner:

So long as effective freedom of exchange is maintained, the central feature of the market . . . is that it prevents one person from interfering with another in respect of most of his activities. The consumer is protected from coercion by the seller because of the presence of other sellers with whom he can deal. The seller is protected from coercion by the consumer because of other consumers to whom he can sell. The employee is protected from coercion by the employer because of other employers for whom he can work, and so on. *And the market does this impersonally and without centralized authority.*

(Friedman 1962: 14–15 [emphasis added])

Such autonomy can be divided into its three dimensions. First, market participants can choose with whom they would like to transact. Partnerships are never forced on people. Second, economic agents are free to accept or to walk away from proffered exchanges. In other words, contracts are struck only by mutual consent. Third, it is entirely up to people whether or not they want to participate in the market. Such freedom of association can be stated in the strongest possible form – the freedom to be a Robinson Crusoe. They can withdraw from the market whenever or wherever they want. *Genuine autonomy should mean that* homo oeconomicus *can be a Robinson Crusoe at will.* After all, an attractive and central feature of the market is that one can choose to trade only when it is in one's own interest. This, of course, includes the option of deciding not to trade at all! Market participation is entirely voluntary. Put in even more succinct terms, an "essentially just society can neither ban nor require capitalist acts among consenting adults" (Gauthier 1986: 341). The same point on the importance of noncoercion in economic participation can be made for the Lockean market society in which people are free to remain, by choice, in their pre-market isolation (Mack 1978: 185).

I argue that we cannot ascribe such a strong freedom of association to market participants. The most obvious shortcoming is the freedom to be a Robinson Crusoe on demand. Trading in the marketplace is no longer merely an option as it was in the era of isolated, self-sufficient feudal communities with minimal commercial activity. The modern industrial

---

21 Friedman (1962: 134–38) cites technological externalities and public goods as examples of such effects.

economy is distinctive for its division of labor in which people specialize in a particular economic undertaking and then procure their other needs from other "specialists" by trading their respective products in the marketplace. Such specialization has been key to the stunning growth in productivity and output in the last 200 years of the Industrial Revolution. However, it has also precipitated a radical reorganization of societal structures characterized by greater interdependence and more impersonal relationships (Polanyi 1944). In other words, for the vast majority of people, there is no other option but to trade in the marketplace. The full-fledged move away from autarky effected with the onset of the modern economy is irreversible. Some degree of market participation and exchange is unavoidable in securing physical survival and basic health in our times. This is true even for the more isolated rural, agricultural pockets of contemporary society.

Granted that we no longer have the freedom to be a Robinson Crusoe at will, proponents of strong market autonomy can still point to the other two elements of the freedom of association: (1) Economic agents are still able to choose with whom they would like to transact, and (2) they are still able to review, negotiate, set, and perhaps even change the terms of contracts to which they commit themselves. I claim that even these liberties are not as absolute or as strong as they appear to be given the realities of the market and the limitations imposed by human nature.

Time utility is an important factor in the consumer's decision in addition to product quality and place utility. In other words, it is not only the product or its quality that is important to the consumer, it is also critical to get these at the right time and at the right place. This is particularly true for those transactions that involve needs rather than mere wants. The impact of not being able to satisfy one's preference for a particular pair of shoes is qualitatively different from not being able to purchase food. There is obviously a time dimension to procuring the latter that lends urgency to locating and completing appropriate transactions in the marketplace that would put food on the table at the end of the day, every day. Such requisite economic exchanges are twofold: having to raise the necessary purchasing power by selling one's own produce or services and having to buy what one needs in sufficient quantities at affordable prices.

Economic agents are compelled to find and complete transactions within a regular, predefined, time period in order to obtain recurring basic human necessities. Market participants do not always have the option of waiting for the most propitious trades because they are bound by an unrelenting, immovable, time constraint of having to eat and be kept warm and sheltered on a regular basis. Only the wealthy with tremendous surplus are able to stay away from trading in the market for a longer period of time, but not even they are always able to choose the kind of contracts they accept or the parties with whom they transact. In other words, market transactors cannot always postpone meeting their needs until another time when a more ideal contract or a better trading partner can be found. They will be occasionally driven to trade with people they would much rather not or conclude market exchanges on terms that are neither to their favor nor liking, simply because of the inescapable reality that many essential human needs are time-constrained and must be filled within a specified interval. Thus, for example, displaced workers who have used up their savings are willing to accept employment that is beneath their professional training and experience.

There are significant limitations to the market's much-touted freedom of association. People simply have to have food, clothing, shelter, and medicine at the right time, in the right quantities, and at the right place on a regular basis. In other words, just like the captain of the wind-tossed ship in Aristotle's example of a mixed action, economic agents may sometimes be forced to trade under less than optimal conditions because of the need to complete an exchange within a specified time period. Or take the case of Zimmerman's (1981a) Q, stranded and starving on the island to which kidnapper A had brought him. Q does not have the option of isolating himself on the island from both A and B à la Robinson Crusoe. At some point, if he is to satisfy his hunger, Q simply has to "bite the bullet" and transact with B or even with unsavory, criminal, A, and at the most unfavorable, exploitative terms at that. This brings to mind Raz's (1982: 112) earlier observation on how individual autonomy is inversely proportional to the urgency of one's personal needs.

The market's freedom of association is limited by the pressing demands of time and place utility; people simply have to go to the market to earn some purchasing power and to procure their basic needs. Only people who do not have to do either of these can be said to enjoy true freedom of association. Thus, in refuting Friedman's claim of extensive freedoms for market participants in his proviso (b) (see above quote), C. B. MacPherson argues: "The proviso that is required to make every transaction strictly voluntary is *not* freedom to enter into any *particular* exchange, but freedom not to enter into any exchange *at all*. This, and only this, . . . would prove . . . to be voluntary and non-coercive" (MacPherson 1973: 146 [emphasis original]).

Atomized economic agency

The perfectly competitive market is the benchmark against which all other market structures are examined and evaluated. An essential feature of this model is that all market participants (consumers, producers, suppliers of factors of production) are price-takers. This means that individual economic agents, acting alone, do not affect market prices in their buying or selling behavior. There are just too many other buyers and sellers in the marketplace.

The upside to this phenomenon is that it precludes exploitative behavior. No one can act as a monopolist in maximizing economic profits by setting prices and quantities that are patently disadvantageous for the rest of the community. The downside to this, however, is the inability of well-intentioned economic agents, acting singly on their own, to change and make market outcomes and processes more fair and in line with larger societal goals. For example, conscientious employers may want to pay their workers a living wage. However, they are constrained by the workings of the market. Should they pay such wages, their cost of production would increase substantially, and they would have to face the predicament of either raising their prices (and driving themselves out of the market) or sustaining large financial losses. Either choice is unappealing; both in fact would lead to the closure of their businesses, to the detriment of the employees themselves who would suddenly find themselves unemployed. These benevolent employers need to solicit the cooperation of their competitors to follow suit and provide a living wage for their own employees. This way, no one is penalized in the market, and everyone is on a level playing field. Unfortunately, not even such an extensive industry-wide cooperation is good enough. In an age of global economic integration, cheaper imports from low-cost areas of the world can easily be brought in to compete with the industry's resulting higher prices. Thus, we are back to square one: benevolent employers having inadvertently priced themselves and their employees out of the market. In other words, only with the cooperation of ever larger circles of people will we be able to effect changes in market outcomes and processes from within the market itself.[22]

In practice, we know that actual markets are far from perfectly competitive. Nonetheless, the atomization of individual economic agency is still readily apparent, especially with the onset of globalization. First

---

22 The quick and easy way of effecting such market changes, of course, is through government fiat.

World unions have been up in arms, bitterly lamenting the loss of their hard-won gains as jobs have moved overseas to cheaper manufacturing sites. Eager to acquire foreign direct investments, many developing nations are believed to have loosened their labor and environmental regulations to give them a further competitive edge in lowering their production costs. This is not even to mention the generous fiscal conces-sions that are lavished on multinational companies, a practice that is common even among states within the United States that are competing with each other for choice foreign-owned factories. Even the Fortune 500, the largest of the world's corporations that are supposed to be the primary beneficiaries and movers of global economic integration, are forced to comply with the regimen of the market, as evident from the constant stream of mergers, acquisitions, and bankruptcies within their ranks. And to bring home the point of the power of markets, observe that not even nation-states themselves are immune from the rigors of the marketplace, as seen in the recent efforts in Europe to curtail long-standing generous welfare benefits in order to stay competitive in international markets (Hirst and Thompson 1999: 163–90). Even countries acting in concert with each other are often unable to defend vital national currencies from disruptive speculative attacks in the foreign exchange markets. These observations support critics of free trade who have long argued that globalization is nothing but a "race to the bottom," a phenomenon that is possible largely because of the atomization of economic agency. Stated in its corollary formulation, the "race to the bottom" is in effect a revealing demonstration, not so much of the relative weakness of individ-ual economic agency, as of the power of the marketplace to discipline and shape the economic behavior not only of individuals, or of corporations, but even of entire sovereign nations themselves. In fact, a positive side to capital mobility is its ability to curtail irresponsible and improvident fiscal policies in developing countries that are dependent on international financing.

In summary, the atomization of economic agency in which people are unable to affect market processes or outcomes singly on their own is a double-edged sword. Such a price-taking feature of the marketplace enhances the freedom of all by precluding monopolistic predatory prac-tices. However, it also cuts the other way. Flawed market operations can be rectified only with the cooperation of a wide circle of economic agents acting in concert with each other. In other words, the expansive autonomy that the marketplace is said to afford *homo oeconomicus* does not include the freedom to redress flaws in market outcomes or processes, nor does it include the liberty to work toward larger societal noneconomic goals. Individual economic agents, acting alone, are compelled to conform to the market's primary and overriding goal of economic efficiency, that is, allocating scarce resources to their most valued uses. Market participants must simply accept the social valuation (prices) of goods and services that they buy or sell, including their own services and assets. These have to be taken as given parameters. And even within imperfectly competitive markets, most economic agents still have very little control over the market prices they face.

Bounded rationality

Both the methodological individualism[23] of neoclassical economics and the broad autonomy it ascribes to *homo oeconomicus* lead to the discipline's view that economic agents know and pursue what is in their best interest and seek to satisfy their preferences within the constraints of their income and market prices. In other words, *homo oeconomicus* is a rational agent engaged in a never-ending cycle of calculations that process a large and constant stream of information; economic behavior and decisions are adjusted accordingly as new data are received, processed, and interpreted. This process is described as instrumental rationality (Heap 1989: 39–55). Economic agency can be likened to a mechanical, mathematical exercise for reaching the optimal solution to a complex, dynamic, maximization problem.

Herbert Simon (1976) is skeptical of instrumental rationality because the sheer volume of information to be considered in a full and genuine optimization exercise far exceeds human computational abilities. There is simply a surfeit of choices in addition to the constant flow of data that must be sifted, understood, analyzed, and then used. There is such a superfluity of alternatives to be weighed that instrumental rationality would have merely paralyzed people into indecision and inaction in the face of a seemingly indeterminate solution to the problem-solving exercise. Moreover, market participants would have had little time for anything else outside of these interminable maximization calculations. Thus, Simon hypothesizes that economic agents "satisfice" rather than maximize. In other words, far from subjecting every decision to an instrumental calculus of gains versus losses, people simply follow predetermined rules and

---

23 Methodological individualism is the view that individuals are the key determinants shaping social phenomena.

procedures. The resulting choices will most likely not be the optimum outcome that maximizes consumer welfare or business profits, but they have immense utility in greatly simplifying and reducing the requisite calculations faced by market participants. People simply follow rules of thumb; Simon calls this procedural rationality.

At its root, Simon's procedural rationality is ultimately about making choices against a larger backdrop of societal custom, law, and usage. After all, it is really these pre-established conventions that streamline and expedite instrumental rationality's endless exercise in optimizing computations; it is these widely accepted norms that avert the indeterminacy given the overwhelming selection of choices available to *homo oeconomicus*. Conventions establish de facto procedures on how people interact with each other in the marketplace. Formal and informal rules arise and shape people's behavior. Equally important is how these emergent standards, whether spoken or unspoken, set expectations. This process can be described as bounded rationality in which economic agents conform to the rules and standards of their social environment.[24]

Markets require prior agreements if they are to work properly. Trading, after all, presupposes common institutions. The seemingly spontaneous emergence of buying and selling is actually supported by an intricate social infrastructure. Historically, the shift away from autarkic feudalism is in large part due to the advent of fairs, banking, laws, and other institutions conducive to commerce (North and Thomas 1973: 134–38; Rosenberg and Birdzell 1986: 113–43). Of note is the need for an enforceable system of property rights if the market is to be viable at all. Thus, while the modern marketplace may seem to be unencumbered on the surface, it is in fact undergirded by a labyrinth of rule-governed and rule-setting institutions. Alan Shipman (2002) traces the necessary legal, epistemological, ontological, organizational, corporate, and financial foundations that lay the groundwork for what is arguably the modern market's most distinctive accomplishment: expansive liberties for *homo oeconomicus*.

In summary, it is paradoxical that markets have such a capacity to empower people with autonomy only because of their (markets') underlying discipline and order flowing from the institutions that shore them up. It turns out that the much-vaunted freedom of market participants is in fact sustained by a strict set of standards. This is significant for our purposes because it reveals how the liberties enjoyed by economic agents

24 See Heap (1989: 116–47) for a more in-depth discussion of bounded rationality.

are in fact very much a function of, indeed delimited by, a wide array of conventions that make market exchange possible in the first place. In other words, the broad autonomy of *homo oeconomicus* is in fact expansive only within the bounds of the marketplace's established rules and conventions.

Instrumental rationality (with its attendant sweeping autonomy) rests on a number of critical premises. In assuming a frictionless economy, neoclassical economics in effect makes completing market transactions costless. Simon's (1976) concerns over the computational limitations and inefficiencies of *homo oeconomicus* are assumed away by ascribing perfect information to perfectly competitive markets. In both cases, there is no longer any need for procedural (bounded) rationality's advantage of lowering the cost of requisite calculations. Moreover, the freedom to exit the market at will and be a Robinson Crusoe is taken as a premise for neoclassical analysis because it assumes an economy that is ahistorical, asocial, complete, and fully informed. The autonomy of *homo oeconomicus* is delimited to the degree these theoretical assumptions are violated in practice.

Pecuniary externalities

Neoclassical economics is the predominant approach to economic analysis and thinking. It is a powerful school of thought that has opened new horizons both in understanding economic life and in devising appropriate policy. However, I submit that one must exercise caution in using neoclassical economics by recognizing the limitations of translating its analytical insights into actual policy and practice, especially when it comes to matters of fairness. In particular, mainstream economics does not deal with the problem of unintended consequences of concern to us because of (1) its criterion of potential, rather than actual, compensation and (2) its differential treatment of technological and pecuniary externalities. Each of these is discussed in what follows. But first, it is necessary to take a closer look at the nature of pecuniary externalities.

As mentioned earlier, externalities are unintended consequences inflicted on third parties and come in two forms: technological or pecuniary.[25] The classic example of a technological externality is that of a factory

---

25 Technological externalities are included in what are sometimes called "'neighborhood effects' – effects on third parties for which it is not feasible to charge or recompense them" (Friedman 1962: 14, 30–32).

discharging its waste by-products into the air and water. Unless it is forced by government or the public to clean up after itself, the offending firm has no incentive at all to curtail or change its polluting industrial processes since it is able to shift the cost to others – the surrounding neighborhoods and villages downstream that have to put up with foul air and water. In calculating its cost of production, the factory fails to account for and incorporate the disvalue of a dirtier environment that results from its operations.[26] The most common usage of the term *externality* pertains to this nonpecuniary variant in which there is a divergence between social and private cost or benefit.[27]

Pecuniary externalities, on the other hand, are unintended consequences that are mediated through the market principally by way of changes in price and quantity. Price adjustments are the very dynamic that brings about allocative efficiency; they are the single most defining feature that imbues the market with its yet unparalleled ability to put scarce resources to their most valued uses. After all, price is the only mechanism that is able to convey a large volume of information efficiently, simultaneously, and in a timely fashion across a multitude of widely dispersed parties. The conclusive failure and subsequent implosion of the Soviet-style economies of the last century provide vivid empirical evidence of the central importance of heeding price signals.

Price adjustments precipitate corresponding changes in the decisions of economic agents, thereby leading to a redisposition of scarce resources within the community. This ability of price to shape individual economic behavior has long been recognized and effectively employed in public policy. For example, taxes have been imposed to dissuade the use of cigarettes, alcohol, gasoline, and carbon fuels; user fees have been successfully employed to relieve traffic congestion in city centers such as London during business hours. In the same way, subsidies for dairy products, the arts, and other merit goods have been used to encourage healthful consumption. Likewise, differential pricing between off-peak and peak hours for electricity, airline seats, toll roads, and bus or subway fares has been a valuable tool for avoiding needless spare capacity and for husbanding resources by smoothing out usage. Deposit-refund schemes have been mandated for bottles and cans to encourage recycling. In other words,

---

26 In the language of economics, there is a disparity between the firm's private cost and the social cost of its activity. Technological externalities, such as pollution, arise because firms do not have to internalize the social cost of their economic decisions unless forced to do so via extra-market mechanisms such as government regulations or taxes.

27 For a quick technical overview of externalities see Scitovsky (1954) and Bator (1958).

price changes have been effective in altering private behavior. At sufficiently punitive levels, such deliberate price adjustments can even compel economic agents to act against their own preferences (as in giving up smoking altogether due to its exorbitant cost). Price adjustments are instrumental, indeed necessary, both in bringing about allocative efficiency and in pursuing public policy through the mediation of the market (as in the US Clean Air Act that allows for trading in emission rights as a way of reducing pollution).

There is a coercive dimension to pecuniary externalities precisely because of the effective ability of prices to induce changes in individual choices. Some of these behavioral changes may be purely voluntary, while others may be of the "mixed action" described by Aristotle in his example of the windswept ship. Thus, during California's energy crisis in 2000–2001, the state's unfulfilled demand for electricity resulted in a sudden increase in energy prices for all other users in the region, forcing most to adopt drastic conservation restrictions. China has emerged as a low-cost manufacturing powerhouse, and its transactions to supply European and American importers with cheaper goods and services have put competing suppliers from many other countries, including the United States and Europe, out of business and in search of alternative livelihoods. Foreign direct investments, seeking higher returns, have been disproportionately pouring into China, thereby leaving very little for other emerging nations. This translates into anemic job creation for countries like the Philippines and Indonesia, compelling many of their unemployed to migrate abroad as domestic servants. The torrid pace of China's economy has resulted in a rapid increase in its oil consumption, leading to much higher petroleum prices for everybody else in the world. All these are examples of pecuniary externalities because it is the marketplace that generates price adjustments that are then transmitted as ripple effects to other economic agents that were not even party to the original transactions that caused the shocks in the first place.

Pecuniary externalities are not peculiar to modernity; rather, they are intrinsic to market exchange itself. Thus, early in the Industrial Revolution, the Luddites lobbied the English parliament to ban mechanization in the textile industry that had deprived them of their livelihoods. Even earlier, medieval guilds went so far as to severely regulate their members' innovative changes to their craft or credit-sales practices. The guilds' interest lay not merely in protecting consumers by imposing some quality control; they were also keenly concerned with preventing craftsmen from imaginative, but disruptive, product improvements or overly generous credit-sales terms that would severely undercut their peers in the market. This was a case of preempting guild members from inflicting hurtful pecuniary externalities on each other.

As mentioned earlier, neoclassical economics does not deal with the unintended consequences of concern to us in this study because of its inadequate compensation criterion and its asymmetric treatment of technological and pecuniary externalities. First, for mainstream economic theory, economic changes are warranted for as long as the gains exceed the losses from such a move. Whether or not winners actually compensate losers is outside the scope of neoclassical economic analysis. It is merely concerned with the capacity to provide theoretical, rather than actual, recompense. Second, observe the unequal treatment of technological and pecuniary externalities in neoclassical economics. Technological external- ities are deemed to be market failures deserving of policy correction because they cause inefficiencies. On the other hand, pecuniary external- ities (such as having to shut down a business due to the influx of cheaper imports or outsourcing) are not a cause for policy intervention because these price or quantity adjustments are mediated through the market and are in fact the very mechanism by which the marketplace achieves its much-heralded strength of husbanding the use of scarce resources.[28] And indeed, the efficacy of the market lies in its ability to optimize the allocation of scarce resources to their most valued uses even in the midst of a constantly changing environment.

Such responsive agility is illustrated in the famous wager between environmentalist Paul Erhlich and economist Julian Simon (Beckerman 1997). Ehrlich took out a bet with Simon that the prices of five metals would increase over a decade as evidence of the world's worsening scarcity of natural resources. Simon won the wager; prices even dropped during this period. But even if the prices had indeed risen, they had a built-in corrective mechanism. As the price of a commodity increases (indicating scarcity), people are encouraged to search for new sources, develop substitutes, or economize on its use through greater engineering efficien- cies. The intensity of the latter efforts is directly proportional to the price increases as a result of scarcity. Thus, price is an effective medium, not

---

28 Hausman (1992: 104) points out that both Scitovsky (1954) and Shubik (1971) observe that pecuniary externalities "disappear in static general equilibrium" and are consequently not of concern for mainstream neoclassical economics. In mixed economies, however, some pecuniary externalities are addressed by policymakers because of their dire consequences. Thus, we have unemployment insurance, workmen's compensation, and trade adjustment assistance programs. These are decisions flowing from political economy, however, and not from the requirements or concerns of neoclassical economic theory.

only for imposing discipline but also for directing effort and attention toward resources' most pressing and valued applications. This is reflective of the market's ability to allocate finite supplies of natural resources efficiently. Pecuniary externalities are not only unavoidable, they are at the heart of what the market is all about. The view of market activity as "a process of discovery" driven by price signals (Kirzner 1990) is testimony to the positive aspects of its unintended consequences.

Nevertheless, for all their positive contributions, I argue that just like their technological variant, pecuniary externalities should not be left unattended and unaddressed by policymakers. These price adjustments effect income and wealth redistributions that often drive people into economic distress. To make matters worse, these burdens are often imposed on the very people who are least capable of dealing with such disruptions.[29]

COERCIVE MARKET OUTCOMES AND PROCESSES

Remote and proximate causes

The second and third sections of this chapter examined the formal characteristics of what constitutes coercion and economic compulsion. The preceding section assessed limitations to the much-touted broad autonomy that the market is claimed to confer on its participants. It now remains for us to put these conceptual insights together and to show why and how it is that market outcomes and processes can beget economic compulsion.

Economic compulsion arises from at least three remote causes (circumscribed freedom of association, atomized economic agency, and bounded rationality) and two proximate causes (pecuniary externalities and economic contingency). As seen in the preceding section, the market plays a large, albeit nonexclusive, role in shaping the opportunities available to economic agents. Recall the following conditions encountered in the marketplace:

1 In a modern economy, no economic agent has the option to be a Robinson Crusoe at will and simply walk away from the market. People have to trade by necessity as they can satisfy their basic needs only through exchanges in the marketplace. [circumscribed freedom of association]

---

29 The next chapter illustrates this regressive phenomenon.

2 Market exchange operates according to pre-established, widely accepted conventions. In other words, market participation implies having to conform to heteronomous rules. [bounded rationality]

3 Market participants are price-takers and cannot change market outcomes or processes through their individual efforts alone. In other words, they cannot readily tailor the terms and conditions of market operations to their own liking or benefit. [atomized economic agency]

These three constraints are foundational for economic compulsion because they define the boundaries of market participants' freedom of action. Economic agents have to participate in the marketplace and, in so doing, live by its rules. And since they cannot influence market operations according to their own benefit or preference, they have to choose from among existing offers in the market. They can select from these available offers, but they cannot choose to opt out completely of the marketplace indefinitely even if the entire selection of alternatives is appalling. Borrowing Albert Hirschman's (1970) language of "exit or voice," I claim that market participants can neither choose to exit from the marketplace nor give voice to their convictions in reshaping the selection of market choices, even in those cases where none of the available alternatives can be considered acceptable by any reasonable person under normal conditions. Thus, these three market features are aptly described as remote causes of economic compulsion. Put in McGregor's (1988–89) framework, *homo oeconomicus* is in a radically inferior bargaining position relative to the market as an institution. In fact, there is no "bargaining" at all since economic agents are price-takers and can only choose from whatever the market offers. But they can neither change the terms of the offers, nor completely forego transacting in the marketplace for an indefinite period of time. At some point, they simply have to accept the least unattractive offer should they find all of them to be disagreeable.

McMillan (2002: 6) describes a market transaction as "an exchange that is voluntary: each party can veto it, and (subject to the rules of the marketplace) each freely agrees to the terms." The degree of autonomy accorded by the market, however, may be more apparent than real. Thus, in the case of the poor, McMillan readily concedes that such a freedom to transact and improve one's lot is quite limited because of what little they bring to the market. I go further than this observation and employ McGregor's (1988–89) insights on disparities in bargaining power to conclude that such delimited autonomy not only applies to the destitute but is also true for all economic agents because they are merely price-takers.

However, McMillan is correct in his observation in the sense that the poor, as price-takers themselves, are in an even worse position than other, average, market participants, who are presumably better able to fend for themselves through their better purchasing power.

The foregoing three remote causes of economic compulsion (circumscribed freedom of association, atomization of economic agency, and bounded rationality) do not by themselves mean that the available choices faced by the economic agent will necessarily be unappealing. All these three constraints require is that *homo oeconomicus* has to make a choice even if all the alternatives happen to be repulsive. Rather, it is the pecuniary externalities that are immediately responsible for shaping the scope and quality of the choices available to *homo oeconomicus*.[30]

As discussed in the preceding section, pecuniary externalities refer to the changes in the prices and economic opportunities that people face in their market transactions; they can be disruptive in their effects. This dynamic is necessary because it is only when price adjustments compel simultaneous and timely changes in the decisions and behavior of widely dispersed economic agents that the economy moves toward an optimum equilibrium in allocative efficiency. This is a strength unique to price signals alone that no other social mechanism is able to replicate. The problem is that there are collateral costs to such a process just as there are attendant benefits. Moreover, such consequent burdens can be regressive in the way they are dispersed across the community (see chapter 2).

Adverse pecuniary externalities are the proximate causes of economic compulsion in addition to the chance and contingency of economic life. Using Raz's terminology, we can refer to negative market ripple effects as "noncoercive interferences" to contrast them with direct and deliberate interpersonal coercive threats.

[N]oncoercive interferences with a person's life and fortunes may also reduce his or her autonomy in the same way as coercive interventions do. The only differences are that *all* coercive interventions invade autonomy and they do so intentionally, whereas only *some* noncoercive interventions do so and usually as a by-product of their intended results. They are *not* direct assaults on the autonomy of persons. (Raz 1982: 122 [original emphasis])

Raz makes the same distinction as I did earlier in differentiating coercion from compulsion in terms of the requisite intentionality for the former. Even more important, observe how his characterization of

---

30 See Bartlett (1989) for an exposition on how market operations can change power relations between people.

noncoercive interferences as inadvertent by-products is a fitting description of the deleterious unintended consequences of market transactions. After all, the intended result of an economic exchange is to improve the welfare of at least one of the transactors; unfortunately, third parties can suffer collateral damage from such transactions due to the interdependent nature of market operations.

By definition, these inadvertent detrimental market outcomes worsen people's choice set. The question is whether the adjustments wrought are so severe as to drive them to forego some of their nontrivial interests. Again, Raz provides insightful observations on human autonomy that aptly describe the nature of economic life:

Autonomy is possible only within a framework of constraints. The completely autonomous person is an impossibility. The ideal of the perfect existentialist with no fixed biological and social nature who creates himself as he goes along is an incoherent dream. An autonomous personality can only develop and flourish against a background of biological and social constraints which fix some of its human needs. Some choices are inevitably determined by those needs. Yet, *harsh natural conditions can reduce the degree of autonomy of a person to a bare minimum just as effectively as a systematic coercive intervention.* (Raz 1982: 112 [emphasis added])

I propose that the marketplace is part of Raz's unavoidable "framework of constraints." After all, as we have already seen, all market decisions are constrained choices. Moreover, the market is among the "natural conditions" that are capable of "noncoercive interferences."[31] Recall that part of a person's social nature is the need to engage in economic exchange with others in order to satisfy personal needs without undue hardship. Unfortunately, such necessary dependence on others can occasionally contract rather than expand personal autonomy. The marketplace can alternate in being exacting or benevolent just like the other "natural conditions" that envelop human experience.

For good or for ill, these unavoidable pecuniary externalities change the all-important baseline of what would have been the normal course of events. The market's subsidiary effects can occasionally damage people's baseline to the point at which any proposal would make them better off, even if it were the most appalling, exploitative, and disagreeable proposition. These harmful pecuniary externalities precipitate what Wertheimer (1987: 233) calls "very hard choices" that leave people in dire straits with unpalatable choices.

---

31 I use the term *noncoercive* only in the sense that these interferences are not intentional. Even if they are unintended, they can nonetheless still give rise to economic compulsion.

In summary, (1) limits to the freedom of association, (2) a bounded rationality that sets the rules for market exchange, (3) an atomized economic agency in which people are price-takers and are consequently unable to influence or change market processes on their own, (4) ceaseless price and quantity adjustments that induce both beneficial and harmful market ripple effects (pecuniary externalities), and (5) chance and contingency are the constitutive elements, indeed, the remote and proximate causes, of economic compulsion.

Revisiting Zimmerman's baseline

Zimmerman's (1981a and b) case of kidnapped and stranded Q is an excellent parallel for the plight of severely constrained market participants. Recall that A kidnaps Q, strands him on the beach, and then offers Q a horrible job knowing full well that Q's only other option is to starve. By both Zimmerman's and Wertheimer's standards, A's proposal is coercive.

Bounded rationality embodies the collective agency of the community; the market can be viewed as a corporate person. According to Zimmerman's baseline, A's proposition is coercive because A is actively delimiting Q's options. Q could have been working in a better job on the mainland had it not been for A's kidnapping Q and bringing him to the island. In the same way, the market could be viewed as irreversibly shaping the opportunities available to economic agents through the path dependence[32] intrinsic to economic life.

The four features of the market just discussed are no different from A's delimiting Q's choices by stranding him on the island and then offering Q an appalling job. *Homo oeconomicus* is in the same situation as Q, completely at the mercy of whatever the market is able to offer. It is the market that determines the prices of the goods and services that *homo oeconomicus* needs. It is also the market that sets the price at which *homo oeconomicus* is able to sell his/her production or services to raise the much-needed purchasing power to procure the means for survival and health. In fact, any proposition that the market provides, no matter how unappealing or exploitative, will always be better than the alternative of starving.

However, there is a limit to how far we can employ Zimmerman's baseline. While the market is directly responsible for shaping the

---

32 Path dependence means that history matters. Earlier events shape later events.

immediate opportunities available to people (just like A delimiting Q's choices), the market is nevertheless *only partially responsible* for the "circumstances" facing economic agents in most cases (unlike A, who bears full accountability for Q's plight in Zimmerman's case). As mentioned earlier, market participants, under normal conditions, are also partly answerable for what they bring to the marketplace based on their previous investments in their own human capital and on their work effort and initiative. Thus, unlike Zimmerman's case, we are unable to go so far as to claim immediately that the market is coercive because it is necessary to weigh first both the distressed economic agents' and the market's fulfillment of their respective obligations. Economic circumstances are the joint outcomes of both the market (through its pecuniary externalities) and the economic agents' striving, both present and past. One's social and historical location is neither always nor purely a matter of accident; personal choices can and often do affect such positioning.

WHO BEARS RESPONSIBILITY FOR AMELIORATING ECONOMIC COMPULSION?

Circumstantial versus interpersonal coercion

There is disagreement over whether circumstances can "coerce" since this phenomenon is by nature interpersonal. Indeed, most of the cases examined in the philosophical literature pertain to coercion between moral agents. For many, it makes no sense at all to talk of circumstances coercing people.

To dispute whether or not circumstances per se can coerce people would divert us from our current study. Instead, I will limit myself to arguing that the circumstances that compel economic agents to give up nontrivial claims in order to satisfy other vital interests are ultimately founded on moral agency, both collective and individual.

First, as seen earlier, economic agents are partly accountable for their purchasing power based on what they bring to the market. Recall that earnings and economic opportunities are partially a function of personal initiative, effort, and past investments in human capital formation.

Second, bounded rationality is largely the result of communal agency. This has significant ramifications for moral discourse. For mainstream economics, the impact of conventions on autonomy is not as important since economics is viewed solely as a pure exercise of choosing appropriate means for specified ends within complete and fully functioning markets (instrumental rationality). How we got to these markets, what processes were involved, and what necessary prior agreements had to be put in place are beside the point. Mainstream neoclassical analysis can get around the problem of accounting for conventions because of its underlying mechanistic, Newtonian view[33] of the economic order.[34] It simply takes these customs as given parameters to be factored in as constraints in the economic agent's maximization exercise. Unfortunately, such a practice is unsatisfactory since conventions cannot be assumed away; they are germane to the market process itself and are pivotal in establishing fairness in the initial, pre-market, arrangements. Because conventions have such a determinative role in market outcomes, it is essential to know who is ultimately responsible for fashioning such established norms.

Bounded rationality suggests that there is an operative corporate agency in the background accountable for the economic circumstances that compel people to make desperate choices. Economic exchange occurs within the bounds of the custom, law, and usage of the institutions that shore up the market, indeed, that make it possible to begin with. In other words, people must conform to the rules of the market if they want to participate in it. However, it is the market participants themselves – together as a group – who are responsible for giving rise to, maintaining, and then further reinforcing such conventions.

While institutions are important in shaping market dynamics and outcomes, there is also a reverse causation in the process. Market activities serve to form and strengthen these institutions. The aggregated effect of the individual actions of economic agents feeds back into developing and entrenching these institutions further through their widespread acceptance and usage. The market has properties of a network externality.[35]

Recall the Dutch contribution to the Commercial Revolution that preceded the Industrial Revolution (North and Thomas 1973: 134–38). At the heart of establishing markets was the need to deal with the transaction costs of searching, bargaining, and enforcing contracts among medieval economic agents widely dispersed across distant and isolated

---

33 See Mirowski (1989) for an exposition on this view.
34 This is in sharp contrast to the evolutionary, institutional schools of economic thought.
35 A network externality is best explained with examples. Take the case of money. A new currency's viability is dependent on its acceptance and adoption by people. Thus, the more the currency is used by market participants, the greater is its attractiveness in serving as a medium of exchange or as a store of value. People would want to hold on to it because it provides ready liquidity. A more recent example of a network externality is eBay. The value of utilizing the site as a venue for buying or selling increases further as more people use it.

communities. Underdeveloped transportation and communications further compounded the difficulties of market exchange. Thus, it is not surprising that animal husbandry (production for onsite consumption rather than for exchange) was the predominant economic activity of the era. Periodic fairs proved to be pivotal in bringing buyers and sellers together. The Dutch took advantage of their strategic location, hosted these fairs on a permanent basis, and put together the rudimentary institutional elements that make a market what it is today. Besides facilitating a transparent and greater flow of information that let everyone know prevailing prices for particular commodities, the market brought with it an additional benefit: network externality. The more people utilized the Dutch markets, the wider was the selection of products made available, the more intense the competition, and the greater the incentive for other buyers and sellers to come and congregate in the market in the subsequent rounds of economic exchange. This latter cumulative effect is an example of a network externality. The repeated use of and conformity to the conventions of the market's background institutions create a demonstration effect for others and also produce the necessary scale that secures these foundations even further. Conventions, after all, are a human creation; this includes the market, notwithstanding its mechanistic order in the neoclassical view of economic life.

One's participation in the market generates the nonpecuniary externality of augmenting its underlying institutions further, even if this result is unintended. This adds an important twist to our examination of the freedom of market participants. It is not merely our own decisions or wants that are relevant to our own personal economic lives. In addition to the pecuniary externalities discussed in the preceding sections, the collective trading patterns and behavior of others also affect us (even if we are not party to their trade) in a second roundabout manner – through their reinforcement of the background institutions that sustain the operations of the market. In effect, their joint market behavior indirectly shapes our own opportunities when we face the decision on where, how much, and what to trade, or even whether to trade at all. Of course, such nonpecuniary, network externality cuts both ways. Our personal economic decisions likewise ultimately affect others through our own contribution in further entrenching prevailing market rules.[36] All this is important

36 In other words, path dependency arising from emerging conventions in the economic order, and, consequently, path dependency in economic freedom, are a function not merely of our own actions, but of others' as well.

because, as already mentioned, conventions impinge directly on the problem of transaction costs in which the expenses of searching, bargaining, and enforcement within the marketplace are determined by its supporting institutions.

Thus, the conventions and institutions undergirding the marketplace are ultimately and properly the shared economic agency of the community. The market is not just some impersonal, amoral institution. It has a corporate personality, and its outcomes and processes can be correctly attributed to human agency. For example, it is the combined effect of consumer confidence that is responsible for the amplitude and duration of business cycles of booms and busts. It is the joint speculative avarice of people that fuels the numerous infamous bubbles in economic history (Cohen 1997). It is consumers' dollar votes that determine the products and services that will be developed and that find their way to the market. Moreover, it is also consumer preferences that assign relative economic value to the societal contribution of various professions. Excessive disparities in the pay of highly sought athletes and entertainers relative to teachers and nurses are ultimately the shared responsibility of a society that has embraced a "winner-take-all" ethos (Frank and Cook 1996).

Such corporate agency is symmetric. In the same way that people can collectively perpetuate undesirable market outcomes and processes, they can also act together to achieve larger, noble, societal goals. Thus, it is also moral agency that is at the heart of changing the unethical marketing practices in selling baby formula in the Third World (Sethi 1994). It is also the consumer dollar votes that strengthen the campaign to improve the harsh working conditions faced by migrant agricultural workers. It is the willingness of economic agents to pay a higher price for coffee that has improved the lot of many farmers dependent on their coffee cash crops (Starnes 2002). It is the unrelenting pressure from concerned students that has prevented many collegiate athletic products from being manufactured in sweatshops (Benjamin 2000; Featherstone and United Students Against Sweatshops 2002). It is the threat of a besmirched name brand that has led multinationals to be more involved in vetting their subcontractors and closely monitoring their employment practices. The list could go on.

The customs, laws, and usage undergirding market institutions are ultimately the responsibility of moral agency – both personal and collective. Even if they are merely price-takers and atomized in their individual economic decisions, people are nevertheless still able to exercise their freedom by banding together. The "voice" (Hirschman 1970) that can reshape market operations may not be possible at the level of the individual, but communal "voice" has proven itself to be very effective. Thus, human agency is liable for acts of omission since aggregated agency can be used for achieving or restoring the good that may have been sullied. More important, it can override the atomization of individual economic decisions and effect changes in market operations either from within the marketplace or through extra-market remedies.

One can use the language and reasoning of neoclassical economics itself to argue for such a concerted venture. There is a convergence between the social optimum and the individual good in perfectly competitive markets in which no one enjoys a "threat advantage" over anyone else and in which people are assumed to know and pursue what is in their best interest. The obverse of this is, of course, the need for a cooperative solution in regimes of imperfectly competitive markets where there are extreme disparities in bargaining strengths or a dearth of information.

> When there is a market failure because of, for example, externalities, the market no longer produces optimal states when participants act to maximize their individual welfare. The presence of externalities leads to divergence between optimality and utility maximization. The difference between the two may be recovered by *cooperation*. Under cooperation each agent's decisions are aimed at a *joint strategy*; the perfectly competitive market, in contrast, is the paradigm of *independent*, non-cooperative choice. People will be motivated to cooperate because they can increase their welfare by doing so.
>
> (McGregor 1988–89: 30 [original emphasis])

The exercise of cooperative moral agency in shaping market outcomes and processes is a necessary condition if we are to avert economic compulsion or redress its ill effects. Thus, as part II argues, uncorrected adverse pecuniary externalities are reflective of a failure of both personal and corporate moral agency.

There is one final point regarding joint moral agency. Wertheimer (1987: 309) considers whether or not we should allow human experiments with prisoners in exchange for rewards, or permit organ sales by the poor. After all, many consider these to be coercive in addition to being exploitative. His response is quite enlightening: "[T]he interesting question is not whether the offers are, in some sense, coercive. The interesting questions are these: Can persons in such conditions make intelligent judgments about their interests? *Does society have an obligation to provide them with better alternatives?*" (Wertheimer 1987: 309–10 [emphasis added]).

The desperate choices of the prisoners or of the poor in the above cases are no different from the millions of migrant workers who have had to leave family and homeland in search of a livelihood, or of children who have had to forego their education to work and supplement their family's meager income. It is no different from people who are driven to accept menial, dangerous, or distasteful employment for lack of better alternatives in the marketplace. Is there a communal obligation to improve the choice set available to these people who have been forced to sacrifice vital interests for the sake of their other unmet nontrivial claims?

CONCLUSION

In recounting a natural history of markets in his book *Reinventing the Bazaar*, McMillan (2002) observes that the market is not a zero-sum phenomenon and can bestow benefits on all parties to an exchange. In fact, this is a particular strength of the market that few other social institutions are able to replicate and make widely available.

> The key feature of markets of all kinds is brought home when we look at the growth of new market mechanisms. Benefiting both buyer and seller, *any transaction creates value.* (Since either party can veto the deal, it must be making both of them better off, in their own eyes, than not trading.) Buying and selling is therefore *a form of creation.* Elementary as this point is, its importance cannot be overstated. There are gains from trade . . .
>
> (McMillan 2002: 26 [emphasis added])[37]

History itself attests to the enormous gains that can be reaped, as evidenced by the past two hundred years of phenomenal economic growth. This accomplishment is possible in large part because of a division of labor and its concomitant expansion of market exchange as people share their produce with each other and, in the process, satisfy their own needs. The impressive gains brought about by the market capture well the dynamics of Adam Smith's (1776) "invisible hand."

Markets create value and confer benefits on many, but not all. In fact, there are numerous instances when market exchange leaves detrimental ripple effects in its wake that are often ruinous of people's lives and livelihoods. Third parties who were not even part of the original

---

37 Of course, there is the issue of whether speculative transactions create or destroy value. Arbitrage helps bring the market to its efficient point and could thus be said to create value. Beyond a certain point, however, such arbitrage can wreak havoc, particularly in the foreign exchange markets, as seen in the Asian financial crisis of 1997–98.

transactions often find themselves having to bear the burden of the inadvertent ramifications of these earlier market exchanges. Moreover, not all market transactions are purely voluntary in the sense of being sought or desired by the parties concerned. People are often driven to consummate market exchanges for lack of better alternatives, and, in many cases, what are at risk are not merely trivial claims but human needs whose satisfaction is integral to individual dignity and personhood. Severe economic necessity begets economic compulsion because it makes the destitute vulnerable to accepting unpalatable (even exploitative) proposals for want of better choices.

The nature and dynamics of market outcomes and processes themselves provide both the remote and proximate causes of economic compulsion. The much-touted expansive autonomy of neoclassical *homo oeconomicus* is in reality circumscribed by limits to economic agents' freedom of association, by their price-taking constraint, and by a bounded rationality that sets the parameters of economic decision-making. In addition to these remote causes, pecuniary externalities (unintended consequences to third parties mediated through the market) and economic chance and contingency both furnish the immediate occasion for economic compulsion. It is these unceasing changes in prices and market opportunities within an extremely fluid social environment that expand or contract economic agents' sphere of autonomy and welfare. These pecuniary externalities can precipitate "very hard choices" among unappealing alternatives.

Economic compulsion is ultimately about moral agency, both individual and collective. Under normal conditions, economic agents are partly responsible for shaping the opportunities they face through their striving, personal initiatives, and past investments in their human capital. Moreover, the rules and conventions that govern market operations are human creations that are developed, refined, and reinforced through continued and widespread usage. They can be changed, for better or for worse, through public choice via market exchange or extra-market interventions.

In conclusion, markets are not intrinsically coercive, but neither are they completely noncoercive as neoclassical economics and some philosophers argue. Markets can be both, depending on the circumstances shaping the alternatives facing economic agents and depending on the vital interests that may be put in jeopardy within the choice set of people in distress. Markets can be coercive depending on the nature and severity of the opportunity costs they generate. Moral agents, both as individuals and as a community, are ultimately accountable for the resulting economic compulsion.

CHAPTER 2

The regressive incidence of unintended burdens

The preceding chapter maintained that negative pecuniary externalities can occasion economic compulsion by the nature of market exchange itself. This chapter goes a step further by arguing that such collateral coercive burdens inflicted by market operations are often skewed in their distribution. Pecuniary externalities merit closer scrutiny because not only are transaction costs different across individuals, they are in many cases regressive. In other words, the incidence of harmful unintended consequences mediated through the marketplace often falls disproportionately on the very people who can least afford to bear them. There are at least three reasons for this phenomenon, namely: variations in personal capabilities, wide disparities in the communal valuation of personal endowments, and differences in the private cost of accessing commodities due to people's dissimilar sociohistorical location. Each of these is examined in what follows. But first, it is necessary to lay out the formal theory undergirding these three factors.

THE THEORETICAL FRAMEWORK: THE MARKET AS AN EFFECTIVE PRICE DISCRIMINATOR[1]

Price discrimination occurs when a seller charges consumers different prices for the same good or service. This practice is possible only if sellers are able (1) to distinguish buyers from each other and (2) to prevent resale among consumers. The most well-known example, of course, is the pricing of plane tickets. By imposing restrictions, such as Saturday-night stayovers and advance purchases, airlines separate business travelers from

---

1 Economists may object to my description of the market as a "price discriminator." Note that I am applying the notion of "price discrimination" to the market only in the sense that it is able to charge every market participant a different "full" price, as I hope to show in the next section.

tourists and charge the former much higher prices than the latter.[2] Price discrimination lends itself well as a theoretical underpinning for the claim that the market can be grossly uneven in its never-ending redistribution of burdens and benefits across the community.

Introductory economics textbooks often begin their description of the economy by describing the circular flow of goods, services, and factor inputs between households and businesses – the two major categories of economic agents. Households purchase the goods and services they need from product markets that are kept well stocked by businesses. On the other hand, businesses purchase their requisite inputs (such as labor and capital) from factor markets whose supplies are furnished by the households. There is a circular flow because the incomes earned by households in factor markets (by selling their services and assets) are then spent by the same households to meet their needs from product markets. Such purchases provide revenues for firms, which in turn use them to pay for households' services and assets in the factor input markets. Thus, the cycle is complete. In both cases, prices play *the* pivotal role in regulating the volume and directing the flow of goods, services, and factor inputs within the economy.

Prices are important to every market participant in two ways: They determine both people's income levels and their purchasing power. In factor markets, household earnings are dependent on the prices of services (e.g., wages and salaries) and assets (e.g., dividends and interest on savings). In product markets, prices shape the size and the quality of the basket of goods and services consumers are able to purchase given their incomes. This dual role of prices can be expressed in simple mathematical terms. Take the case of households:[3]

$$
\begin{aligned}
\text{household income} &= \text{household spending} \\
\text{wages} \times \text{hours worked} &= \text{price} \times \text{quantity of commodities}
\end{aligned}
$$

Prices matter for households in their capacity both as consumers (affected by the price of merchandise in product markets) and as sellers of factor inputs (e.g., in the wages they can obtain in exchange for labor services).

In a perfectly competitive market, everyone faces the same price for similar goods and services. After all, in perfectly competitive markets, all

---

2　The second condition of no resale is satisfied by disallowing interpersonal transfers of purchased tickets in the wake of terrorist threats.

3　For this brief exposition, I assume there are no savings, and all incomes are spent. Thus, the household earns no income from capital assets.

economic agents have perfect information (people possess the same data), there are no costs to moving goods and factors of production (perfect mobility), all goods and services are homogeneous, and the presence of so many buyers and sellers precludes monopolistic control of prices. Price discrimination is not possible; the law of one price prevails.

The neoclassical assumptions for perfectly competitive markets are, of course, never achieved in practice. Actual markets carry an entire spectrum of goods and services that are differentiated from each other, thereby enabling sellers to play on consumers' brand loyalty and charge different prices. Information is costly to obtain, process, and use; it is consequently incomplete and asymmetric across economic agents. This opens the door for profit-making opportunities in which people use information that is not widely available to buy cheap and sell high (arbitrage). Goods, services, and factors of production are not perfectly mobile because there are costs incurred in moving them around from one sector to another. In other words, perfectly competitive markets are assumed to be completely frictionless; they are not. In fact, they entail substantial frictional costs. For example, the cost of living is much higher in Alaska and Hawaii than in the rest of the United States because of the considerable expense of transporting merchandise to these far-flung states. Moreover, imperfect mobility impedes ease of entry and exit in industries, thereby allowing some degree of monopolistic or oligopolistic control of prices.

The violation of key neoclassical assumptions for perfectly competitive markets means that the law of one price is never truly observed in actual markets. Imperfect mobility, asymmetric and incomplete information, and proprietary product differentiation give rise to real ancillary costs in searching, negotiating, concluding, and enforcing economic transactions. These transaction costs are added to the cost of production and in fact this marketing cost often comprises the bulk of the final selling price consumers pay. After all, getting the right goods to the right consumers at the right time at the right place and in the right quantities and quality is an expensive undertaking in an actual economy of imperfect information and imperfect mobility.

Market participants do not all face the same set of transaction costs. Economic agents that have access to better data and are adept at processing and using such market information have lower transaction costs compared with people who have neither of these two advantages. More savvy economic actors negotiate better sales terms and prices for themselves. The same holds true for those with a wide and excellent network of friends and acquaintances. Better educated and more seasoned transactors weather economic disruptions better. People with better human capital enjoy greater socioeconomic and geographic mobility compared with those who have minimal skills and confidence. In other words, *transaction costs vary across market participants and are a function of these economic agents' personal attributes and their social and historical location.* Thus, the full price consumers pay for the same goods and services is different depending on the concomitant frictional costs that are incurred. These latter costs are largely, though not exclusively, person-specific.

This phenomenon of person-specific transaction costs can be formalized using the household production model of Gary Becker (1965) and Kelvin Lancaster (1966). The traditional formulation of consumer theory involves people maximizing their utility[4] from their consumption of goods and services subject to their budget constraint.

Maximize : Utility   =   f (apples, movie tickets, books, haircuts, etc.)
subject to : Income   =   price × quantity of goods/services

Observe how goods and services enter directly as arguments in the utility function people maximize.

Becker's and Lancaster's seminal contributions lie in their reformulation of the model describing how economic agents behave. People consume goods and services not for their own sake, but for their characteristics. For example, food is consumed not as an end in itself but for its instrumental capacity to dispel hunger and provide nutrients. People watch movies, spend time in the museum, or go to the theater not as ends in themselves, but to derive recreation, aesthetic pleasure, fellowship, and rest. Students do not buy books or matriculate in schools for their own sake, but for the knowledge they acquire from these resources. In other words, consumers desire the attendant qualities these goods and services provide, and not the goods or services themselves. Becker and Lancaster call these much-sought qualities "commodities" to distinguish them from the actual goods and services that are purchased in the market. It is these commodities that are directly incorporated into the utility functions that people maximize. Goods and services purchased and consumed in the process enter the utility function only in an indirect manner. Thus, rewriting the traditional consumer utility function, we have:

4 A utility is a measure of people's satisfaction.

Maximize : Utility = f (nourishment, rest, fellowship, knowledge, etc.)
where
nourishment = f (food, time for cooking, time for eating, etc.)
rest, fellowship = f (movie-theater tickets, time, etc.)
knowledge = f (books, school tuition, time for studying, etc.)

To draw out these much-needed qualities, people require at least three key resources: (1) goods and services purchased from the product market, (2) personal time, and (3) skills. All three are needed as inputs in "producing" the aforementioned commodities. Thus, it takes both food and time (for cooking and eating) to assuage one's hunger; it takes movie/theater tickets and time (to watch the movie or play) to derive pleasure, recreation, rest, and fellowship. In other words, for Becker and Lancaster, individuals (or households) ought to be viewed not merely as consuming economic agents but as individual "microfirms" producing assorted commodities (qualities) for their own consumption and enjoyment. They buy goods and services from the market as inputs, which they then process with their personal effort, skills, and time to produce these Beckerian-Lancasterian commodities. Hence, this approach is aptly called the household production model.[5]

Becker's and Lancaster's models are ground-breaking for their incorporation of time as a requisite input in utility maximization. However, their contribution goes much farther than this initial implication. It turns out that the temporal dimension they introduce also opens the door to analyzing the critical role that human capital plays in such production-consumption. The time expended is an excellent indicator of the ease and efficiency with which individuals "produce" the commodities they require. Such efficiency is largely a function of people's personal skills and sociohistorical location. Personal capabilities matter. For example, a gifted student needs less time than an average classmate to "produce" the commodity of learning or to earn the same grade. This corresponds to what Amartya Sen (1981a, 1984) later describes as economic agents' "functionings and capabilities." The ease or difficulty with which market participants procure for themselves the requisite commodities of nourishment, learning, recreation, fellowship, and so forth is dependent on their

---

5 A further necessary modification of the model has to do with the income constraint. The traditional model's income constraint is changed to a full income constraint that includes total time available to the person (household). Since I can make my point without unduly weighing down readers with technical details, I refer interested readers to the original articles of Becker and Lancaster for an exposition on the notion of full income.

"functionings and capabilities." Sociohistorical location also matters because it directly shapes both the economic opportunities and the prices (including wages) people face in the market. For example, in societies marred by racial and gender biases, women and minorities often have to expend more effort and time to attain the same level of accomplishment as the rest of the population and rise above their disadvantaged position. They are paid less for the same jobs or are barred from prized occupations. In other words, these individual (household) production functions are unique to every person and are shaped by (1) their personal human capital and (2) their socioeconomic history and position within the community. Both of these factors determine individuals' (households') opportunities, wages, and access to communal goods and services. These are the key determinants of the costs people incur in participating in the market.

In summary, the price of goods and services (including wages) is not the only relevant variable to consider in the marketplace; the other critical price is that of the time employed, effort expended, and ease with which one produces Beckerian-Lancasterian commodities. Both are constitutive of the set of prices people encounter in economic life. The expenditure of time and effort is dependent on the efficiency and skill with which people combine their personal time with purchased goods and services to produce the much-desired qualities of the activity (Beckerian-Lancasterian commodities). Moreover, the requisite time and effort are also dependent on the hurdles that must be overcome given people's place in society.

This set of time- , skill- , and location-related prices is properly subsumed under the transaction costs described earlier since they partly arise from the violation of the assumptions of perfectly competitive markets. Nonetheless, it is important to make a distinction. The term *transaction costs*, as it is used in the literature, pertains to the nominal cost expended in searching, bargaining, concluding, and enforcing coveted exchanges in the marketplace. For the rest of the book, I refer to *full transaction costs* or *person-specific transaction costs* to include not only the aforementioned nominal expenses but also the time- , skill- , and effort-related costs to producing and consuming Beckerian-Lancasterian commodities. These *full transaction costs* incurred by people in the marketplace are largely, though not exclusively, shaped by their personal endowments and sociohistorical location.

The key implication to highlight from these findings for purposes of this chapter's thesis is that people face different "full" prices for the same Beckerian-Lancasterian commodities they produce and consume in the face of variations in their human capital and sociohistorical position within the community. In fact, we can make this statement even stronger by saying that people face *unique* prices for the commodities they produce and consume given their dissimilar levels of human capital and personal histories. Since the latter factors are particular to every person, we expect *full transaction costs* to be person-specific as well. Where people have been and where they currently are in the marketplace determine the set of full prices they face.[6] Such person-specific transaction costs enable the market not merely to be a price discriminator (charging different prices for the same commodity), but an *effective* price discriminator in which *every* market participant pays a distinct full price for their production-consumption of Beckerian-Lancasterian commodities. It is this phenomenon of effective price discrimination that opens the door to the skewed distribution of some of the market's unintended consequences. It is to actual instances of such that we now turn our attention.

PERSONAL CAPABILITIES

Successful market participation depends heavily on personal aptitudes such as innate intelligence, emotional maturity, interpersonal social skills, education, sociability, and other specialized skills and talents. Given the central importance of personal capabilities, market outcomes can often be lopsided.

There are different schools of thought regarding market processes (Boettke and Prychitko 1998). The dominant one, of course, has been the neoclassical school's view that economic life is akin to physics in the mechanistic regularity and stability of the laws that govern its operations (Mirowski 1989). Given such a Newtonian backdrop, economic life is seen as revolving around optimum points of equilibria that bring order to the cacophony of disparate preferences and decisions of a wide diversity of economic agents. In contrast to such a deterministic view of economic life is the evolutionary approach. The economy is not predetermined but is open-ended both in its results and in its processes. Within this evolutionary school of thought, market operations have been viewed as exciting processes of discovery (Kirzner 1990) or of creation (Buchanan and Vanberg 1991).

This is not the place to contrast the finer points of these competing schools of thought. It is sufficient for our purposes to observe that these

---

6 Path dependence is at the heart of these differential prices. Human capital is largely a function of people's past investments and efforts in improving their own skills. Current social and historical location is largely, though not exclusively, determined by past rounds of economic activities.

different approaches converge in one important respect: Personal capabilities of economic agents play a significant role in these market processes. The focus of neoclassical economics is on working out the proper solution that brings about the desired optimum equilibria. More often than not, however, economic agents are faced with disturbances that are exogenous to their decisions. Moreover, the unintended consequences of others' economic transactions (pecuniary externalities) require a realignment of one's own economic decisions. Such an adjustment process is constant given the ever-changing parameters of a dynamic economic life. In other words, the economic state of affairs is more often one of disruption than a steady-state equilibrium. Faced with such disequilibria in a setting of risk and uncertainty, economic agency is a never-ending stream of repeated calculations and a ceaseless reallocation of one's resources. Nobel laureate Theodore Schultz (1975) astutely observes that the ability to deal with disequilibria is a function of human capital.

In the Hayekian world of evolutionary economics, individual liberty and initiative are paramount if discoveries are to be made (Kirzner 1990). These discoveries are at the heart of the economy's strength and dynamism since it is through the private efforts and enterprise of economic agents that inefficiencies are eliminated, and consumer needs and wants are met in the most resourceful, most cost-efficient, and least intrusive manner. Buchanan and Vanberg (1991) would go even further than this and say that economic activity is about more than just uncovering what is already there waiting to be discovered; it is rather about creating something new – something that was nonexistent.[7]

Common to these different approaches to market processes is the pivotal importance of human capital. Personal qualities are the defining determinants that ultimately shape the outcomes of economic actors' market activities. Schultz (1975) reviews a wealth of empirical studies on the impact of education and observes that schooling invariably improves the lot of economic agents, not only because they are more efficient and productive in their work, but, more important, because they have better allocative skills. Dealing with disequilibria, and perhaps even bettering one's position on account of such disruptions, is largely determined by how well one is able to reallocate the disposition of one's resources – a

---

7 Buchanan and Vanberg's (1991) point is that to view economic agency merely as one of discovery is to presume a predetermined Newtonian order waiting to be uncovered. Thus, it is at its root no different from the neoclassical "equilibrium" approach to market processes. In contrast, to regard economic activity as a creative process is to be truly open-ended in whatever direction and however the economy may evolve depending on the decisions of market participants.

skill that is in turn a function of one's human capital. By extension, if human capital is so vital for timely and innovative responsiveness, how much more for discovery and creative work? Schultz's observations, flowing from a neoclassical world view, apply with even greater force in a Hayekian evolutionary economy. The findings and theses of these different schools of thought take on even greater significance in the current globalized knowledge-driven economy compared to the industrial era of the preceding two centuries.

The central role of personal capabilities often leads to unbalanced outcomes from unfettered market processes. The uneducated and the unskilled find themselves even further marginalized in the marketplace. They are unable to cope with necessary agile reallocations to adjust to new economic conditions, nor are they likely to be in a position to properly read economic signals and seize opportunities for discoveries or for creating something new. Moreover, the capacity to sift, analyze, and then use information from the vast quantities of data produced and exchanged in the postindustrial economy requires a high degree of learning, training, and experience. With the onset of the knowledge-based economy, constant disequilibria and a market that is chock-full of possible discoveries and creative breakthroughs are to the benefit of the highly skilled and the well educated. We expect to see a worsening relative inequality.[8]

Extra-market interventions are necessary to prevent the further marginalization of those who are unable to keep up with the rising "entry cost" of participating in the marketplace. This only goes to highlight even further the importance of Sen's (1981a, 1984) "functionings and capabilities" as alternatives to the neoclassical choice of individual preference satisfaction as a measure of welfare and as the object of maximization in economics.

These insights on the fundamental importance of human capital can be generalized for all economic agents, both personal and corporate. As we see in the following sections, the ability of a nation to weather shocks or to take advantage of new opportunities in a dynamic economic environment is largely a function of its composite human and social capital, analogous to the aforementioned personal capabilities at the level of the individual economic agent.

---

8 There is clear and strong empirical evidence of an earnings gap between college and high school graduates (Coleman 1993). In household studies, there is also convincing data on how better-educated mothers have healthier children because they are better able to use health and nutritional inputs. For example, education is an important determinant of a mother's ability to supplement breastmilk without deleterious effects on the health of the infant (Barrera 1991).

SOCIAL VALUATION

The cost of market participation is partly conditioned by the size of the agent's purchasing power, and, as we see later in this chapter, the well-to-do tend to have better access to information, education, and economic opportunities. These wealth advantages are in turn determined by the degree to which society values people's assets, contributions, or services. For example, exceptional athletes, first-rate managers, and computer-savvy entrepreneurs are highly sought out and remunerated well by society for their perceived contributions to the community. Social valuation matters greatly in market outcomes and processes.

Given that information is imperfect, such social valuation is often based on bounded rationality, that is, on widely accepted norms, perceptions, informal rules, and customs within society. Bounded rationality is particularly important in cases in which the basis for valuation is not tied to clear objective measures (like productivity) but to subjective standards like taste.[9] In fact, Samuel Bowles and Herbert Gintis (2002) argue that community governance (defined as "small group social interactions") complements both the market and the state in determining market outcomes.

Objective valuation

Neoclassical economics values work effort and output according to its *marginal productivity theory of factor payments*. Factors of production are paid according to what they are able to produce and contribute to the company's revenues (their marginal productivity[10] multiplied by the market price of their work output). For example:

for labor : wages = price of output × marginal product of labor

for capital : returns to capital = price of output ×

marginal product of capital

Sen (1985: 15–17) is critical of this approach. In the first place, factor payments are not really based on the last unit of output produced (marginal productivity), but on average productivity. Second, this theory represents only the demand side and does not consider the supply of the

---

9 Examples of this kind of valuation include the pricing of concerts and collectibles.
10 Marginal productivity is defined as the incremental output produced per incremental input (such as labor or capital) added.

factor; equilibrium price after all is determined by the intersection of both the demand and supply curves. Third, it is difficult, in practice, to break down total output into the constituent marginal productivities of its different factors.

Nevertheless, despite misgivings about this theory, it cannot be ignored because it is appealing and makes intuitive sense in its normative implications. There are numerous possible distributive criteria, to wit: distribution according to productivity, talent, merit, effort, equality, need, and social utility (Rescher 1966: 73–83). Neoclassical economics falls along the lines of distribution according to productivity. For this reason, J. B. Clark (1899) argues that the marginal productivity theory of factor payments is also about justice and fairness since people are paid according to what they have contributed to the larger society. In contrast, Christian thought has a long-standing tradition of calling for distribution according to need.

This chapter is not the place to assess the morality of these different criteria. I would rather simply describe the regressive dynamic of distribution according to contribution (marginal productivity theory of factor payments) relative to a distributive criterion according to need (e.g., the Christian preferential option of the poor).

Whether or not factors of production are indeed paid along the lines of the neoclassical formulation of the marginal productivity theory of factor payments, what is important to note is that factor payments are based on the market price of these factors' output. Thus, immigrant agricultural workers picking strawberries and grapes in California are paid far less than Silicon Valley software programmers. From a purely economic point of view, this is rational since the value created and the services provided by the latter group to the community are much more substantial and carry far wider ripple effects than those provided by agricultural workers. Nevertheless, the dynamic of such a distributive criterion according to contribution can have a regressive impact because of the poverty trap that it fails to breach.

While some agricultural workers ultimately achieve upward social mobility and become small-scale landowning farmers themselves, most are caught in a poverty cycle. They are poorly paid because of the relatively low economic value of the output they produce for society. However, on account of such poor earnings, they are unable to invest further in themselves (for example in education and training) and improve their productivity. And since they are unable to upgrade their skills, they are stuck with menial, low-paying work. In other words, there is a long-term regressive feature to a distributive scheme according to contribution because those who are in most need of further improvement through investment in personal human capital are precisely the ones who are unable to do so because of their inadequate earnings. This is particularly true for the hard-core unemployed with minimal skills or poor work habits. Unfettered market operations will not always succeed in breaking such poverty cycles because they are primarily interested in allocative efficiency and not remedial income redistribution or human capital formation.[11] Extra-market interventions are often needed to get around these poverty traps and provide assistance to those who can benefit the most from the upward social mobility that the modern economy has made possible.

Subjective valuation

The market's valuation of work effort and output is neither always nor solely based on objective value or factor contribution. After all, economic value is determined not merely by the objective cost of production but also by the subjective satisfaction that consumers derive from such goods and services. In what follows, I argue that there are certain cases of regressive subjective valuation that are often embedded within the customary practices of the market.

Race- and gender-based valuation

A primary example of such a dynamic is an unfettered market's low valuation of the services of certain castes, minorities, and women. Left on its own without legislative relief or other forms of extra-market intervention, a free market would simply effect and even strengthen established societal norms and biases in the way it allocates scarce social goods and assigns value to work output and effort. Thus, prior to the grassroots clamor of "equal pay for equal work," women were paid less than men for comparable work and were shut out from certain careers that had been traditionally viewed as the exclusive domain of men. "Glass ceilings" defined limits to how far women might be promoted to positions of authority and responsibility.[12] The same phenomenon holds true for minorities. Such discriminatory valuation is regressive in its impact since

---

11 In fact, allocative efficiency is a necessary, though not a sufficient, condition for sustained economic growth and long-term economic viability. To be a sufficient condition, it must be complemented by an equitable distribution that leads to human capital formation. See, for example, Fei, Ranis, and Kuo (1979).
12 See, for example, Remick (1984) and Burstein (1994).

women and minorities are among the largest groups below the poverty line. Without deliberate extra-market relief and mediation that change the attitudes and behavior of freely acting economic agents, the market will simply carry out society's practice of assigning a low valuation to the work effort and output of these groups, thus effectively relegating them to inferior roles and pay. This is true for the castes of South Asia to this day and during the time of South African apartheid. Great care must be exercised lest the unfettered market be an instrument and a venue for reinforcing pre-existing biases and sustaining improper subjective valuations.[13] Thus, affirmative action programs for both employment and the awarding of contracts have been initiated as remedial measures to reverse such deleterious market practices.[14]

Numerous other examples abound that illustrate how the market's pricing of work effort, output, or personal skills and endowments can be skewed in its valuation without being overtly discriminatory. For example, there is ample empirical evidence of environmental inequities in which the nuisance and health costs of dirty industries or waste disposal sites are disproportionately borne by minorities (Downey 1998; Hockman and Morris 1998). Or take the case of the Larry Summers memo that generated much bitter recrimination (Hausman and McPherson 1996: 9–22). As chief economist of the World Bank, Summers observed that there were rational economic arguments for the exportation of dirty industries from industrialized to developing countries. One argument provided was the lower economic cost of morbidity in emerging nations given their lower wages; there were smaller forgone earnings from getting sick in poorer countries. In effect, the value of health was purely a function of economic earnings.

Labor market compensation
The labor market provides another instance of a regressive dynamic in social valuation. The disparity in the compensation of top executives versus rank-and-file workers is a perennial matter of debate and concern. Whether from a strictly pecuniary or an ethical point of view, most would agree that justice and efficiency both converge on the same conclusion: Compensation packages cannot be equal across jobs given differences in their responsibilities, requisite skills, and contribution. However,

---

13 See Blank's (2003: 452–54) theory #4 on poverty and on how markets can be used by political interests for noneconomic goals.
14 See, for example, Mills (1994).

disparities in such pay are not based purely on objective factors alone. If they were, there should be no appreciable variance in the compensation structures of the OECD countries. As it is, pay disparity in the United States is many times that experienced in Europe and even more so when compared to Japan. One can only infer from this that there is a large element of subjective valuation (e.g., long-standing industry practices) involved when it comes to determining how much more executives ought to be paid relative to ordinary workers.

Such subjective valuation makes regressive market outcomes more likely. For example, observe the differential retirement and severance packages of top executives vis-à-vis those of rank-and-file workers.[15] Those who have less of an economic nest egg to begin with and are in need of a more secure safety net are precisely the ones who have to bear the brunt of necessary cost-cutting measures, in contrast to top executives whose compensation packages and "golden parachutes" are secure. This again is an illustration of the earlier point made on how the disposition of mutual advantages from market exchange is largely a function of the sociohistorical location of the parties involved and their resulting bargaining power.

Similarly, take the plight of Third World farmers. Compared to their urban counterparts, rural populations are at greater risk of economic disruptions given the vagaries of their agrarian occupation. Moreover, they are poorer. Despite this relatively greater need for a social safety net, it is ironic that health insurance and social security programs are better and more comprehensive among urban rather than rural workers, if they are available at all to the latter. Such an uneven dynamic is also seen in the disproportionate amount of investments funneled into the urban rather than the rural areas. There is a particularly acute disparity when it comes to both physical and social infrastructure. Sectoral gaps in educational and health investments, for example, have long been a matter of concern among development practitioners.[16] This pattern is true not only in the Third World, but even in the First World. Note the difficulty of getting doctors to serve in the rural areas of the United States. Unfettered economic transactions seek the highest returns possible, and better-situated economic agents are in a far superior position to appropriate these gains for themselves. Those who can truly benefit from such

15 See, for example, *New York Times* (2003).
16 Some of these patterns are driven by objective rather than subjective valuation. As explained in a later section, there are objective, rational economic reasons why it is more remunerative to invest in the urban, industrial sectors of the economy rather than in agriculture.

free-market activities are precisely the ones who face formidable hurdles to participating in the marketplace.

In summary, these deficiencies in endowment valuation should not be taken as a sweeping critique or condemnation of the market. After all, one must remember that compared to the pre-modern feudal and guild restrictions on economic and social mobility, the modern market has proven itself to be egalitarian in the way it has opened opportunities for advancement for everyone on the basis of hard work and enterprise. Nevertheless, the quality and scope of people's market participation are determined largely by the economic value of their personal assets and endowments. Such economic valuation is ultimately set by established societal norms, tastes, and customs that find expression in and are often reinforced by market operations. Social networking can greatly ease and facilitate economic advancement within the marketplace; sociohistorical location matters when it comes to positioning oneself in the market.[17] Whether at a microeconomic or macroeconomic level, extra-market mechanisms and incentives are often needed to get around the workings of the market and redirect societal valuation in ways that bring investments and programs to disadvantaged groups and improve the economic value of the work effort and output of populations who are in greatest need.

ACCESS PRICING

The "entry cost" to market participation depends heavily on people's sociohistorical location. Social placement is a critical factor in shaping one's access to communal goods, capital, markets, and technology. The following sections examine this feature of the marketplace.

Credit markets

As mentioned earlier, markets are distinctive for their ability to allocate scarce resources to their most valued uses. Such a strength, however, has a downside to it in the additional costs it imposes on economic agents who

---

17 A similar phenomenon has been observed in development economics. Educational attainment is often used as a way of rationing scarce jobs even for those positions that do not require a high level of education. Moreover, Glaeser, Laibson, and Sacerdote (2002) note that the neoclassical rational choice model can be used effectively to show how social location is partly a matter of individual choice for utilitarian ends; people make decisions on how much they would like to invest of themselves and their resources in social interaction. Furthermore, economic agents' ownership of positional (Hirsch 1976) or dominant (Walzer 1983) goods determines the value of their endowments and the prices they face.

are in dire need of these scarce resources but are unable to ante up the necessary price to bid them away from their alternative uses. This "auction" is, of course, what gives the market its unique flexibility and ability to gather, process, and disseminate enormous amounts of information rapidly and efficiently and adjust people's decisions accordingly.[18]

Take the case of small- and medium-scale farmers, a large proportion of the world's poor.[19] If farmers want to break out of their isolated shell and participate in the market, they have to go beyond mere animal husbandry (farming for one's own consumption) and produce a surplus that can then be exchanged for their other needs in the marketplace. This, however, requires essential investments in upgrading farming methods and equipment. Development economists are well aware that a significant cause of rural poverty is low agricultural productivity due to farmers' outdated technologies and inadequate facilities for storage and marketing. These obstacles can be largely addressed through appropriate capital expenditures that are in turn heavily dependent on the availability of credit. Unfortunately, farmers in developing nations face major hurdles in competing against the industrial sector for such scarce funds because of the high transaction costs in credit markets.

As noted earlier, transaction costs are expenses incurred in the threefold tasks of searching, bargaining, and enforcement that are essential to completing any economic exchange. In capital markets, these costs necessarily include an assessment of the borrower's assets, income, credit history, and risk of default. There is a variety of legitimate and rational economic reasons why unregulated credit markets are regressive in the way new or needy entrants face higher costs in tapping capital financing.

First, agriculture, by its nature, carries greater risks and uncertainties relative to industry. This is evident in the greater price volatility of primary goods compared to manufactures. Climate changes can precipitate either lean or abundant harvests, leading to wide and harmful price swings. To make matters worse, farmers are vulnerable not only to the weather in their local area, but also to the climatic conditions experienced by their competitor-farmers in other geographic areas. For example, the price coffee growers in Central America get for their crops is also a function of how well or how poorly coffee growers in South America and Asia fare. Climatic shifts half a world away may ultimately determine

---

18 In technical terms, this is the Walrasian auction.
19 In what follows, I use "agriculture" to refer only to small- and medium-sized family-run farms and not to industrial farming.

whether a local farmer makes a profit or not. Bumper harvests in one locality can be a bane not only for the local farmers but also for other farmers in another continent. Relative to the industrial sector, agricultural enterprises carry the extra burden of being highly vulnerable to sudden worldwide shifts in weather patterns. On top of this, of course, is the unpredictable and often catastrophic nature of animal diseases and crop blights.[20]

Second, of the three major sectors of the economy – agriculture, industry, and services – farming offers the least robust set of opportunities for vibrant innovations and rapid growth.[21] This has long been evident in empirical work. Modern economic growth has been generally accompanied by a shift in a country's economic center of gravity from agriculture to industry and then to services. Industry and services eventually replace agriculture as the predominant sectors in terms of output and employment (Kuznets 1966). Moreover, as the long-run terms of trade move in favor of manufactures, farmers are increasingly unable to get a good price for their primary goods relative to industrial products.[22] Consequently, industry and services attract more investments than agriculture. These two sectors also get the lion's share of complementary physical and social infrastructure projects that are critical for the conduct of business, such as roads, ports, electricity, water, schools, and hospitals. Thus, on average, industry and services produce far greater profits than agriculture.

Third, interest rates for credit necessarily reflect the cost of administering such loans, which includes the expenditures in time, money, and effort in evaluating and monitoring borrowers' activities. Since industry and services are for the most part located in urban areas, lenders enjoy economies of scale in servicing loans to these sectors. Moreover, transportation and communications are much better and cheaper in urban settings compared to far-flung rural family farms spread over a wide geographic area. This disparity is particularly true in developing countries.

Fourth, unlike urban industrial or service enterprises, small family-run farms are rarely in a position to post highly valued collateral to cover their loans. Land is about the only asset they can provide as surety; crops are

---

20 Note the mad-cow crises, hoof-and-mouth disease, and avian flu of the last decade.
21 This is not to downplay the enormous technological achievements in agriculture throughout history. Take note of the Green Revolution in the last century. I am simply stating that the breadth, scale, and pace of technological change in industry and services are relatively better compared to agriculture.
22 See, for example, Singer, Sapsford, and Sarkar (1998) for a quick review of the Prebisch-Singer thesis.

perishable and farm equipment is often not much to speak of. In contrast, the capital, plant, equipment, inventory, and raw materials of industry and service enterprises serve as excellent sureties. The availability of assets that can be used as a pledge affords better credit terms for the potential borrower.

Fifth, new entrants to the marketplace have no credit history at all, thereby aggravating their risk profile. Asymmetric information in credit transactions is a particularly vexing problem encountered in credit markets. Lenders are unable to observe the motivation and the work effort of the borrower. Given such incomplete information, the lender's recourse is to rely on the credit history of the borrower; reputation gleaned from previous debt performance is a second-best solution. An established track record leads to a lower risk profile that translates into better credit terms. Unfortunately, new entrants to the marketplace do not have such a credit history; they have minimal or no credit standing at all and are consequently charged a higher risk premium, if they can borrow at all.

Sixth, since loans to small farmers are unlikely to be sizable, it may be unprofitable for banks to extend such loans in the first place. The cost of monitoring and administering small farm loans may exceed lenders' revenues from such lending unless banks are permitted to pass on the cost to farmers and charge prohibitive interest rates or extra fees as a consequence.[23]

Given these conditions, it is not surprising that loans from formal credit markets are often not even available for agricultural and rural areas since lenders would much prefer to serve the industrial and service sectors that are predominantly in urban centers. And even if such loans were available to farmers, they would be expensive. In the face of the uncertainties intrinsic to agriculture, it makes economic sense for creditors to charge an extra risk premium in lending to this sector, due to its higher probability of default given its susceptibility to weather shifts, its lower growth prospects, and the higher cost of administering its loans.[24]

---

23 There are minimal costs to monitoring and servicing microenterprise loans patterned after the Grameen Bank (Hossain 1988; Wahid 1993). The community and one's peers serve as guarantors against a loan default. This solves the problem of asymmetric information between the borrower and the lender since villagers know each other's strengths and weaknesses well, thereby minimizing the moral hazard problem.

24 Markets generally process information well. Even when it comes to sovereign debt, poorer, less organized, and less disciplined nations have to pay higher premiums on their financing from international capital markets. After all, they pose a greater credit risk.

This phenomenon of farmers getting "crowded out" of formal credit markets by their industrial and service counterparts is replicated in many other situations. Not only do lenders favor industry and services over agriculture, they also have a marked preference for large enterprises over small- and medium-scale businesses, and the non-poor over the poor (Bernstein 2004; Ranieri 2004). Not only are the latter charged a higher price for their loans, they are often not even able to get credit at any price in the regular, formal, credit markets. Scale and established reputation are needed to access cheaper financing.[25]

If these funds are not at all forthcoming from the formal markets, farmers and small- and medium-scale enterprises are compelled to borrow from the underground economy (e.g., loan sharks) at even higher and often usurious rates. They are a "captive market" since they have no other funding sources. The lack of formal credit markets for small farmers and entrepreneurs creates monopolistic opportunities for the black market, to the detriment of those who can ill afford such higher rates to begin with.

In either case, whether in the formal markets, if available at all, or in the underground economy, farmers and small- and medium-scale entrepreneurs find themselves paying a higher price for financing compared with industry, services, or large-scale enterprises. In other words, there is a regressive nature in the manner credit is priced: Economic actors who need it the most and can least afford it are precisely the ones who are compelled to pay a higher price.

Many policymakers are familiar with this disturbing feature of unfettered credit markets. Thus, legislation has often been used to mandate extra-market assistance for rural financing (Lim 1993). In other cases, government acts as a co-guarantor or subsidizes the cost of borrowing by these at-risk economic agents. Of course, an excellent testimony against the skewed dynamic of unfettered credit markets is the success of the microenterprise loans pioneered by the Grameen Bank in Bangladesh (Hossain 1988; Wahid 1993). Readily available credit at affordable prices and at reasonable repayment terms has been instrumental in giving the poor and the small vendors a chance to contribute to and partake of the benefits of a market society.

Lest I leave readers with the impression that this regressive feature of unfettered credit markets applies only to less developed countries, it is

---

25 Such preferential treatment is evident in the differential rates charged to customers. Banks reserve their prime rates for their most valued and reliable customers, a sound practice no different from other businesses.

important to be reminded of the practice of red-lining in the United States (Wray 1995). Left on their own, banks and insurance firms avoid serving blighted communities, thereby compelling their residents to go without insurance[26] or to cash their checks at neighborhood stores for a fee.[27]

Moreover, consider differential car insurance premiums. There is a higher incidence of property damage and car thefts in inner cities compared to suburban areas. Thus, it makes economic sense for insurers to reflect such a pattern in differential insurance rates. Of course, an unfortunate consequence is that inner-city residents, generally the working poor who do not have the wherewithal to flee to the safety of the suburbs, are forced to pay a higher premium for their car insurance relative to suburban residents.

In addition to the inadequacy of banking and insurance services, residents are unable to procure housing, car, or other durable goods loans that are essential both for creating jobs within the community and for improving inner-city neighborhoods. And even if funds for credit are available, minorities and the elderly tend to get worse mortgage terms (Barta 2003). Thus, federal bank regulators have provided both incentives and sanctions in an effort to encourage banks to expand lending in low-income communities in accordance with the Community Reinvestment Act passed by the US Congress in 1977.[28]

In summary, the literature in development economics abounds with empirical evidence that, left on their own, farmers and small- and medium-scale entrepreneurs in less developed countries are "crowded out" of credit markets. They cannot usually get loans from formal markets, and even if they do, they are charged a higher rate because of their perceived risk. There is a perfectly rational economic explanation for why the cost of borrowing is (1) lower for the urban industrial and service sectors compared to rural agricultural farms, (2) lower for large enterprises compared to small- and medium-scale firms, and (3) lower for the nonpoor compared to the poor. Farmers, small firms, and the poor have a higher probability of default and are more expensive to service and monitor. Unfortunately, it is these groups that cannot afford the higher cost of borrowing to begin with. Even worse, credit is often unavailable to

---

26 See, for example, Thomas (1999), Treaster (1996), and Warfel (1996).

27 Note how the poor have to pay for services, such as cashing checks, that are costless for many others.

28 Lacy and Walter (2002) argue that such mandated lending imposes additional costs on middle- and high-income borrowers.

them, thereby driving them into the underground economy where the cost of borrowing is even higher. Such an uneven state of affairs feeds on itself to create a self-sustaining malevolent cycle. Poor small-scale farmers or entrepreneurs are unable to access formal credit markets because of their low productivity. However, they are unable to improve their productivity due to lack of funds for capital improvement. This unfortunate dynamic to unfettered markets makes for a poverty trap. Thus, legislative relief or other extra-market mechanisms (such as credit cooperatives) are needed to break this deleterious cycle through appropriate interventions in market operations.

Foreign direct investments

This regressive phenomenon also occurs at the macroeconomic level on a global stage.[29] Take the case of foreign direct investments (FDIs).[30] Such cross-border capital movements are highly sought because of their potential for improving the economic lot of entire communities. They create jobs, and their wide ripple effects can pull along the rest of the economy by reinvigorating or perhaps even creating new profit centers within the nation. This is particularly true for small Third World countries. The forward and backward linkages of foreign direct investments often set the stage for future dynamic growth and further economic development. Thus, foreign direct investments produce the greatest marginal benefits in the poorest countries. The prime example of all these positive effects is, of course, the transformation of China in the last two decades due to the large infusion of foreign direct investments it has received.

Ironically, the biggest recipients of FDIs are the developed countries – Europe, Japan, and the United States. And even for the residual that goes to developing countries, there is also a skewed pecking order in which the bulk of Third World-bound FDIs end up in China or Brazil. Smaller, less developed countries (LDCs) have to content themselves with limited capital flows; moreover, they have to offer even more generous tax concessions, long-term land leases, and exemptions from local regulations in an effort to lure FDIs. The price for attracting investments for these

29 The household production model of Becker (1965) and Lancaster (1966) does not merely apply to the individual or the household but can be extended to any economic agent at any level of aggregation, including an entire country or group of nations. The essential mechanisms and the operative dynamics governing the conceptual framework remain unaffected by scale.
30 Foreign direct investments are funds used to purchase capital, plant, equipment, and other real, tangible assets in another country.

smaller emerging nations is relatively higher than for the bigger, more developed countries in the Third World.

There is a self-reinforcing dynamic to this condition. FDIs tend to cluster together because of complementarities and scale effects. For example, investments that develop a country's manufacturing base attract other investments that improve the physical (roads, rails, ports, energy sources), financial (banking, insurance, financial services), commercial (shopping centers, office rentals), and social infrastructure (residential development, schools, hospitals) of the recipient nation. Besides these complementary capital expenditures, there are also investments in the ancillary industries that supply parts, equipment, and materials to these emerging manufacturing and construction sectors. In other words, there is a cascading effect, a herd effect, so to speak, of mutually reinforcing foreign direct investments that produce economic growth and advancement over a wide front.[31] Moreover, since different sectors of the economy provide markets for each other, there are resulting economies of scale that furnish such a country with a pronounced cost advantage in competing in the global marketplace. All these effects make the host country that much more attractive for further foreign direct investments. This is double trouble for smaller LDCs. First, they would find it even more difficult to compete in export manufacturing in the global marketplace, given the cost advantages accruing to the larger LDCs that are successful at drawing foreign direct investments. Second, their cost disadvantage makes it that much more difficult for the smaller LDCs to compete for FDIs in the subsequent rounds of economic activity. Both of these lead to an ever-widening inequality. An example of this is the case of China relative to the rest of Asia and the case of Brazil relative to its neighbors. The gap is even worse between industrialized countries and small emerging nations.

Of course, unfettered markets should not be blamed for this uneven dynamic because they are meant to operate in such a manner as to produce the greatest economic returns, that is, the most valued uses for scarce resources. Foreign direct investments understandably go to countries with a more stable and developed socioeconomic infrastructure (Mallampally and Sauvant 1999; United Nations Conference on Trade and Development 1998). Not surprisingly, countries face different prices for attracting FDIs. Markets are supposed to maximize returns rather than

---

31 This is exactly the balanced-growth strategy to development proposed and debated in the mid-twentieth century (Nurkse 1953; Rosenstein-Rodan 1943) in contrast to the unbalanced-growth strategy to development.

"satisfice"[32] according to some larger, non-economic, social objectives like poverty alleviation. Nonetheless, as a descriptive exercise, it is important to be aware of how this feature of the market can produce a regressive impact.

Financial liberalization

Trade has brought along enormous economic benefits. Scholars and policymakers have consequently pushed for greater openness in capital markets as well in the hopes of replicating the same benefits. Capital controls in developed countries have come down since the 1980s, leading to a more integrated global financial marketplace today. Less developed nations have been urged to do likewise and to open their capital markets. It is believed that such capital market liberalization will attract much-needed funds for their development. Empirical evidence supports the claim that sustained growth in this new era of global economic integration requires both trade and financial market openness (Dollar and Kraay 2001; *The Economist* 2003b).

Unfortunately, such requisite capital market liberalization makes countries more susceptible to macroeconomic shocks (Dobson and Hufbauer 2001; *The Economist* 2003b and c). No country is exempt from this as both industrialized and emerging countries have had their share of monetary and exchange rate instability. However, there is a marked difference in the ability of nations to contain global financial disorders from spilling over borders and inflicting damage on their domestic economies (*The Economist* 2003b: 8). Given their deeper financial resources, industrialized countries are in a better position than less developed nations to ride out such volatility (Prasad et al. 2003). Poor countries have had to pay a higher price for financial liberalization. Such higher costs often come in the form of severe cuts in social services, a stricter fiscal regimen, and a more restrictive monetary posture, in order to restore macroeconomic balances as part of structural adjustment (Cornia, Jolly, and Stewart 1987). Note, too, the relatively fleeting impact of the foreign exchange crises in the last two decades in Europe compared to the deep and devastating effect of those experienced in Russia, East Asia, Mexico, Brazil, and Argentina.[33] Of course, many of the latter cases are aggravated by chronic domestic fiscal improvidence and weak institutions. Nevertheless, the

32 Simon (1959).
33 See, for example, *The Economist* (2003b).

uneven impact of such global financial disruptions is in large measure a
function of the depth and development of the financial infrastructure of
these countries. Emerging countries are more likely to suffer from international monetary contagions given their underdeveloped financial
systems.[34]

In summary, empirical evidence suggests that there can be sizable costs
that must be incurred before enjoying the benefits of financial liberalization (*The Economist* 2003b). These costs (financial and exchange rate
instability and contagions) are inversely proportional to the depth of a
country's banking and financial infrastructure. Poorer, less organized, and
less disciplined nations face a higher price for participating in global
capital markets. Greater financial openness has resulted in greater economic volatility, which tends to hurt the poor more than the wealthier
nations (Prasad et al. 2003).

Missing or incomplete markets

The preceding sections examined the skewed impact of unfettered market
operations. However, the same phenomenon also occurs at the opposite
extreme of missing or incomplete markets. My description of the regressive impact of unfettered credit and financial markets should not be read
as a sweeping condemnation of the market. Far from it. The modern
economy has not only supported the largest population ever seen in
human history, it has also sustained such larger numbers of people at
the highest per capita income ever.[35] Market openness has been instrumental in breaking the poverty trap for many. Consequently, scholars
have long viewed inadequate access to markets as among the principal
causes of poverty.[36] Many rural families often wallow in destitution and
are unable to avail themselves fully of the benefits of trade either because
of their isolation (World Bank 1990) or because of missing or incomplete
domestic markets.

34 Global markets for primary goods (agricultural crops and minerals) are also prone to cyclical
   swings. Many less developed countries are not diversified enough in their exports or in their
   customer base and are consequently extremely susceptible to disturbances in global trade. We find
   numerous cases of poor countries dependent on a narrow range of agricultural and mineral goods
   exports. Trade can effect both significant benefits and costs, and emerging nations are less able to
   handle the negative side of global markets.
35 Market operations are in large part responsible for such a dual achievement by separating
   economic life from the restrictive constraints of pre-modern political control that had so stifled
   private initiative. Contrast, for example, the feudal manor's economy of precarious survival with
   the modern industry's economy of accelerating abundance (Rosenberg and Birdzell 1986).
36 See Blank (2003: 449–51), for example, for this theory of poverty.

Incomplete or missing markets impose costs, and these burdens are likely to be uneven in their impact because people's ability to get around the ill effects of such absent markets is dependent on their sociohistorical location and the quality of their economic infrastructure. This is unfortunate since nations that are poorly prepared to deal with such economic gaps are precisely the very countries that are more likely to suffer a greater prevalence of missing or incomplete markets. Moreover, missing markets partially account for disparities in the economic performance of nations (*The Economist* 2000a; Olson 2000).

Compare, for example, the most significant determinants of long-term growth and development in First and Third World countries. Advanced education is the key factor in a knowledge-based economy. In contrast, good health is one of sub-Saharan Africa's most urgent needs for economic well-being.

In the United States, the market for college student loans is an effective way of addressing its most pressing requirement for further economic development. On their own, poor students would not be able to procure a college education for themselves. However, through student-loan programs, they are in effect able to borrow from their future stream of earnings in order to finance the education that will make their future earnings possible in the first place. This is an illustration of a strength of the market in being able to smooth out the budget constraints in a person's life cycle. It is the market that enables people to have the resources to invest in and develop their skills and aptitudes today by "drawing" from the future income derived from such a well-developed human capital.

In contrast, one could view the absence of a market for tropical drugs as a case of a missing market, the inability to borrow from the future. There are few pecuniary incentives for pharmaceutical companies to invest in the development of such medicines because most will not pay for themselves. There is no market for these drugs despite the enormous toll tropical diseases are taking in terms of human morbidity and mortality (Chase 2003; Trouiller and Olliaro 1998; Trouiller et al. 2002). The real medical need for such drugs has not turned into economic demand because the affected populations are simply too poor to have the kind of purchasing power that assures producers recovery of their investments in developing drugs for tropical diseases.

Such inadequate purchasing power can be partially attributed to the high incidence of morbidity and mortality. Thus, we have another poverty cycle and trap. We could break out of this dilemma if only there were a market in which sub-Saharan Africans were able to borrow from their future earnings (given good health and a longer life expectancy) to pay for tropical medicines today. What is critical is being able to pay the price of investing upfront to get around tropical diseases and allow for better health and life expectancy, which in turn should be able to pay for themselves through better future productivity. Indeed, missing markets can be regressive in their impact; unlike their poorer counterparts, wealthier countries are often able to get around missing or incomplete markets.

One final comparison is worth highlighting. Substantial upfront cash expenditures are often necessary for certain purchases, such as houses and cars. Most consumers in both developed and emerging nations need to borrow from their future streams of earnings in order to effect such durable goods purchases. The higher rates of home and car ownership in the more developed countries are partly due to the existence of markets for home mortgages, second mortgages, and car financing. Such markets are not as common in poorer countries given their underdeveloped financial infrastructure. In effect, compared to their OECD counterparts, residents in emerging nations face a steeper price in borrowing from their future incomes, if this is possible for them at all, in order to even out their consumption across their life cycle. The success of the Grameen initiative in providing credit to microenterprises, its extensive replication in Asia and Latin America, and its subsequent wholehearted adoption by multilateral agencies, such as the World Bank, provide evidence and highlight even further the higher prices the poor often face because of missing or incomplete markets.

Markets are geared toward producing the highest pecuniary returns. That they have not spontaneously arisen and are missing or incomplete in meeting clearly legitimate needs is indicative of market failures that require extra-market ameliorative measures.[37] Unfortunately, poor nations are precisely the ones that are ill equipped to design and implement such extra-market interventions.

Unrestricted labor markets

The labor market also illustrates a regressive dimension to pecuniary externalities. People engage in market transactions to improve their

---

37 An excellent example of this is the initial limited success of a vaccine for malaria that was developed as part of the Malaria Vaccine Initiative funded by the Bill and Melinda Gates Foundation (McNeil 2004). Nongovernmental organizations can be instrumental in addressing the problem of missing or incomplete markets.

welfare. Consequently, one can describe market exchange as being about securing mutual advantages.[38]

The distribution of such mutual advantages is, however, dependent on disparities in the transaction costs faced by economic agents. As we know, transaction costs consist of the expenses associated with searching for the appropriate good or service, bargaining over the terms of the exchange, and then enforcing the agreement. Each of these is a function of people's social networking, personal capabilities, and wealth. Thus, we expect *full transaction costs* to vary across economic agents because of differences in personal attributes and circumstances. Moreover, we would also expect people who are better situated, have a wider circle of social contacts, are more skilled, and have deeper financial reserves to be in a better position to extract more gains for themselves from market exchange relative to their weaker trading partners; the former should face fewer hurdles than the latter when it comes to getting the most out of the marketplace. In other words, less better situated, less better connected, and poorer economic agents face higher *full transaction costs* in the marketplace.

The labor market provides numerous examples of the uneven impact of differential transaction costs across economic agents. Unregulated labor markets ultimately lead to a skewed distribution of burdens and benefits between employers and workers. Recall, for example, the unsupervised labor markets of the early stages of the Industrial Revolution.[39] Working conditions deteriorated to the point where nineteenth-century England was forced to enact social legislation to curtail abusive practices. Extra-market measures specified a maximum to hours of work, a minimum age for child labor, and mandatory safety standards. To this day, labor markets, even in the most capitalistic economies, are regulated in varying degrees precisely because of the uneven playing field between employers and workers. Appropriated gains are largely a function of bargaining power. Left on their own, the weaker party faces steep barriers to getting its share of mutual advantages from economic transactions. After all, calculated bargaining and constant repositioning are the defining features of a free market (Walrasian auction). Thus, as we saw in chapter 1, McGregor (1988–89) has been emphatic in pointing out that the formal characteristic of what constitutes coercion can be found not in the normalcy criterion of

---

38 This is a criterion that is implicit in pareto optimality in which no one can be made better off without making somebody else worse off.

39 See, for example, Cooke-Taylor (1891), Hutchins and Harrison (1903), and Kirby (2003).

predetermined baselines, but in the glaring disparities in bargaining advantages between parties in a market exchange.[40]

Dealing with volatility

As we have seen earlier, Schultz (1975) argues that the ability to deal with disequilibria is a function of people's human capital. To this we might add that, in many cases, the ability of economic agents to ride out the volatility of markets is also largely a function of their nest egg, that is, their accumulated financial reserves.

People need to even out their cash flow to cover their consumption in the face of exogenous shocks that interrupt their stream of earnings. However, there is a cost to smoothing out such fluctuations and synchronizing cash flow with consumption requirements. For example, laid-off workers who have substantial savings to tide them over are able to wait patiently and search for another suitable employment opportunity. In contrast, the poor who have no cushion to fall back on are pressured to accept just about any offer that comes along, even those that do not pay as much or are a step down in job responsibilities. The poor do not have the luxury of staying unemployed for long.

People with substantial savings are also in a better position to ride out fluctuations in earnings without having recourse to credit sources. In contrast, the poor who have little or no financial cushion to lean on are driven to borrow at whatever terms are available given their immediate need for cash. Thus, they are more prone to unfavorable credit terms and to predatory lenders because they have no other choice.

Another way of illustrating the poor's relatively greater vulnerability is to compare the consumption baskets of the poor and the wealthy. The poor have a larger proportion of their budget spent on basic needs. This means that they are at greater risk from interruptions in earnings. They have more urgent unmet needs and are therefore more vulnerable to shocks from the marketplace.

In summary, the differential ability of economic agents to ride out volatility is a function not only of their human capital but also of their

---

40 Beyond labor markets, we find a similar pattern in the case of World Trade Organization (WTO) negotiations. Less developed countries have complained that despite their substantial concessions, the benefits of the multiple rounds of negotiations have been skewed in favor of the developed world. For example, LDCs face the additional expense of implementing the agreement on trade-related intellectual property rights (TRIPS) (whose primary beneficiaries are the developed countries), even as developed countries in their own turn have kept delaying requisite reforms in agriculture (which would have greatly benefited LDCs). For the latter, see Lankes (2002).

financial resources. The same is true at a macroeconomic level. As noted earlier, there is a difference in the socioeconomic costs incurred by First and Third World countries in weathering financial and currency crises. The poor face a higher set of prices and are more prone to the aforementioned instances of economic compulsion.

Insights from the poor and the ultrapoor

One could cite many other examples of a skewed dynamic to economic life by observing the plight of the poor. Access to basic needs, such as fuel and water, is also regressive in the prices paid by the poor relative to the rich. Urban slum dwellers in Port-au-Prince (Haiti), for example, are reported to pay a hundred times more for piped water than the wealthy (*The Economist* 2000b). As a proportion of their full income (that is, in terms of both time and money), the rural poor also pay a disproportionately higher price for water and fuel, given the enormous amount of time spent by women and children collecting water and firewood.[41] The poor bear a higher cost in securing basic needs by whatever measure is used — money, time, morbidity, or mortality.

In a synthesis of poverty studies, Michael Lipton (1988) notes that, left on their own, the poorest of the poor seem to be unable to benefit from poverty alleviation programs. This is true even among the poor in more developed countries. For example, in 1997, less than 20 percent of poor small farms took advantage of US agricultural farm program payments compared to over 75 percent and 60 percent for large and very large farms, respectively.[42] Moreover, eligible, poor farm households avail themselves less of food stamp and Medicaid programs than other eligible, nonfarm, families (Gundersen and Offutt 2003).

One can only surmise from these findings that the ultrapoor face additional hurdles relative to their less impoverished peers. Quoting Dorothy Day, Robert Kuttner (1997: 153) observes that "the poor are not poor just in money, but in organization, knowledge and self-respect." They are fatalistic, pessimistic, and consequently disengaged in the

---

41 One could conceivably argue that this is a case of under-investment in a public good. Some, however, would view this as a case of incomplete markets; privatizing water resources in Argentina, for example, has been found to reduce childhood mortality by 8% and even as much as 24% in the poorest areas (*The Economist* 2003a; Galiani, Gertler, and Schargrodsky 2003).

42 Gundersen et al. (2000: p. 19, Table 9). Small poor farms are defined as having an annual income of less than $20,000 and gross sales of less than $100,000 compared with large farms (sales revenues between $250,000 and $500,000) and very large farms (sales of over $500,000) (ibid. p. 5).

promotion of their own well-being (ibid.: 154). Thus, in economic terms, we could describe the ultrapoor as facing higher prices even in the poverty alleviation programs that are targeted at them to begin with.[43] If such is the case for extra-market interventions that are already specifically designed to assist the ultrapoor, how much more for regular market operations? In other words, the ultrapoor most likely face even higher prices in participating in the marketplace.

Other examples

International trade can in many ways be viewed as paradigmatic of the nature of market exchange in both its strengths and its weaknesses. The greater hurdles and higher costs faced by the poor in participating in global trade illustrate how market operations can often be uneven in the distribution of the burdens and benefits of economic exchange. For example, trade leads nations to shift their production toward the activities they do best (their comparative advantage). This transition is often skewed in its impact. In the more developed countries, it is the unskilled and lower-skilled manufacturing workers who bear the immediate brunt of low-cost imports. These displaced workers will find it even more difficult to find alternative employment as industrialized nations move ever higher in the technological chain of products in which they presumably have their comparative advantage. It is not surprising that trade has always been a contentious issue throughout history because it disrupts people's livelihoods and lifestyles.

The impact of gentrification is yet another example of the skewed impact of pecuniary externalities. Property values rise as commercial businesses and the wealthy move into, invest in, and improve urban centers. The resulting increase in rentals and property taxes drives away long-time residents who are in effect forced to move to more affordable but run-down sections of the city where they may also face the additional expense of longer commutes to work or to access essential social services. Silicon Valley in the dotcom bubble of the 1990s was a case in point, in which even the middle class themselves were "crowded out" by commercial renters and wealthier households which could afford to

---

43 A plausible explanation for the higher prices that the ultrapoor face is their lack of complementary assets to properly use government assistance. For example, the more educated are most likely better able to navigate through the maze of requirements for some of these programs. See Barrera (1991).

pay the ever ratcheting rents and property taxes.[44] Such displacement represented a real increase in the array of prices (time, convenience, and money) faced by those who had been negatively affected by the unintended consequences of gentrification and the real estate bubble.

SUMMARY AND CONCLUSIONS

History provides convincing evidence of the enormous gains from market operations. Contrast, for example, the feudal economy of precarious survival with the industrial economy of accelerating abundance. The key factor that accounts for this difference is the relatively greater freedom accorded economic activity in the modern era. This in turn has spawned specialization and market exchange among economic agents. Price signals are the principal mechanisms that orchestrate a spontaneous order from the resulting diversity of transactions and decisions unleashed by unfettered private initiatives. Price adjustments, however, inflict unintended consequences on unsuspecting third parties.

Pecuniary externalities reallocate burdens and benefits across different economic agents. Such market-driven redistributions of gains and losses can often be regressive in that the poor often end up facing higher "entry costs" to participating in the marketplace. This phenomenon arises because the set of prices that people face is largely a function of their personal capabilities and their sociohistorical location. *Full transaction costs* are not equal across the board but are in fact individualized. It is this disparity and diversity in capabilities and social position that make the market an effective price discriminator in the way it imposes transaction costs that are specific to each market participant. In understanding why and how sociohistorical location and personal capabilities matter, we gain insights into how we can design extra-market interventions to correct for the regressive impact of pecuniary externalities.

The market, left on its own, will do what it does best: allocate scarce resources to their most valued uses by seeking the highest returns. The distinct benefit in this is the attainment of allocative efficiency that lays the groundwork for sustained long-term growth and development. The success of the modern market for the past two centuries speaks for itself, in which a larger population base is readily provisioned, and at a higher per capita income, than at any time in human history. Nevertheless, there

---

44 See, for example, Conlin and Robson (2001).

is also a downside to this dynamic: a regressive incidence in the *full transaction costs* attendant on market operations.

Viewed strictly from the goal of allocative efficiency, the skewed incidence of the burdens of market adjustments is an unfortunate and unintended, though understandable, collateral effect of putting scarce resources to their most valued uses. Free market exchange, after all, is concerned merely with creating the highest possible total gains, and not with how such created value is distributed among the transactors, or even whether they are mutually advantageous to all.[45] Ameliorative measures are necessary to correct such a market feature.

45 Pareto optimality is merely about improving someone's position without making anybody else worse off. Thus, it is possible to have economic agent A reap all the benefits of a market transaction without any gains at all for economic agent B, as long as the latter is not made worse off. Alternatively, using the compensation criterion, all that is needed is for winners to be able potentially to remunerate losers, without having actually to provide such recompense.

PART 2

Setting the moral baseline and shaping expectations

CHAPTER 3

Economic security as God's twofold gift

The preceding chapters examined the nature and dynamics of the economic compulsion precipitated by the adverse unintended ripple effects of the market. Is economic distress morally significant? If so, why? Christian ethics has much to contribute to answering these questions.

This chapter argues that economic compulsion ought to concern Christians because it goes against God's proffered gift of economic security and is prima facie evidence that we, both as individuals and as a community, have not lived up to the obligations attendant on such a benefaction. Economic security is a twofold gift because God not only supplies our needs but also uses our mutual responsibility for each other as a channel for bestowing such provisions on us. In other words, God provides for us through each other; God elicits human participation in effecting divine providence. This initiative is yet another unmerited divine favor.

Within Christian ethics, I submit that the divine gift of economic security could be defined as (1) access to the requisite goods of life (2) within the nurturing care and support of the community, and (3) through the individual's own efforts, to the extent possible. Privation in any of these three constitutive elements is sufficient to give rise to economic distress. Failure in the first condition means a deprivation of basic needs essential to survival and health. Disorder in the second requirement reveals a collective inability to live up to duties of mutual assistance. Deficiency in the third reflects a state of chronic dependence. I examine each of these in the following historical review.

ECONOMIC SECURITY IN THE HEBREW SCRIPTURES

The book of Genesis provides scriptural grounds for the claim that God provides for the material needs of human beings. The accounts of creation describe God's overwhelming sovereignty over all life. Moreover, they affirm divine solicitude for humans as the earth is entrusted to their stewardship to meet their needs. Thus, commentators, such as the patristic writers,[1] cite the Genesis narratives of creation as a basis for the belief that God provisions us with great liberality.

All three aforementioned essential conditions of economic security as a divine gift can be inferred from the book of Genesis. However, I propose that the biblical accounts of the liberation of Israel from slavery and oppression and her formation as a nation provide even more vivid scriptural foundations for the claim that human economic security is intrinsic to God's intended order.

Thomas Ogletree (1983: 79–80) notes that historicity and sociality are the two distinctive enduring legacies of Hebrew thought to moral understanding. In the following sections, I argue that both historicity and sociality can be used effectively in understanding why economic security is a gift from God, what its indispensable elements are, and how such divine bequest is effected.

Historicity

God broke into human history to liberate Israel from oppression and slavery in Egypt. But there was more. It was not merely the gift of emancipation that was proffered, significant as it already was. YHWH went further by also imparting the gift of abundance. Not only were the Hebrews freed from servitude, they were also led by God to a land they could rightfully possess and call their own, a land where they no longer had to be aliens at the mercy of others for their livelihood, a land where God was the owner. No longer did the Hebrews have to live in trepidation, dependent on the goodwill of their overlords, for YHWH was now their landlord and patron. A double gift of freedom with prosperity for the nation Israel followed in the wake of God's in-breaking. The Lord of nature – the Creator of the heavens and the earth, the provider of all living creatures – was revealed to be also the Lord of history. And as the Lord of history, God had given Israel the Promised Land, a "land flowing with milk and honey," even at the cost of dispossessing its previous occupants (von Waldow 1974: 496).

Eberhard von Waldow (1974) and Christopher Wright (1990) examine at length the centrality of land not only in God's creation but also in Israel's election to be the Chosen People of YHWH. In fact, the role of

---

1 For example, Basil and Gregory of Nyssa.

land in Hebrew history is so fundamental that von Waldow (1974: 493) even goes so far as to claim that if Israel's relationship with God has to be described in a single phenomenon, it has to be "Israel and her Land" rather than "Israel and her Covenant." Wright (1990: 4) observes that land is a perennial factor in Hebrew history from God's promise of land in the call of Abraham in Genesis; to its conquest and division in Joshua; to the numerous precepts governing life on the land in Exodus, Deuteronomy, and Leviticus; to the wars fought by David and Saul to secure the borders of Israel; to the land's pillage and loss in the Exile; to its subsequent return to the remnants in the post-exilic period of reform, renewal, and rebuilding. The life of the Chosen People revolves around land. Land is the concrete particularity that serves as the terrain upon which Israel's relationship with YHWH unfolds.

Land has two dimensions; it is both symbolic and functional. Land took on a symbolic role because it served as the tangible sign of the Hebrews' election to a special bond with YHWH. It was a relationship unique to Israel alone, God's Chosen People. The Promised Land stood as clear proof and testimony of their special favored status before God. Land was of central importance to the family-clan, the basic unit of Hebrew society. Land ownership was the basis for their sense of "belonging" as an integral part of the nation. Indeed, landholding was a necessary condition of full membership within the community; it was the basis for their claim to be treated as an equal by others (Wright 1990). Thus, it is completely understandable why land return and redemption (Leviticus 25) occupy such a cardinal place in the Law. The loss of ancestral land due to economic insolvency, and its subsequent return, are also found in the other nations surrounding Israel (Chirichigno 1993: 350; Fager 1993: 25). However, in the case of the Hebrews, there was added urgency to regaining their family inheritance because the latter was their link to and the sign of their special relationship and status before God.

Of interest to us in this study, however, is the earth's functional role. Land is not merely symbolic, but it also fills an actual need, and an important one at that. In an agrarian culture, landholding is the source of wealth and power.[2] Land guarantees the household's independence because it provides family members with a livelihood that is not contingent on the will or whim or permission of anybody else. Moreover, land provides families with the means to discharge their cultic, military, and juridic obligations to the rest of the community (Wright 1990: 97). It was

---

2 In contrast, capital can arguably be described as the source of wealth in modern industrial society, while knowledge serves this function in the postindustrial economy.

land after all that provided the family-clans with the first fruits that were offered in sacrifice; it was land that furnished the material means that were needed to sustain them through the requisite fallows and Sabbath rests; and it was land that provisioned them with the plenitude that could then be shared in the communal feastings, tithings, gleaning, and alms-giving. In other words, besides being the tangible sign of Israel's election to Covenant responsibility, land also filled an important practical role by providing households with the economic security that satisfied not only their own needs, but also those of the larger community and those who were unable to fend for themselves.

The accounts of the division of the Promised Land (Josh. 18:1–10; Num. 26:52–56) also suggest that land served not only a symbolic role but a very real practical function. Note the attention given to how the land proportions were set according to family size and the fertility of the plots. If land were merely symbolic, there would have been no need to go through all this trouble. As it is, however, the Hebrew writers emphasize the great care and thought that must have been accorded to land division and allocation since the earth and its fruitfulness ensured the economic viability of each household clan.

The substance of the argument I am making (that God envisioned an order of creation and human affairs in which no one was in want) transcends the issue of whether the accounts of the occupation of the Promised Land and its subsequent division are truly historical and fact-ually accurate, or merely allegorical. For example, the Promised Land has been repeatedly described as "a land flowing with milk and honey" (Exod. 3:8, 17; 13:5; Lev. 20:24; Num. 14:8; Deut. 6:3; 11:9; 26:9, 15; 27:3; 31:20; Josh. 5:6; Jer. 11:5; 32:22; Ezra 20:6, 15). Von Waldo (1974: 499) cautions that this should not be read literally because the people (and the writers of the Hebrew Scripture) were most likely overwhelmed in their gratitude toward God and carried away accordingly in using such extravagant imagery to describe their blessings. It is sufficient for our purposes to note, however, that whether historical or metaphorical, God's grant of land is perceived by people as a de facto gift of economic security. Norbert Lohfink (1987: 43–42) points out that ancient cultures use such language to refer to the land of the gods overflowing with plenitude. That the Hebrew writers ascribe these same characteristics to their own land is merely to affirm their conviction that God did not will for them to be in want but provided for all their needs.[3]

---

3 The same also applies to the accounts of the manna and quail as they crossed and wandered through the desert (Exod. 16).

The gift of economic security as part of divine providence can also be inferred from the Sabbath (Deut. 5:12–15), the sabbatical-related legislation of the fallow (Exod. 23:10–12; Lev. 25:1–7, 18–24), and the Jubilee (Lev. 25). Patrick Miller (1985), Robert North (1954: 230), and Adrian Schenker (1998: 37) ascribe a messianic or eschatological typology to these sabbatical rests, releases, and feasts. There are no class divisions in the shared feastings; master, servant, aliens, the rich, and the poor are all equals partaking of the bounty provided by God. Together with the rest from toil provided for all, these sabbatical pauses are a foretaste of the eschatological banquet in which there will be no distinctions in status and where there will be plenty for all. Schenker (ibid.) goes so far as to claim that they are in fact a retrieval of the "original condition." Furthermore, the rest called for during the Sabbath, the sabbatical fallow, and the Jubilee is a de facto statement of faith: that YHWH, the Lord of nature, provides for more than enough to allow for such extended respites from labor. This is particularly true for the Jubilee year in which there is need to store two to three years' worth of provisions. Hebrew writers are acutely aware of this practical consideration and are quick to assure the people that YHWH will indeed furnish the requisite increase (Lev. 25:18–22). It does not matter whether or not these sabbatical laws were actually implemented to the letter. What is important for our study is the people's perception: (1) that divine provisions are adequate to discharge whatever YHWH is asking, and (2) that God's intended order is one of a shared superfluity and rest from toil for all.

We arrive at our first conclusion: Economic security is embedded within God's intended order in creation and in human affairs. What is not at issue for this study is the people's belief that YHWH is the Lord of nature who can provide bounteously and that YHWH is also the omnipotent Lord of history who does in fact bestow such plenitude. Regardless of whether the Hebrew accounts of liberation, conquest, and settlement are factual or metaphorical, what is not at issue here is the historicity of God breaking into human affairs and being a part of them. What is not at issue here is that from God's in-breaking flows a concomitant gift of economic security: freedom and prosperity, that is, freedom from oppression and freedom from want.

Sociality and conditionality

Another important undercurrent in the Scripture's account of God's in-breaking is the centrality of human response to YHWH's initiatives and fidelity. The Hebrews were acutely aware that their tenure on the "land flowing with milk and honey" was dependent on their dedication to YHWH; they were to discharge all that was required of them in their election to responsibility as God's Chosen People (von Waldow 1974: 503–506). Such expectations were articulated by the Law. They were to live upright lives, just as YHWH had been righteous in dealing with them as a nation. And an essential feature of living in such righteousness was for them to care for each other.

The gift of economic security attendant on God's in-breaking was merely conditional and not absolute. In other words, the Chosen People would be able fully to savor God's gift of freedom and abundance only to the degree that they truly took responsibility for each other. Thus, note, for example, the Covenant Code (Exod. 20:22–23:33), the Deuteronomic Code (Deut. 12–26), and the Code of Holiness (Lev. 17–26) and their extensive list of statutes and ordinances pertaining to economic life. Israel was to build a nation characterized by an economy of mutual assistance and equality in which no one would be in want. Hebrews would lend food or money to each other in hard times (Deut. 15:7–10; Lev. 25:35–37) without charging any interest at all (Exod. 22:25; Deut. 23:19–20; Lev. 25:36–37). They were to cease working periodically in order to rededicate themselves in sabbatical rest and celebrate festivals as equals (Exod. 23:10–12; Lev. 25:1–7, 18–24). A Jubilee year was to be proclaimed every fifty years during which land was returned to its original owners, debt was written off, and those in bondage were released (Lev. 25). Landowners were not to be over-thorough in harvesting their fields and vineyards, but were to generously leave enough for the marginalized to glean (Deut. 24:19–21; Lev. 19:9–10; 23:22; Ruth 2). Moreover, they were to tithe from their produce and bounty (Deut. 14:22–29). Debt was to be held only for six years and then forgiven on the seventh (Deut. 15:1–3). Slaves were to be freed after six years of service (Exod. 21:2–6; Deut. 15:12–18). Alms were to be freely given to the distressed. Widows, orphans, and strangers[4] were to receive preferential treatment and be singled out for special assistance because they were beloved of YHWH (Ogletree 1983: 56); it was primarily for their benefit that Israel was bound to a long list of economic ordinances as part of the Covenant. The widow, the orphan, and the alien

---

4 Von Waldow (1970: 182) refers to them as the *personae miserabiles.* See also Pleins (2001: 50–54) for the special place of the disenfranchised in the Law.

exhibit a common feature: They were landless and completely at the mercy of others for their protection and basic needs.

These economic statutes explicitly state the requirements for living in the "land flowing with milk and honey." Better yet, these precepts governing economic life describe the means by which the "land flowing with milk and honey" can be actualized (Deut. 28; 4:1; 5:31; 6:1–3; 11:8, 31; 12:1). Regardless of the scholarly debates and disagreements on the dating[5] and sequencing of these laws, one thing is clear: Common to all of them is the understanding that a hard life of want and destitution is not what God had envisioned for Israel, but one that is free, just, and compassionate in a Promised Land of material and spiritual bounty. These gifts are meant to be accepted, maintained, and internalized by the Chosen People, and then allowed to bear plentiful harvest. These economic ordinances describe a people struggling to ameliorate the chance and contingency of socioeconomic life in their desire to care for each other, especially those in severe economic distress, and thus live up to their special election in the Covenant.

All these fall within Ogletree's (1983: 79–80) observation that sociality is another legacy of Israel to moral understanding. We are truly responsible for each other. Thus, we are led to our second conclusion: God effects the divine gift of economic security (of freedom and abundance) within the human community through mutual cooperation and self-giving. It is a divine grant reserved not only for a few, but to give a comprehensive material security for all, without exceptions, even for the stranger and the alien. These are very high standards requiring much sacrifice. But Israel is able to embark on that which is difficult and exacting because, as the motive clauses[6] (Gemser 1953; Doron 1978) repeatedly remind the Chosen People, they are merely being asked to extend to others and to each other the signal favors bestowed on them by YHWH in their own moment of need and desperation.

This communal feature constitutes the second dimension of the gift of economic security. God provides more than just basic necessities for survival and basic health; God also provides humans with the signal opportunity to participate in, indeed *to effect and incarnate*, divine righteousness in the here and now in human affairs. This, I submit, is the

---

5 See, for example, Chirichigno (1993: 17–29); Gamoran (1971: 132, n. 45); Pleins (2001: 88, n. 63); Schenker (1998: 40, n. 32); von Waldow (1970: 182–83); Wright (1990: 58).

6 Motive clauses are the addenda to the statutes that articulate the rationale for such precepts.

added gift of human instrumentality. It would have been so easy for
God to provide directly for Israel without the need for human cooperation. Nonetheless, God is going to provide for them as a Chosen People
in the measure that they truly care for each other. God provides for us
through each other.

Individual effort

Historicity, conditionality, and sociality all converge on yet another
constitutive element of the divine gift of economic security: the importance of personal effort and striving. As individuals, Hebrews located their
self-identity in their common life as a nation. Despite this strong corporate personality, the basic social unit in Hebrew life was nonetheless still
the household (Wright 1990: 97). It was through their families that
individuals discharged their obligations and drew benefits from the larger
community. Thus, for example, note how all the preceding discussion on
the importance of landholding revolves around the household-clan and
not the individual or even the nation as a whole. The gift of economic
security is actualized at the family level.

It is not good enough that the extensive array of economic ordinances
provides a safety net for those in dire economic straits. The Law goes
beyond this and seeks a further goal: the restoration of families as
independent functioning social units. The next chapter examines at length
the principle of restoration embedded within the Law. For now, it is
sufficient to highlight a special character in the legislation on debt remission, slave manumission, interest-free loans, mandatory lending, and land
return. These are all meant not only to provide relief to people who have
fallen on hard economic times, but, more importantly, *to restore* distressed households as landholding families that are able to function
independently once again and supply their own needs.

The economic precepts on almsgiving, tithings, shared festivals, and
gleaning would all have been sufficient if the goal of the Law were merely
to satisfy the basic needs of people. The other aforementioned economic
ordinances would have merely been redundant; but they are not. In fact,
the main thrust of the statutes governing economic life is both relief and
restoration. The end (*telos*) of mandatory lending, interest-free loans, debt
reprieve, slave release, and land return is to reinstate and rebuild the
afflicted household's capacity to do what it is able to do for itself. The
goal of these restorative economic laws is to ensure that families are able to
sustain themselves on their own and take their places once again in the

larger community as equals, as landholding families that are able to bear their share of the common juridic, military, and cultic obligations.[7]

Again, one finds ample support for this claim of a restorative goal to these economic laws by looking at the care with which land had been divided and allocated (Josh. 18:1–10; Num. 26:52–56). In making the size of the land allotment a function of household size and the plots' fertility, the people implicitly acknowledged that an essential community goal was providing the best conditions for maintaining the independence and the economic viability of each household. In other words, there was a need to ensure that people were able to accomplish what they should be doing for themselves. The same can be inferred from the Hebrew writers' description of how YHWH ceased to provide the Chosen People with manna as soon as they reaped the produce of the Promised Land (Josh. 5:10–12).[8] Indeed, the divine gift of economic security has a third constitutive element: While access to basic needs is effected within and in cooperation with the larger community, it presupposes personal effort and striving, to the extent possible, as a necessary condition.

Summary

The narrative of God's in-breaking in human history provides an excellent exposition of the dynamics of economic security as a divine benefaction. The conclusion that economic security is a gift intended by YHWH for the Chosen People as part of the restoration of due order in human affairs goes beyond the question of whether the biblical accounts of the formation of the nation Israel in the Promised Land are historically accurate or merely allegorical, or a mixture of both.

This divine gift of economic security has three essential features: (1) the capacity to access and procure the means of life (2) within community and (3) through personal enterprise, to the extent possible.[9] Given these foundational elements, we can discern two parts to God's gift of economic security: (1) the gift of life and its necessary provisions and (2) the

---

7 Described in contemporary language, these laws advance the principle of subsidiarity, that is, the principle that higher bodies ought not to arrogate to themselves functions that lower bodies are able to discharge themselves (Pius XI 1931: #79.)

8 Again, the point that YHWH was not going to do for the Hebrews what they were able to do for themselves transcends the issue of whether these accounts are factual or figurative.

9 This latter qualification is important since the aged, the infirm, and the orphans can only do so much in procuring basic necessities for themselves. Moreover, there are those who are trapped by socioeconomic circumstances and are unable to provide for themselves.

gift of participating in God's providence, of God providing for us through each other.

Lohfink (1987: 5–15) eloquently describes this twofold dimension to the gift of economic security. He is emphatic that while God does indeed have a special solicitude for the poor, it is a mistake to glamorize poverty because it is an aberration of God's intended order of creation. It is likewise an error to depict God as an otherworldly divinity aloof and far removed from the seemingly mundane struggles of creaturely life and concerned merely with the affairs of the spirit and the ethereal. Far from these misconceptions, our God is a God "interested in the here and now," "interested in material things," and "interested in plenitude and riches." God created human beings, not that they may wallow in destitution and hardship, but that they may enjoy the fullness and the joy of divine creation. And this enjoyment is not limited to some eschatological time and place in the future when everything will be made right; it is meant for the temporal present. Plenitude is not reserved for the messianic banquet alone; rather, God envisions a life of material abundance even during our journey, even as the trajectory of salvation history unfolds. And to cap it all, Lohfink (1987: 12–15) observes that this burning interest on the part of God "unleashes a drama." It is the drama of YHWH breaking into human history to liberate an oppressed people, form them into a nation like no other nation, and then put them in a land of their own where no one will be in want.

The drama unleashed in God's in-breaking continues; it is ongoing. For God has commissioned us to carry on the work of restoring due order in human affairs. For this reason, Lohfink (1987) has vigorously argued that at the heart of the historicity in Israel's narrative is a systemic reform that not only provides relief for the poor but also addresses the root causes of their destitution and want. Thus, we have the exacting collection of economic ordinances in Hebrew Law; Israel is to be an active participant in the unfolding drama God has unleashed. Israel is not merely going to be a passive recipient of YHWH's saving act, as she herself is to be an agent for extending such divine initiatives to others who have yet to taste and experience for themselves the plenitude intended by God in the here and now. Material prosperity is merely the tip of a much deeper and more significant gift of participation in divine providence and righteousness.[10]

---

10 For a more extended treatment of the Old Testament economic ordinances as an invitation to participation in God's righteousness and providence, see Barrera (2005: chapters 4 and 5).

ECONOMIC SECURITY IN THE NEW TESTAMENT

Access to basic needs

Matthew 6:25–34 and Luke 12:22–31 clearly point to the bounty of God's intended order. Procuring the material means for survival and health ought not to be cause for anxious concern because of the certainty of divine beneficence. Such Matthean and Lucan assurance finds its warrants within the larger witness and theology of the entire New Testament. In the first place, this confidence in material sufficiency stems from the conviction that human beings are deeply loved by God above all other creatures to the point where every moment of human existence is ever present before a solicitous divine gaze.[11]

Second, even as the incarnate Word of God has come to preach and win hearts and minds, Jesus nevertheless takes an active role in ministering to people's physical and material needs as seen in the many miracle accounts of healing and feeding. Jesus is not an otherworldly God aloof from the daily struggles of people; rather, he immerses himself in the difficulties encountered in living in a material world.

Third, belief in the certainty of human provisioning is validated too by the faith community's acknowledgment and appreciation of God's characteristic liberality. We see this generosity in the evangelists' accounts of Jesus preaching on how he came that we might have fullness of life. We observe this munificence in the parables that speak of a prodigal Father of endless chances and forgiveness (Luke 15:11–32; Matt. 18:21–35). We encounter this divine quality in the miracle narratives in which human needs are met, and always to superfluity (Matt. 14:13–21; Mark 6:34–44; Luke 9:12–17; John 2:1–11; 6:1–15). Even if these miracle stories are about much larger theological points (such as the messianic plenitude in the miracle of the wine at Cana and the Eucharist in the feeding of the multitudes), rather than chronicles of actual historical events, we nevertheless still arrive at the same point: The evangelists understand that ours is a God of unbounded beneficence. And this applies to both our spiritual and material welfare.

The faith community and the evangelists see a self-revealing God who takes an active interest and role in meeting humans' temporal and transcendent needs and invariably satisfies these with characteristic benevolence. This conclusion goes beyond the scholarly debates on whether

11 See, for example, Matthew 10:29–31 and Luke 12:6–7.

the preceding accounts are truly factual or merely allegorical. And, of course, the paradigm of such unstinting outpouring is the passion and death of the incarnate Word on Calvary. Indeed, even as Lohfink (1987: 5–15) describes the divinity that broke into human history to liberate an enslaved people in the Hebrew scriptures as a God "interested in the here and now," "interested in the material world," and "interested in plenitude and riches" for humans, I argue that such a divine profile rings just as true in the New Testament. Jesus fits Lohfink's characterization of such an engaged divinity well – of how God is profoundly concerned and involved with bestowing plenitude and riches on God's children in the temporal here and now. The Gospel of Christ calls for and celebrates a poverty of spirit, not destitution; the latter is not part of God's intended order, as Matthew 6:25–34 and Luke 12:22–31 assure us.

The social character of economic security

Just as we find in the Hebrew Scripture, such proffered material sufficiency is merely provisional. The passages in Matthew 6:25–34 and Luke 12:22–31 themselves lay out the stipulation that following the will of God is a precondition; indeed, it is the very means by which humans are able to benefit fully from creation's bounty. Thus, in examining how the early Christian tradition deals with economic needs, Barry Gordon (1989a: 43–58) describes the New Testament's succinct solution to the problem of scarcity as one of seeking the Kingdom of God.

From an economic point of view, the pursuit of the Kingdom of God entails a mixed array of both precepts and counsels. There are admonitions against turning wealth into an idol (Matt. 6:24; Luke 16:13), against keeping others in subservient dependence through patron–client relationships (Moxnes 1988), and against the pursuit of position and honor driven by an inordinate, selfish desire to be above everybody else (Matt. 20:20–28; Mark 10:35–45). There is also the call for radical voluntary divestment for the sake of greater personal perfection in Christian discipleship (Matt. 19:16–22; Mark 10:17–31; Luke 18:18–30). Then, there are the duties of honest work and of living up to the positive economic obligations we owe each other. Only the latter two are relevant for our issue, and, accordingly, only these will be examined in what follows. The other precepts and counsels are beyond the scope of the present study.

Just as in the Old Testament, there is an unavoidable social component to actualizing economic security in the new dispensation. In the first place, the enjoyment of the fruits of the earth to fulfill our basic needs is a divine gift intended for all. This is clear from the preceding section's exposition on how Matthew 6:25–34 and Luke 12:22–31 fit in within the larger testimony of the entire New Testament. Second, we are responsible not only for our own personal economic needs but also for the unmet needs of our neighbors. We see this in the parable of the rich man dressed in purple and Lazarus (Luke 16:19–31). We are reminded of this duty in the strongest possible way in the parable of the separation of the goats and the sheep (Matt. 25:31–46). In other words, we are indeed each other's keepers; we are truly responsible for each other's welfare. This is not merely a counsel of perfection but a precept, for we are told in no uncertain terms that we are going to be held accountable for failure to fulfill this positive obligation we owe each other.

The common economic life of the early Church is likewise an affirmation of the social character of economic security. Luke describes how people divested themselves of their properties and entrusted the proceeds to the apostles to be used for the benefit of the entire community. And no one was said to have been left in want (Acts 4:32–37), just as in the envisioned Covenant model of community for the nation Israel. This communal dynamic intrinsic to economic security is also illustrated in the Pauline collection for the poor of Jerusalem undertaken throughout the churches he had established (1 Cor. 16:1–4; 2 Cor. 8:1–15; 9:1–15). Besides providing real relief for the destitute of Jerusalem, such an offering was also meant to convey and affirm the Gentile Christians' solidarity with their suffering Jewish brethren.

Both in theory and in practice, the ideal economic order in Kingdom discipleship is effected through the generous self-giving and mutual sharing of the followers of Christ. There is an inescapable social component to economic security, a divine gift given to society as a whole and actualized by the community itself in the way people care for each other. There are ample warrants in the New Testament for the claim that embedded within the proffered divine gift of economic security is the added benefaction of human participation in divine providence.

The requisite personal contribution

Paul's work ethic is the most articulate and compelling New Testament expression of the third constitutive element of economic security: the need for sincere personal effort and exertion in providing for our own needs and those of others. A distinctive undercurrent in Paul's writings is his sense of urgency driven by a conviction about the imminent return of

Jesus Christ. Thus, he is emphatic that people should take immediate and decisive steps in reorienting their priorities and direction in life in preparation for the looming *parousia*. Whatever time is left should be devoted entirely to assiduously collecting themselves in a manner befitting people who are about to meet the Lord. Indeed, more than anyone else, Paul has a keen appreciation that anything else outside such preparatory activity is a waste of precious time and effort.

Despite the sense of immediacy in his appeals to people to put themselves in a high state of readiness for the approaching return of Christ, Paul is nonetheless attentive to the realistic demands of daily living. He severely rebukes those who, in anticipation of the *parousia*, saw no further reason to apply themselves in toil and had simply reneged on their responsibilities to themselves and their dependents by giving up work. Paul tells the Thessalonians to have nothing to do with these people (2 Thess. 3:6–12). Even as worldly tasks and affairs pale in comparison with the supernatural new age about to dawn, personal work is nevertheless still an obligation that must be fulfilled during this period of expectant waiting. We should not let others shoulder the burdens that are properly ours to bear to begin with. Moreover, through such labor, we are able to provide assistance to those who are genuinely unable to support themselves (Eph. 4:28).

Paul lived up to what he preached. As an apostle of the Lord, he was aware of his right to demand material support and sustenance from the churches to which he ministered (1 Cor. 9:1–15). Notwithstanding such a duty on the part of the faithful, Paul voluntarily ceded his claim for recompense and worked as a tentmaker for his own upkeep (Acts 20:32–36; 1 Thess. 2:7–9; 2 Thess. 3:6–12; 2 Cor. 11:7–9). Thus, in both his written instructions and in his own life, Paul affirmed the obligations of a proper work ethic that requires us to do what we are able to do for ourselves and for those who are truly unable to care for themselves.

Pauline preaching and example provide direct and unequivocal validation of a characteristic feature of economic security: the need for personal enterprise, labor, and contribution, to the extent possible. Furthermore, there is also an indirect attestation to this element of economic security, and this one can be described as an argument from silence. There is a glaring contrast between the Gospels and Pauline writings regarding possessions. The evangelists, especially Luke, highlight the great value attached to complete and radical personal divestment as a precondition of a more perfect discipleship (Matt. 19:16–22; Mark 10:17–31; Luke 18:18–30). In fact, Luke records the voluntary poverty embraced by the early Church in Jerusalem (Acts 4:32–37). In contrast, there is a complete absence of such teaching in Paul (Dahl 1977: 22–39).

To account fully for this disparity is beyond the scope of this study. However, we must briefly consider Gordon's (1989a: 77–81) explanation as it provides additional corroboration to my claim that personal initiative is a third constitutive element of economic security. Gordon hypothesizes that Paul had witnessed firsthand the disastrous consequences of the Jerusalem community's experiment in decapitalization and common property ownership. The ensuing impoverishment compelled Peter, James, and John (Gal. 2:9–10) to ask Paul to solicit assistance for the poor of Jerusalem as he preached to the Gentiles. Against this larger backdrop, one gains a better understanding not only of the need for the Pauline collection but also as to why Paul diverges from the evangelists when it comes to radical voluntary dispossession.

At no stage does Paul advise his congregations to emulate the practice of the mother church. Quite the reverse. The communities for which he feels responsible are not to make their incorporation in Christ an occasion for a plunge into experimentation with economic relationships. Not only are their members to maintain steady and devoted application to work, but also they are not to engage in any dramatic liquidation of capital. Nowhere does Paul even suggest common ownership or pooling of possessions. (Gordon 1989a: 78)

The complete absence of any teaching or even passing reference to radical voluntary dispossession in Paul is a jarring contrast with the Gospels, and lends much credence to Gordon's thesis. It cannot be simply dismissed as an oversight since Paul's letters reveal an eye for details (e.g., household rules). Nor can the question of economic life and private property ownership be said to be a minor point; it is not, considering the repeated treatment it receives in the subsequent writing of the Gospels that reflects the teaching's relative importance within the tradition. This conspicuous silence on the part of Paul can only lead us to infer the need for personal labor to attain economic security not only for oneself but for others as well. Private property is essential to such personal enterprise.

In conclusion, scholars have long warned of the risks of gleaning a homogeneous ethics from the New Testament because of its broad diversity (Hays 1996; Matera 1996; Schnackenburg 1965; Schrage 1988; Verhey 1984). The preceding discussion does not pretend to be an exhaustive synthesis of New Testament insights regarding economic security. The only point I am making is that there is enough in New Testament literature to substantiate my characterization of the nature and dynamics of economic security as a divine gift. We find a clear affirmation of the bounty of God's providence and the need for both a corresponding personal and communal response to enjoy its fruitfulness.

ECONOMIC SECURITY IN PATRISTIC LITERATURE

Despite the wide range of patristic writings that are so different in their theological concerns and emphases and so varied in their cultural, geographic, and temporal contexts, it is remarkable to see complete agreement over the harsh condemnation of the unaddressed detrimental effects of the marketplace.[12] Moreover, the wealthy are deemed to bear primary responsibility for such sad states of affairs, whether through their sins of omission or commission.[13]

Access to the gifts of the earth

The starting point of the patristic doctors' blunt censure of the rich lies in their deep conviction in the goodness of God's providence; scarcity is a man-made phenomenon. Creation is a gift from God that has been made so bountiful in order to meet the needs of all humans. The aversion of many of the patristic writers to private property ownership can also be traced to this fundamental belief in the whole of creation's being given as a gift to all of humanity for their common use.

Gordon (1989a: 102–105) points to the Greek Fathers' unwavering confidence in the depth of God's love for the human person; such divine love necessarily entails the same omnipotent God's ensuring that nothing essential for human flourishing is ever withheld from or found wanting in those who are beloved of God. Basil sees nature's abundance as an affirmation of how God, the paradigm of the virtue of *philantrophia*, looks after us and provides for our needs. Gregory of Nyssa pictures humans as guests in the world, with God as the perfect host who ensures that we receive the very best of hospitality (Gordon 1989a: 102).

As mentioned earlier, Lohfink (1987: 5–15) is emphatic that ours is a God interested in plenitude and riches for the temporal here and now.

---

12 Note that "detrimental effects of the marketplace" is a modern description of the problem and is not something any of the Fathers would have ever said.

13 The patristic corpus is vast, and going through the original literature is an undertaking that is in itself a separate major project. Thus, for purposes of this section, I have had to rely on the syntheses and commentaries of others, to wit: Avila (1983); Giordani (1944); Gordon (1989a and b, 1994); Phan (1984); Ramsey (1982); Viner (1978); and Walsh and Langan (1977).

This is echoed by Clement of Alexandria, who finds nothing to celebrate about indigence:

For neither great nor worthy to be desired is the state of one so lacking in possessions that he does not have the wherewith to live; for if it were, then that whole swarm of proletarians, derelicts and beggars who live from hand to mouth, all those wretched cast out upon the streets, though they live in ignorance of God and of his justice, would be the most blessed and the most religious and the only candidate for eternal life simply because they are penniless and find it hard to live, lacking the most modest means.

(*Who Is the Rich Man That Shall Be Saved?*: XI)[14]

In other words, there is nothing intrinsically meritorious in being destitute. Such a condition has no part in God's intended order of creation and human affairs. On the contrary, God is keen on providing abundance in the here and now, and not merely after some unknown apocalyptic time in the future.

Of course, the basis for all these claims is Genesis 1:28–30 in which humans are given dominion over all creatures so that they may satisfy their needs for survival, growth, and development. Human beings are beloved of God, and it would have been a self-contradiction for God to have created humans in the divine image and likeness without providing all the necessary means to thrive and to live up to this particular gift that makes them different from all the other creatures. Augustine is also quick to note that original sin did not alter creation's copious endowment. Nature itself is not subjected to transformation on account of human disobedience.

[T]he material world lies under no curse, is afflicted with no stain, no subjection to Satan, is not alienated from God because of man's sin. It shares neither the guilt nor the *poena* of man. It does not groan for liberation; it awaits no redemption, no judgement, no purification. (Clarke 1958: 150)[15]

To the patristic mind it is self-evident that God has provided enough, and for the benefit of all. *Economic security for everyone is a corollary of divine creation.* The earth is a bequest shared by all. This foundational premise has far-reaching ramifications not only for patristic thought but for the entire social tradition itself. In the first place, the steadfast belief in

---

14 Quoted in Gordon (1989a: 86).
15 We find corroboration for this position in Aquinas's divine attributes. Since God is Pure Act and has no potency, God must be immutable. Furthermore, there is no time in God. Thus, the bounty of creation cannot be said to have been taken back by God as punishment for human sin. As I argue in a later section, humans are chiefly responsible for material want.

the abundance of creation is instrumental in the reversal of pagan values regarding poor relief and responsibility for the marginalized. Walsh and Langan describe this phenomenon well:

The repudiation of pagan notions about happiness and the transformation of values . . . clearly depend on a new conception of God's nature and his activity in the history of salvation. *The Greek apologists stress the fact that belief in the existence of an all-bountiful God has resulted . . . in a new breed of men and women who refuse to abandon the poor and the helpless to fate,* but who rush to their assistance in times of crisis. (Walsh and Langan 1977: 117 [emphasis added])

Indeed, there would have been less urgency to taking responsibility for the destitute if the world had been created by divine design with an intrinsic insufficiency of goods to meet human needs. Fate would have the final say on who lives comfortably and who dies from want. Poor relief would simply be a futile exercise that goes against nature. Consequently, belief in the plenitude of creation is essential, lest we be fatalistic about destitution and leave the poor to wallow unaided in their plight.[16]

Walsh and Langan (1977: 147) allude to a second ramification in their conclusion on patristic social consciousness. The certitude regarding the abundance of God's creation serves as the basis for what has come to be known in our own day and age as the principle of the universal destination of the goods of the earth (John Paul II 1991: #31). Modern Catholic social documents have consistently used this as a key principle in addressing many of the social questions of the last century (Barrera 2001: 193–205).

In summary, the starting point in patristic economic thought is the claim that God endowed the earth with a sufficient abundance to satisfy human needs out of love for humanity. Moreover, the fruits of the earth are a gift meant for all and are, consequently, to be shared by all.

---

16 Walsh and Langan's (1977) point on the significance of belief in the abundance of God's intended order is important. Take the case of the Reverend Thomas Malthus in his celebrated *Essay on the Principle of Population.* The last two chapters of the first edition of this work (1798) grapple with a theodicy that accounts for why a benevolent, provident God would permit a world of dire subsistence living. He concludes that scarcity is instrumental to the formation of the mind. Material want is essential to prodding humans to exertion and effort; they would have otherwise languished in torpor and inactivity. William Paley (1802) and John Sumner (1816) share the same view on the functional role of scarcity in forming human character as part of God's order of creation. Consequently, it is not surprising that Malthus, Paley, and Sumner are against social ameliorative measures as these simply go against nature (Waterman 1991). The patristic writers have a diametrically opposed position – that ours is a bounteous world to begin with; destitution is an aberration in God's order of creation that requires remedial action. For a critical examination of the Malthusian theodicy of scarcity, see Barrera (2005).

Corporate effort

From the patristic point of view, the gift of economic security that is implicit in God's creation comes with a significant social dimension. This is evident in their keen understanding of the nature of the earth as a shared inheritance, in the manner by which they propose people ought to deal with the vicissitudes of economic life, in their reaction to the consequences of rival consumption as an economic phenomenon, and, finally, in their theological understanding of what it is to be a community of faith. The patristic writers clearly see economic security as a communal endeavor.

First, as I mentioned in the preceding section, there is a deep-seated conviction not only of the abundance of God's creation but also of the common stewardship of such plenitude. Both claims clearly come to the fore in the various syntheses of patristic social thought (Giordani 1944; Gordon 1989a and b; Hengel 1974; Phan 1984; Ramsey 1982; Viner 1978; Walsh and Langan 1977). Furthermore, observe another clear pattern in the writings of the early Church Fathers: The proffered divine benefaction (of supplying for our needs) brings with it the concomitant obligation to share such blessings. The blessings of divine providence carry attendant duties.

There is no consensus among the Church Fathers on whether or not God had intended private property ownership in human affairs.[17] For example, Chrysostom sees common ownership as the only permissible form of proprietorship since the world can be likened to a single household in which all receive "equal allowances" because all are brothers and sisters (Gordon 1989a: 102; 1989b: 117–19). On the other hand, Clement of Alexandria and Ambrose accept private property ownership as a legitimate institution in God's order of creation. Regardless of their competing positions on the nature of private property rights, patristic writers nevertheless arrive at the same conclusion: There is a distinction between ownership and use (Avila 1983: 33–46; Gordon 1989a: 85, 114). Augustine subscribes to a "'right use' theory of legitimate ownership" in which the title to hold property is contingent on its proper use (Gordon 1989a: 124). The obligations of just use are satisfied only in the measure that the property benefits not only the owner but the widest possible circle of people. In other words, there is a compelling social mortgage; the ownership may be private but the fruits from its usage must be shared. This, of

17 See Hengel (1974) and Avila (1983).

course, is based on the aforementioned understanding of how the blessings of divine providence bring with them corollary obligations.

Second, the social character of patristic economic thought can be seen in their views on how chance and contingency in nature and in economic life ought to be ameliorated. For example, Basil and Chrysostom account for the observable geographic differences in nature's fertility as part of God's intended order rather than as a flaw in divine providence. In particular, they see disparities in the productivity of different lands as the occasion by which humans interact and cooperate with each other in their economic life. Nature itself occasions cooperation through the economic exchange that allows people mutually to benefit from each other's labors (Gordon 1989a: 103).

The repeated call for almsgiving is an even better illustration of the social dimension to the patristic understanding of economic security. The need to share not only of our surplus, but even of our substance, is a constant refrain in their admonitions on economic life.[18] In fact, Gordon (1989a: 106–109) notes that charity is the early Church Fathers' solution to the problem of scarcity. This persistent summons to share is founded on the aforementioned tenet that the earth is bequeathed to all. The bounty of the earth is not an end in itself but is meant to serve human development. Moreover, the unmet needs of our neighbors are the measure of how much we should share of ourselves and our means.

Third, patristic teachings are permeated with a social dimension because of their appreciation of how economic life is primarily a moral phenomenon. Since God as Creator is omnipotent and since God as provider is lavish and benevolent, how then do we account for the empirical realities of material want and destitution? Sin. In other words, patristic writers view economic deprivation as completely man-made (Gordon 1989a: 104–106, 126); it is a gross distortion of God's intended order. In particular, conspicuous consumption, avarice, and the diversion of resources to satisfy the whims of the wealthy few deprive many of their rightful legacy from God. The fruits of the earth are indeed plentiful because of God's lavish generosity; nevertheless, they are still finite. Rival consumption is unavoidable in the material world: Person A's consumption or use of a scarce, finite good Y leaves that much less of good Y for the use or enjoyment of person B and everyone else. However, the phenomenon of rival consumption can cut both ways: It can either inflict pain or destitution on others (as in the hoarding or gluttony of some), or

18 See, for example, Phan (1984) and Ramsey (1982).

it can ennoble ourselves and others (as in sacrificial almsgiving). Thus, Clement of Alexandria, Cyprian, and Basil see detachment from wealth as an indispensable virtue not only for the personal holiness of the person, but for the welfare of the entire community.

Finally, the social dimension in patristic economic thought is very much in evidence in its theological understanding of the nature of the Christian community as forming a single unity (Walsh and Langan 1977: 134–46). As one living organism and as the Body of Christ, all members are affected and hurt if a single member is in distress (ibid.: 137). In the final analysis, this is perhaps an even stronger warrant for mutual assistance and almsgiving than the earlier point on the end (*telos*) of the fruits of the earth. Christian fellowship is a community of love and mutual sharing, a "symbiosis" (ibid.: 135) that produces a whole greater than the sum of its individual parts, a whole that is able to achieve that which its separate components are unable to attain singly on their own.

Personal work

In contrast to Chrysostom's fierce antipathy toward private property ownership, Clement does not believe that the solution to scarcity lies in common ownership. Instead, unlike many of the other patristic writers, Clement sees the value of entrepreneurial initiative in providing not only for the self but even for others. He suggests that there are better alternatives to merely providing alms and argues that how well Christians are able to provide relief to the marginalized is in large part a function of how well they employ their capital productively (Gordon 1989a: 86–87).[19]

Clement of Alexandria would go so far as to say that *autarkeia* is a purpose of property ownership. In his *Paidagogos*, Clement notes: "Those concerned for their salvation should take this as their first principle, that all property is ours to use and *every possession is for the sake of self-sufficiency* [*autarkeia*], which anyone can acquire by a few things" (Avila 1983: 35 [emphasis added]).[20] This passage is significant because it highlights the third essential feature of economic security: providing for our own needs through our own exertions and initiatives, to the extent possible, in order

---

19 Viner (1978: 23) is critical of the early Church Fathers for not considering the possibility that capital, instead of being liquidated and given away as alms, might be better utilized as an enduring form of assistance by providing employment for the destitute. Viner overlooks Clement of Alexandria's position on property ownership.
20 See also Gordon (1989a: 85).

to avoid being an unnecessary burden on others and in order to avoid crowding out those who are genuinely helpless and in need of assistance.

Ambrose echoes Clement on this point. In speaking of agriculture, Ambrose appreciates the hard work it entails. Such labor produces personal gain without harming others (Gordon 1989a: 117–18). Moreover, in putting their private property (land) to good use, farmers enhance not only the earth but their own virtue as well. Thus, not only does Ambrose encourage the proper use of private property, he also highlights the authentic and tangible contribution of private enterprise and initiative to the community's well-being.

The patristic writers grapple with the problems of idleness and dependency. Clement of Alexandria, for example, deals with the question of early Christians regarding the difficulty of distinguishing those who truly need alms from the slackers. His response is that it is better to be taken advantage of and benefit the undeserving rather than miss the opportunity of doing good (Walsh and Langan 1977: 136). Chrysostom acknowledges the complaints of the rich regarding the vices and the indolence of the poor. Nevertheless, he urges greater forbearance from the wealthy in the face of their own spiritual lassitude (ibid.: 141).

Despite their unremitting calls for almsgiving, the early Church Fathers are in no way brooking idleness. There are repeated teachings on the value of work and personal effort. In sharp contrast to the prevailing Greek and Roman disdain for manual labor as reserved only for slaves and lower classes, the patristic literature views work as noble and as intrinsic to Christian discipleship. Furthermore, they are hard on the lazy by asserting that there is no obligation to feed or to give them alms. Moreover, work is essential for the person's development because of the dangers of sloth. So significant is this concern that the fourth-century Apostolic Constitutions devotes an entire chapter to the topic and aptly entitles it "The Idle Believers Must Not Eat." Tertullian takes pains to disabuse people of his time of the claim that Christians are lazy; he lists all the occupations and places in which Christians are hard at work. We find this appreciation for hard work and the condemnation of indolence across the entire spectrum of patristic authors and writings: Chrysostom, Tertullian, Clement of Rome, Epiphanius, Ambrose, Clement of Alexandria, the *Didache*, the *Didascalia apostolorum*, and the Apostolic Constitutions (Giordani 1944: 279–97; Phan 1984: 34–35). It is precisely the arduous personal toil that goes into tilling the soil that leads Ambrose to conclude that there is no shame at all in the personal wealth that is earned from agricultural enterprise (Gordon 1989a: 117–18).

Augustine views work as natural to human beings; it has never been punishment for sin despite the toilsome nature it took on after the Fall. We find human labor right in the Garden of Eden itself. Hence, there is no reason to associate work with disgrace, as in Greek, Roman, and Stoic thought. Gordon (1989a: 125–28, 132) notes that Augustine is quite "innovative" compared to the other Church Fathers when it comes to understanding the nature of work. For Augustine, honest personal labor is ennobling because it provides a livelihood with which to meet one's needs. Moreover, it can bring enjoyment, is spiritually meritorious, frees one from the dangers of idleness, and provides the resources with which to assist the poor. Augustine differs from other patristic authors by going so far as to describe human work as "assisting God," especially in occupations in medicine, agriculture, and navigation. Moreover, while others frown on the legitimacy of trading as an occupation, Augustine welcomes merchants as rightful participants in the economic order.

To illustrate further the great premium accorded by the early Church Fathers to supporting oneself through one's own means, observe the limits that Augustine sets when it comes to almsgiving, arguably one of the most important tenets of patristic social thought. One should not give to the point of impoverishing oneself. Furthermore, Augustine even goes so far as to make concessions and allow the wealthy to determine that which is superfluous in their income on the basis of the standard of living to which they are accustomed (Gordon 1989a: 128). This is in sharp contrast to the prevalent harsh patristic condemnation of the wealthy and their opulent lifestyles.

In all this, we can glean a patristic understanding and appreciation of the value and role of personal striving in effecting God's vision of economic security for all. Not only does work lead one to take responsibility for one's own upkeep, it also affords the person the means to provide the truly helpless with the selfless assistance that is so highly and uniformly valued in patristic social thought.

Summary

In contrast to the Hebrew Scripture, the patristic writers do not call for systemic change nor do they advocate institutional ameliorative steps to address poverty. Instead, they rely heavily on personal conversion and almsgiving. Economic life, far from being prosaic, turns out to be a unique opportunity to grow in holiness. Observe, for example, the following from *The Epistle to Diognetus*:

[I]f a man will shoulder his neighbor's burden; if he be ready to supply another's need from his own abundance; if, by sharing the blessings he has received from God with those who are in want, he himself becomes a god to those who receive his bounty – such a man is indeed an imitator of God.

(quoted in Walsh and Langan 1977: 116)

Cyprian, in his treatise *On Works and Almsgiving*, also argues that, through generosity, we can imitate God the Creator who has spared nothing to provide for us equally (Walsh and Langan 1977: 126–27). Indeed, we can become God-like through our economic behavior. We lend ourselves as divine instruments as God alleviates the indigence of the needy through us. We can choose to become channels of God's grace and righteousness.

The dual nature of economic security is reflected well in patristic writings. It is understood as twin gifts of God providing for our needs and God affording us the opportunity to partake of divine activity. Walsh and Langan succinctly capture this dynamic well in their summary of the nature of the created universe:

Thus we find that in the mainstream of patristic teaching the things of the earth are created by God and so they are good. Human persons then have a right to possess and to use material goods. But these goods are to be used to meet the needs of all human beings, the poor as well as the rich, and *their owners have the opportunity and the responsibility to imitate the goodness of God, who is both Creator and Father.* (Walsh and Langan 1977: 129 [emphasis added])

Thus, there is a double blessing in the divine benefaction of economic security.

ECONOMIC SECURITY AND THE SCHOLASTIC JUST PRICE

Scholastic economic thought is extensive, and I will limit myself to illustrating how the biblical notion of economic security is consistent with one of the more significant teachings of the era: the doctrine of the just price. Inferring economic security from the scholastic just price is straightforward. The difficulty lies in justifying which interpretation of the just price doctrine to use for this purpose. Consequently, for this section, I depart from my usual threefold division[21] of materials, and briefly explain instead the account of the just price doctrine that I employ.

---

21 Note that I have a tripartite division (access to basic needs, personal effort, and sociality) in presenting materials from the Hebrew, New Testament, patristic, and modern periods, but not for the scholastic era.

Much has been written on this subject, and there is no agreement as to what precisely is the nature of the just price.[22] On one side of the debate are scholars who believe that the just price is about effecting a reciprocal equivalence in the value of that which is exchanged in the marketplace. In other words, it is primarily concerned with commutative justice. This stress on attaining parity in exchange can be traced back to Aristotle's influence on Aquinas's thought on the just price. An alternative interpretation of the just price doctrine is that of ensuring that the community provides an adequate livelihood for workers and their dependents. This is sometimes called the social-status theory of the just price (Spengler 1968: 224–27). In this case, satisfying the demands of distributive justice is paramount. Without going into great detail, it is important to note the distinction between these two views of the scholastic just price since only the latter of these approaches pertains directly to economic security.[23]

In the scholastic just price theory, exchange value is not derived from the intersection of competitive demand and supply functions as we find in modern economic analysis. Instead, it is governed by custom, law, and usage. Proponents of the view of the just price as "equivalence in reciprocal exchange" argue that such custom, law, and usage pertain to the community's determination over time of what constitutes a fair exchange between different kinds of goods. This eventually becomes the prevailing exchange value in the marketplace and is the just price. On the other hand, advocates of the view of the just price as "just income formation" see custom, law, and usage as the community's judgment of what its members ought to receive as a proper recompense for their labors given their contributions to, and role in, society. Thus, the exchange value of goods and services is ultimately founded on the community's determination of what a reasonable and fair livelihood is for the workers or providers of such goods or services given their social status in the community.[24]

The claim that the scholastic just price is ultimately about ensuring proper income formation cannot be readily dismissed. In the first place, one must remember that this was an era that unquestioningly accepted the view that people are born into, inherit, and stay within their social roles and status. Great premium is attached to preserving and maintaining the

---

22 See, for example, Baldwin (1959).
23 See Barrera (2001: 63–66; 90–92) for a brief description of these two competing interpretations. In modern economics, these two approaches roughly and respectively approximate (1) price as set by consumer satisfaction and (2) price as the cost of production plus a mark-up.
24 Viner (1978: 84) ascribes this position to nominalists and rejects it.

status quo in such a hierarchical world view. This organic model of community has implications for economic life. For example, in defining superfluous income for purposes of determining how much to give as alms, Thomas Aquinas (1947/8: II-II, q. 32, a. 6, reply) argues that superfluity is that portion of the income that is not needed to maintain one's social standing in the community.[25] The assertion that the just price is about the provision of a livelihood appropriate to people's station in life fits within the larger medieval mind frame.

Second, there is a circularity in reasoning to say that the just price is the prevailing exchange value in the marketplace, which in turn is founded on custom, law, and usage. How were these formed in the first place and on what grounds? How did they become standard practice in the community to begin with? We cannot simply argue that custom, law, and usage are culled from the long-standing value people assign to different goods and services. There has to be a deeper standard (explicit or implicit) that accounts for why and how people assigned prices in the way they did in the marketplace. To define scholastic just price as that price that prevails in the market is simply tautological. Moreover, what is the point of having a distinct concept of the just price if it is nothing but a description of the prevailing behavior in the marketplace? What function is served by the just price doctrine if it simply calls on people to pay the price that the market sets? Langholm (1998: 86) himself admits that "the market estimate is in a sense redundant when the market is, in fact, operating normally, because the just price will then establish itself automatically." Commutative justice would have been purely about compliance with a community valuation that did not have an objective basis at all (such as just income formation) beyond the satisfaction or utility it gave to people.[26]

Even if we were to grant, for the sake of argument, that the just price is about attaining equivalence in exchange based on the market price, to my mind, the two positions are not mutually exclusive but in fact complement each other. After all, people's common sense of what constitutes parity in the exchange value of disparate goods and services must ultimately be founded on some observable objective criteria that everyone readily experiences. And what better and readily available standard is there than people's perception both of the labor that went into the good and of the differences in the income levels needed to sustain different

25 Leo XIII (1891: #36) adopts this definition as late as *Rerum Novarum*.
26 This is akin to modern pricing theory based on consumer utility.

offices and roles in the community? In the medieval organic view of community, reciprocal equivalence in exchange based on the prevailing price in the market was most likely informed by people's perception of what a fair income was for work effort and for the upkeep of the providers of such goods and services given the duties they had to discharge in the community (Spengler 1968: 224–27). Commutative and distributive justice are inseparable. In fact, one could go so far as to claim that commutative justice must satisfy the requirements of distributive justice; the latter is a necessary condition for the former.

Given these distinctions, I argue that the scholastic just price doctrine is ultimately about ensuring economic security for people given their roles and responsibilities in the community. All three constitutive elements of economic security are present in the scholastic just price. If my interpretation of the scholastic just price as a livelihood maintenance program is correct, then it is clear that the just price is about ensuring that people are provided with an income that secures access to their basic necessities. Recall that this is the first constitutive element of economic security.

In the cost-of-production interpretation that I am using, the just price is in effect the remuneration that the entire community provides workers for their societal role. The just price is the outcome of a social process because it is a communal estimation of what justice requires for the upkeep of workers, and it is paid for by the entire community. This is reflective of the second condition, that is, the necessary social character of economic security, since the just price is essentially about a division of labor, mutual interdependence, and fairness.

In my choice of the social-status theory of the just price, the value of the workers' goods or services is based on the common estimation of the economic worth of their roles and contribution within the community. This presupposes personal work effort and striving, the third condition of economic security. After all, one would have to produce something first before one could sell anything in the marketplace.

ECONOMIC SECURITY IN MODERN CATHOLIC SOCIAL DOCUMENTS

Modern Catholic social teachings do not form a single or systematic, homogeneous corpus because they are either ad hoc documents that address pressing social questions of their day or commemorative reaffirmations of earlier teachings. Nevertheless, it is possible to infer economic security (and its three constitutive elements) as a much-desired end in the ideal social order sought by this papal social tradition. This is so because modern Catholic social documents are predominantly about political economy. I use the modern Catholic social principles in the following sections to show how the biblical-patristic vision of economic security has made its way to the present era.

Meeting basic needs

Despite discontinuities in the modern Catholic social tradition (Curran 2002: 21–51, 53–100 and 101–107), an unchanging theme is its fundamental belief that the goods of the earth are meant for the benefit of all regardless of how titles of ownership are distributed (Barrera 2001: 193–205). This has come to be known as the principle of the universal destination of the goods of the earth; its provenance in the patristic understanding of the nature of creation is readily evident. Through all the disparate social questions of the past century, these documents invariably appeal to this principle in resolving many of the competing claims encountered in the modern industrial economy. Various names given to this norm include: the principle of the common use of goods, the right to life and subsistence (John Paul II 1981: #82), the law of the common destination of earthly goods (Vatican Council II 1965b: #71e), and the universal purpose of created goods (Paul VI 1967: #22). The proximate goal of this principle is to ensure that people are able to access and procure for themselves all the necessary means for their survival, basic health, and development.

The significance and utility of the principle of universal destination of the goods of the earth in a modern economy is best illustrated in Leo XIII's (1891) *Rerum Novarum*. In seeking to diffuse the explosive tension between labor and management in the aftermath of the Industrial Revolution, Leo XIII deftly balances the competing claims of workers and capitalists. Unlike the radical solution of dismissing capitalists' claims by abolishing private property ownership, and unlike laissez-faire capitalism's preferential protection of employers' rights, Leo XIII simultaneously affirms both the right to private property ownership and the right to a living wage. The balance is struck through Leo XIII's assertion that just ownership does not automatically confer just use. This is a distinction that flows from the principle of the universal destination of the goods of the earth. In other words, even while exercising the right to enjoy the profits of their capital, employers are nonetheless obligated to ensure that their possessions also benefit others; in this case, workers. This entails the provision of both gainful employment opportunities and a living wage for those who do not own property and depend on others (capitalists) for a livelihood. Note how these objectives are clearly about letting people enjoy economic security through their own exertions.

Observe how *Rerum Novarum's* staunch defense of private property ownership is also a call for economic security. Leo XIII lists practical reasons why the right to own property is innate to human nature itself. Using teleological reasoning, Leo XIII argues that private property ownership meets some of the deepest yearnings and needs of people: in providing a bequest for loved ones, in having a nest egg for a rainy day, in affording workers the possibility of upward mobility by being proper-tied themselves in the future, in conferring a peace of mind that comes with knowing that one owns the means to satisfy the family's recurring needs (such as the roof over their heads), and in serving as an alternative, remunerative, means of keeping hard-earned savings (Leo XIII 1891: #7–23). All these reasons are ultimately about providing workers and their dependants with economic security.

The economic security that flows from being able to access the material means of life without great or undue hardship is clearly an unspoken but self-evident goal of *Rerum Novarum* for workers. This is reflected in Leo XIII's calls for the provision of employment opportunities at a living wage and in his practical arguments why private property ownership cannot be abolished by the state. Subsequent documents reaffirm both of these positions with varying degrees of emphasis and urgency depending on the social questions of their day. The economic security sought for workers in this seminal document is eventually expanded in scope to include the economic welfare of nations.[27]

Laborem Exercens is another social document that illustrates the cen-trality of economic security in this modern tradition. John Paul II offers a theological and philosophical reflection on the nature of work and pro-poses the primacy of labor principle. He asserts that the price of goods and services in the marketplace must be high enough to afford workers a living wage. In other words, workers must not be treated or remunerated as if they were just factors of production no different from capital, plant, and equipment. Market price must be sufficient to provide people with a viable livelihood. Besides this call for a living wage, the encyclical reiterates the moral imperative of providing substantive employment opportunities.

27 See, for example, John Paul II (1987, 1991), Paul VI (1967) and Vatican Council II (1965b).

These two examples do not exhaust everything that can be gleaned on economic security from the modern Catholic social documents. That is a separate project in itself. It is sufficient for our study merely to note that the principles of the universal destination of the goods of the earth and the primacy of labor both reflect how the concern over the satisfaction of basic needs is still very much a part of the modern social tradition.

The social dimension

The social character of economic security is likewise evident in these modern Catholic social documents. This tradition assigns both a personal and a social character to everything in political economy: labor, capital, and the fruits of the earth. Take, for example, the changed definition of what constitutes superfluous income. Leo XIII provides the superfluous income criterion as an example of the just-use obligation attendant on wealth and property ownership. Under this norm, people are obligated to use that which is superfluous in their income for the benefit of others. Leo XIII (1891: #36) follows Aquinas in defining superfluity as that part of one's income that is not needed to maintain one's social standing in the community. Seventy years later, John XXIII proposes a different benchmark: Superfluity in one's earnings is determined by the relative unmet needs of one's neighbor.[28]

John XXIII's formulation moves the focus from the self (maintaining one's own social status) to a concern for the welfare of others. It has a patristic ring to it, given the strength of the claims that others have on us, even to the point of requiring great sacrifice on our part to satisfy these obligations. This reappropriation of an earlier, stricter, social tradition only goes to reiterate the communal nature of economic life. That it should come from John XXIII should probably not be a surprise at all considering one of his key observations in *Mater et Magistra*: the phenomenon of socialization.

Writing in 1961 to commemorate the seventieth anniversary of *Rerum Novarum* and to reflect on how Christianity can better serve modernity, John XXIII calls attention to the issue of socialization, in which society has come to be so complex and interdependence so profound that tasks that used to be easily performed by individuals and smaller bodies now require the collaboration of many others and the use of ever-larger groupings of people. As a consequence, John XXIII acknowledges the

28 See Vatican Council II (1965b: part II, chapter 3, footnote #10).

need for a larger and more active role for government in socioeconomic life. In what Bryan Hehir (1998) subsequently calls the principle of socialization, higher bodies have an obligation to assist lower bodies and even perform what these smaller bodies are unable to do for themselves for the sake of the common good.[29]

John Paul II's (1981: #67) proposal in *Laborem Exercens* for alternative work arrangements (co-ownership, profit-sharing, and co-management), and his call to ensure a broader participation for all, also illustrate a growing appreciation for the heavily communal character of economic life. And of course, there is also his principle of solidarity that calls for an active and genuine concern for the welfare of others (John Paul II 1987). The repeated calls for relative equality (Christiansen 1984) and for cross-border assistance between nations (John Paul II 1987; Paul VI 1967; Vatican Council II 1965b) echo the strong prophetic and patristic admonitions on how we are truly responsible for each other. Thus, the preferential option for the poor has been a staple of this modern tradition (Dorr 1983). This stress on mutual sharing has made many commentators uncomfortable to the point where the *Wall Street Journal* refers to *Populorum Progressio* as warmed-over Marxism (O'Brien and Shannon 1977: 311). Or note, for example, Bauer's (1984) quip on the tradition as "Ecclesiastical Economics: Envy Legitimized." Both are serious misunderstandings.

Vatican Council II's (1965b) *Gaudium et Spes* is the single most important document of this modern tradition that articulates the social dimension of economic security. Part I of this constitution examines what it is to be a person and a human community. Moreover, it argues that far from being intrinsically at odds with each other, the individual and the community are complementary, indeed, necessary conditions for each other's good. Part II of this document presents an application of this theological reflection, and its extended sections on economics, politics, and the common life of nations stress the essentially social nature of political economy.

I believe that the most eloquent proof of this modern social tradition's firm understanding of the social character of economic security is articulated in the opening lines of *Gaudium et Spes*:

The joys and the hopes, the griefs and the anxieties of the men [and women] of this age, especially those who are poor or in any way afflicted, these are the joys and hopes, the griefs and anxieties of the followers of Christ. Indeed, nothing genuinely human fails to raise an echo in their hearts. (Vatican Council II 1965b: #1)

29 This is essentially the corollary of Pius XI's (1931: #79–80) principle of subsidiarity.

Personal effort

In addition to their pronounced emphasis on the social character of economic life, the modern Catholic social documents nonetheless also stress the importance of personal effort. In his theological and philosophical exposition on human work in *Laborem Exercens*, John Paul II (1981) outlines the value of work for human self-realization: as an outlet for creativity and self-expression, as a means of earning a livelihood, as a venue for sharing in the sufferings of Christ, as a channel for contributing to the common good, and most of all, as an opportunity for sharing in the creative work of God. Such an understanding of the nature of work situates the principle of the primacy of labor in its proper context and prevents its misuse. This principle is not merely about asserting the working person's claim against employers and society; equally important, it is also about personal obligations to give one's level best in honest labor and effort.

Of course, an important expression of the need for personal initiative in attaining economic security can be found in Pius XI's (1931: #79–80) principle of subsidiarity, which states that higher bodies ought not to arrogate for themselves functions that lower bodies or individuals are able to discharge for themselves. In other words, private initiative has to be protected, nurtured, and encouraged. The immediate context of this principle demonstrates the place of personal effort in attaining economic security. Pius XI issued *Quadragesimo Anno* in 1931 out of concern over the glaring and worsening disparity evident in the small pockets of great economic and political power amidst a vast sea of poverty and helplessness. Instead of appealing for direct relief and immediate intervention from governments, Pius XI proposed to reorganize society along the lines of industry-level vocational groupings. Each industry was to be reconstituted into groups of employers and workers, which were then to negotiate with each other, as equals, on all matters that affected the industry and their mutual interests, including wages and working conditions. It would have been so much easier to ask governments to step in and curtail corporate power. As it was, however, Pius XI sought to lay the foundations for better cooperation by counterbalancing one concentration of power (the employers') with another concentration of power (the workers'). This proposal was never implemented because it was impractical and unworkable. However, its value lies in its underlying rationale, to wit: the principle of subsidiarity in which both workers (as a group) and employers do what they are able to do for themselves instead of running to the government for remedies.

The goal of ensuring that people are able to access the material means to satisfy their needs through their own labor is evident in the modern Catholic social tradition. In addition, it is clearly understood that such economic security is achieved within a community that provides both assistance, where necessary, and the appropriate social conditions that are conducive to personal growth and development.

SUMMARY AND CONCLUSIONS

Economic security is constitutive of the intended due order in God's creation. It has three necessary elements and results in the provision of two divine gifts. Economic security is about (1) the satisfaction of one's basic needs (2) with the nurturing assistance of the community, and (3) through one's personal effort, to the extent possible. The satisfaction of all three conditions unveils two divine gifts: material sufficiency and participation in divine providence.

The underlying understanding in Genesis that the earth is the Creator's gift to meet human needs and the nation Israel's appreciation of the Promised Land as a "land flowing with milk and honey" both speak of God's benefaction of economic security: an envisioned human life that is not burdened excessively with the difficulties of procuring the means to satisfy basic material needs. But there is a second dimension to this divine blessing – the gift of human participation in effecting and then maintaining such economic security not only for themselves individually but for everybody else. In other words, there is the additional gift of instrumentality. Thus, adverse unintended consequences of market exchange ought to be the subject of moral discourse. After all, chronic economic compulsion (defined as the privation of economic security) reflects humanity's failure to live up to its obligation of stewardship both of the gifts of the earth and of the gift of each other.

Nowhere in the entire tradition is there a single treatise on the notion of economic security as a divine gift, much less on the insight that it in fact embodies a set of twin gifts. In this chapter, I have had to glean through the literature. Nonetheless, despite such reliance on inferences, there are ample warrants to be able to advance the following claims:

1 God's intended order of creation includes provisioning us with all we need in conjunction with our personal and communal effort and striving.

2 God adds a second gift within this initial grant: the invitation to partake in divine governance by serving as an instrument through which God provides for us through each other.

The starting point of economic security as a divine gift is the account in the book of Genesis of how the earth was created and then entrusted to the human community.

[W]hile it is true that human beings are meant to change this world, they are to change it into an image of a heavenly model in harmony with the work of the first six days. This alteration is to make it possible for God to dwell among human beings. *It is not human beings, but God's dwelling among them, that, according to the priestly document, is "telos, end and goal of world history."*
(Lohfink 1994: 17 [emphasis added])

To my mind, this captures well the ultimate significance of the gift of participation set within economic security. As instruments that effect God's providence and righteousness in providing for our needs, we also make God's work and presence incarnate in our midst.

To go back to the original question: Why should Christians be concerned with economic compulsion? Because it goes against God's vision of economic security for all. Even more important, chronic economic distress that is left unattended is an indictment that we, as individuals and as a community, have squandered the second gift embedded in the divine benefaction of economic security either through our failures of omission or commission, or both.

If heeded seriously and taken to heart, Christian ethics can prevent the unavoidable chance and contingency of economic life from degenerating into economic compulsion. The biblical vision of economic security is an effective and essential corrective to the exigencies that imperil our common enjoyment of God's gift of a bounteous and flourishing life in the here and now.

CHAPTER 4

Retrieving the biblical principle of restoration

Harmful market ripple effects are not peculiar to modernity.[1] This chapter argues that the Hebrew economic ordinances were in fact a response to the pecuniary externalities and the economic chance and contingencies of their era. Moreover, there was a rehabilitative intent in these norms governing economic life. The challenge for contemporary Christian ethics is to reappropriate this earlier spirit of generosity and mutual sacrifice and adapt it to the dilemmas of our postindustrial age.

LAW CODES

We discern and comprehend more of God's self-revelation and initiatives as we grapple with and try to make sense of our own human experience – its joys, its hopes, its difficulties, and even its tragedies. A sphere of such divine–human encounter is economic life. We can best appreciate the role of economics as a venue for human participation in God's righteousness by reflecting on how we have coped with the exigencies of economic life. The Hebrew experience sheds much light in this regard because it was a dynamic process of economic disruptions evoking determined moral responses.

As seen in the preceding chapter, there is an impressive array of economic precepts in the Covenant (Exod. 20:22–23:33), Deuteronomic (Deut. 12–26), and Holiness (Lev. 17–26) Codes of the Hebrew Scripture. Of immediate interest to us are the provisions on debt legislation, slave manumission, and land return. These laws were written, edited, and further developed to even tougher standards over the span of several centuries from the formation of the nation to its post-exilic

---

1 A good part of this chapter has been published previously as "Unintended Consequences and the Principle of Restoration Retrieved" in the *Journal of Catholic Social Thought*, 2(1): 85–124 (2005).

period. These codes arose in response to rapidly changing socioeconomic conditions.

Believed to have been written at a time when the tribes of Israel were gradually transformed from an itinerant way of life to settled agriculture, the Covenant Code preserves the nomadic ethos of mutual assistance as people began to live in permanent settlements. In a precarious economy with little surplus, if any, coming to each other's aid and easing each other's losses is the only way of ensuring mutual survival. Thus, it should not come as a surprise to have customs, such as lending without interest to a distressed neighbor, codified early on as part of this nascent nation's laws.

The Deuteronomic Code evolved amidst the deteriorating socioeconomic conditions of the monarchial era and is believed to have further humanized the Covenant Code.[2] Many were impoverished and driven to debt and slavery given the heavy royal fiscal exactions, even as others benefited from the centralization of power, market expansion, international trade, and urbanization. An impoverished underclass emerged even within the ambit of a new-found, growing, national wealth. Thus, we have the prophetic indictments calling the nation back to the original vision of an economy of equality as part of the Covenant struck with YHWH.

There is no consensus on the dating of the Holiness Code. Some view it as early legislation, at about the same time as the Covenant Code.[3] Others, however, favor a much later composition of the Holiness Code, during the post-exilic era.[4] It was a period when the nation Israel, newly freed from her Babylonian captivity, struggled to reappropriate for herself a way of life more in line with the Covenant. I subscribe to this later dating in what follows.

In summary, these law collections were being codified, edited, and made even stricter precisely during periods of great social transformation. In other words, they were in part a response to the unintended consequences of a rapidly changing socioeconomic life. Moreover, of even greater interest for this study is the restorative spirit animating the economic ordinances of these codes.

---

2 Chirichigno (1993: 113–30, 139–42); de Vaux (1965: 72–74; 166–67); Mays (1987: 148–49); Neufeld (1955: 376–78).
3 For example, Wright (1990: 126) and Eichrodt (1961: 96).
4 For example, Brown, Fitzmyer, and Murphy (1990: 78) and Lowery (2000: 57).

THE RESTORATIVE THEME

Debt legislation

There are four key elements to the debt legislation found in Hebrew Law: the provision of interest-free loans (Exod. 22:25; Deut. 23:19–20; Lev. 25:36–37), mandatory lending (Deut. 15:7–10; Lev. 25:35–37), debt remission (Deut. 15:1–3), and restrictions on the type of collateral that might be demanded as surety (Exod. 22:26; Deut. 24:6, 10–13). The Chosen People were obligated to lend without cost to their neighbors who had fallen on hard times. This was true for both money and grain loans, or for any other lending that usually carried interest charges. In doing so, not only did they provide mutual assistance to each other at a time of great distress, they also refrained from profiting from each other's misfortunes.[5] On top of this, loans might not be secured by taking as a pledge any tool or household article that was essential for the livelihood or survival of the debtor. Lenders might not take any surety at all from the poor. Moreover, debts were written off after six years to halt the continued slide of the distressed into ever deeper impoverishment. Of course, creditors could completely avoid putting themselves through these troublesome impositions by simply refusing to lend their surplus. However, a subsequent redaction of the law corrected for this loophole by turning lending to a needy neighbor into an explicit moral obligation (Deut. 15:7–10).

The restorative value of these statutes is best appreciated by understanding the degree to which the marginalized of that time were subjected to economic compulsion. Scholars believe that most of the debts incurred in the period were consumption-distress loans (Gnuse 1985: 19; Lang 1985: 99; de Vaux 1965: 170–73). In other words, unlike in the industrial economy, most people did not avail themselves of loans to finance their production, engage in business, or consume non-essential durable goods. Rather, debtors were compelled to borrow money or grain to meet their basic needs and survive; they were driven to procure loans because of some exigency. Thus, scholars call these hardship, consumption-distress, loans.

The prevalence of consumption-distress loans can be inferred from the reported socioeconomic conditions of the period. Mesopotamian monarchs decreed debt write-offs whenever the economy ground to a halt because the general population was weighted down by too many debt

---

5 Foreigners might be charged interest for their debts.

liabilities that had to be repaid (Lohfink 1986: 224). Unlike the nation Israel, neighboring Near Eastern countries did not have a regular schedule for debt forgiveness.

The ban on charging interest to a fellow Israelite also indirectly suggests the widespread need to procure consumption-distress loans. Meislin and Cohen (1964: 266) believe that this prohibition was defensive in nature because it prevented the loss of its citizens to neighboring rivals. Should Hebrews borrow from foreigners and be unable to pay back the loan, their resulting enslavement represented a serious drain of labor from the nation. This was especially alarming in the event of war. Thus, interest-free loans are believed to have been a way of ensuring that Israel did not lose valuable manpower to surrounding countries because of debt defaults. If this thesis is correct, it would suggest that both consumption-distress loans and debt delinquencies were routine to the point where the community was obliged to take the drastic step of banning the charging of interest for loans for its own national self-preservation.

Besides the pervasiveness of such loans, it is also important to observe the gravity of the economic duress experienced at that time. One can infer this from the prevailing interest charges in the credit markets of the era. Interest rates for money loans in the Ancient Near Eastern countries varied from 20 percent to 25 percent on average, although they could run as high as 50 percent; for grain loans the average was $33\frac{1}{3}$ percent but it could go as high as 100 percent (Gnuse 1985: 19; Maloney 1974; Neufeld 1953–54: 194, 197).[6] The more scarce the funds and the more pressing the demand for such loanable surplus, the greater the required interest premium. If interest rates of 20 percent to $33\frac{1}{3}$ percent are burdensome even in a modern economy of accelerating growth, how much more for an ancient economy with relatively limited growth prospects? After all, these people were driven to borrow in the first place because they were unable to produce enough to supply their own needs. Hence, tacking on an additional third or a quarter of the loan to the principal must surely have been an onerous burden imposed on borrowers. That punitive interest rates and harsh repayment terms were even tolerated at all can only mean that debtors must have been in desperate straits. The degree of economic coercion at that time is also reflected in the widespread infraction of the law on usurious lending (Neh. 5:1–13; Ezra 18:5–8, 10–13, 17; 22:12; Hab. 2:6). In this regard, even the other Ancient Near Eastern nations were

6 All interest rates for this chapter are per annum.

ultimately compelled to cap interest charges, most likely because of runaway rates and widespread abuse (Neufeld 1953–54: 195).

Examining the total size of the debt is another way of inferring the severity of the economic hardships that pecuniary externalities and economic contingencies could inflict at that time. Despite not having to pay interest for their loans, many Hebrews still succumbed to a debt trap as they sank further into arrears. Thus, Chirichigno (1993) suggests, for example, that the Jubilee legislation is descriptive of the process by which a household head went ever deeper into insolvency – having to borrow in the first place, then losing one's land, and finally being compelled to sell oneself into slavery. Debt could be accumulated to the point where it even exceeded the total value of one's ancestral land, thereby necessitating the debtor's sale into slavery. Examined in another way, liabilities could balloon even to the point of exceeding twelve years' worth of wages.[7] That people were driven to borrow such large sums and be caught in a downward spiral of ever-deepening penury even without the burden of having to pay a compounding interest only goes to highlight the catastrophic privation that could befall economic agents of that age.

Both the ubiquity of needy borrowers and the size of their loans suggest the severity of the economic compulsion encountered in the Hebrew marketplace. The constitutive elements of the nation's debt legislation exhibit a common restorative function. First, in mandating the provision of loans to a fellow Israelite, these statutes ensured that people who had fallen on hard times need not be driven to borrow at excessively harsh terms from foreigners; recovery would be much easier. Second, debt reprieve not only stopped the person's downward slide into further indebtedness, it also wiped the slate clean to provide the distressed with a new beginning that was unencumbered by outstanding obligations. Third, restrictions on the type of collateral that might be obtained (in particular, restrictions on taking millstones and cloaks) and the ban against taking any surety from the poor (Exod. 22:26; Deut. 24:6, 10–13) prevented the cost of securing supplementary finances from being prohibitive; obtaining some measure of relief from cash flow problems should not come at the expense of losing one's means of livelihood and

---

7 Limiting debt slavery to a maximum period of six years of service was in effect a de facto cap on the amount of the loan that the lender might retrieve from the borrower through the latter's indentured service. Note, however, that the implicit wages assigned to slave labor were only half of that accorded to free labor (Deut. 15:18). Thus, the total value of services rendered by the debt slave before release was equivalent to twelve years' worth of free labor. This, of course, must be discounted to account for the cost of feeding and housing the slave.

sustenance. Fourth, the interest-free nature of these loans meant that the marginalized were relieved from having to incur an additional cost for procuring some liquidity or from borrowing from their future income, which was meager to begin with.

These provisions of Hebrew debt legislation share a common feature of shielding people who had fallen on hard economic times from additional burdens. The goal was to restore their capacity to partake of the communal economic life as free men and women. Distressed economic agents were provided with the vital means, *at no cost*, to keep on participating in the marketplace despite the harsh contingencies that drove them to debt in the first place. The community was in effect affording them some breathing room, and an unencumbered one at that, to recover from whatever harmful pecuniary externalities might have caused their economic troubles to begin with. An approximate idea of the extent of the restorative relief provided can be gleaned from the opportunity loss (20 percent to $33\frac{1}{3}$ percent interest) sustained by lenders in the mandated interest-free loans. This is not even to consider the possibility of having to write off these debts after six years. The obverse of this high opportunity cost is, of course, a measure of the concessionary grant received by the distressed and needy borrowers in the effort to restore their ability to partake of the shared economic life as full partners. Hebrew debt legislation has a restorative function in the manner in which it replenishes people with the necessary cash flow (or grain in the case of food loans) to weather economic distress while staying as active, viable participants in the marketplace.

Slave manumission

Debt, rather than war, was the principal cause of bondage in Israel (de Vaux 1965: 83, 172). Debtors and their families were sold into slavery to cover arrears or in the aftermath of a debt default. However, there was a maximum term of six years of service after which debt slaves were to be given back their freedom, and all outstanding obligations were wiped clean. In Exodus 21:2–6, only the male slaves enjoy the benefit of such a reprieve. By the Deuteronomic reform, not only is this ordinance extended to women, but a further obligation is imposed on masters to generously provision freed slaves (Deut. 15:12–18). The Jubilee Law takes this a step further by inviting the Chosen People to take in fellow Hebrews who have fallen on hard times, not as slaves but as hired hands or as tenants (Lev. 25:39–40). Moreover, all who are held in bondage are to be given their freedom in the year of the Jubilee.

De Vaux (1965: 83–84) notes that the number of debt slaves at that time is unclear and is really a matter of conjecture. Based on their calculations of the costs and wages of that era, Leon Feldman (1972: 39–41) and A. Kahan (1972: 1269–70, 1275) conclude that there was no economic incentive for families, except for the wealthy ones, to keep slaves because it was cheaper to hire free labor than to put up and maintain an additional member of the household. This is not even to mention the risk of the slave running away and the manifold restrictions regarding the proper treatment of slaves.

In contrast to these views, evidence from the scriptures suggests that debt slavery was not only commonplace but was also an economic boon. At the time of the edict of restoration, a total of 49,647 captives returned to Israel from Babylon; of these, 7,337 were slaves (Ezra 2:64–65; Neh. 7:67). This is 15 percent of the total population of returnees. Most of these are likely to have been debt slaves rather than prisoner-of-war slaves since the period of Israel's victorious wars was long past. With respect to the remunerative nature of holding slaves, note how King Zedekiah had to cajole people to release their slaves in accordance with the Law. After having agreed, they reneged on their promise and seized back the freed slaves (Jer. 34:8–22). The Hebrews would not have been so obstinate and reluctant to part with their slaves if the latter were more of a hardship than a source of profit. Gnuse (1985: 23) would even go so far as to claim that slave release was never practiced at all.

Moreover, it is believed that the unusually long period of fifty years between cycles of slave manumission in the Jubilee Law was a compromise with masters in an effort to win better treatment for indentured servants whom they had no intention of releasing anyway (de Vaux 1965: 83). In other words, the legislation was a second-best solution. Furthermore, the prevalence of debt slavery can also be indirectly inferred from references to the extended family's obligation to redeem an enslaved kin (Lev. 25:47–55). In addition, observe the numerous passages dealing with the proper treatment of slaves (e.g., Exod. 21) and the development of legislation regarding slave emancipation across different codes spanning many centuries. If debt slavery were not truly prevalent in the culture, then why is so much attention and care devoted to the proper protection of slaves? Finally, that enfranchising slaves is not unique to Israel but is codified even in other Ancient Near Eastern laws (Chirichigno 1993) provides further indirect evidence of the rampant nature of indentured bondage during that era. All these suggest that debt slavery was not only common but was also lucrative.

Regardless of which hypothesis is correct regarding the state of debt slavery in Israel, what is clear is that manumission not only provided relief but also restored those previously held in economic servitude as full and equal partners in the community. Over time, there was a clear progression toward ensuring that the discharged slave had a fighting chance of holding on to that restored freedom. Deuteronomy 15:12–18 is an improvement over the stipulations in Exodus by calling on the master to furnish the freed slave generously with provisions. Leviticus goes a step further by returning land to its original owners. Such recovery of ancestral land was a tremendous help for emancipated slaves because it provided them with the best chance of maintaining their independence by having a sure and stable source of livelihood. On top of this, some interpret Leviticus 25 as the abolition of debt slavery altogether, in which those who have fallen on hard times are no longer to be treated as slaves but as equals – as hired hands or as tenants (Lowery 2000: 45). This is restorative in the sense of maintaining their dignity and place in society by accepting them as members of the household, as free men and women, rather than as indentured servants. Thus, their liberty is preserved despite economic failings or misfortunes. Over time, we see increasingly humane and more generous terms in the reconstitution of former slaves as free members of the community with no outstanding obligations.

It must also be noted that the six-year maximum service for debt slaves was a de facto cap on the amount of debt that might be recovered. Regardless of the size of the loan, six years of service was the maximum length of time that a debt slave might be held in bondage in lieu of debt repayment.

Again, the degree to which such slave manumission was a restorative mechanism can be inferred from the severity of the prevailing economic compulsion in that period. That people would voluntarily choose to become slaves in perpetuity (Exod. 21:5–6; Deut. 15:16–17) rather than be free but have to fend for themselves is reflective of the hardships in the cut-and-thrust environment of the marketplace. In fact, Kahan (1972: 1269–70, 1275) suggests that the high unemployment rate in the Hebrew economy drove many to see perpetual slavery as a more palatable alternative.

Land return

The Jubilee Law (Lev. 25) is a radical economic reform that simultaneously effects not only the forgiveness of debt and the manumission of slaves but also the return of ancestral land to its original owners. In effect, land is never sold in perpetuity but is transferred only as a long-term lease until the next Jubilee. The value of land is based on the number of harvests that can be reaped from it until its scheduled return. No monetary value may be assigned to its intrinsic worth, as land belongs to God.

The restorative value of the Jubilee Law in both its theological and practical functions is fairly self-evident and well known. In the first place, land is the principal source of livelihood and wealth creation in an agrarian economy; it also ensures that relative inequalities within the community are kept within limits. Second, as mentioned in the preceding chapter, land was the means by which the Hebrew household satisfied its cultic, juridic, and legal obligations to the community and constituted the grounds for the household's membership in the nation. Third, land lay at the core of the Hebrew self-identity as it was the direct and tangible sign of their election as the Chosen People of God. Land was their bequest from God and was a sacred trust received from their parents and grand-parents and meant to be preserved and passed on to their own children and grandchildren. Finally, there is always the problem of economic coercion. In the Code of Eshnunna (39 A3), there is a right to repurchase a home that had been sold at a time of financial difficulty (Lohfink 1991: 37, fn 11). This reflects the moral conviction that people ought not to lose that which is essential or valuable for their upkeep or future (land or house) on account of economic setbacks.

The loss of ancestral land seems to have been a widespread phenom-enon at that time, as suggested by similar rehabilitative practices in the surrounding Ancient Near Eastern nations (Eichrodt 1961: 96; Greenberg 1972). Moreover, the repeated and lengthy references to the practice and obligation of land redemption among kin (Lev. 25:23–34; Ruth 4:1–11; Jer. 32:7 ff.) are indirect evidence that the forced sale of hereditary land was much too common an experience. In fact, the recovery of ancestral land is believed to have been the *raison d'être* of family groups.

The "kin group" was a major constituent in the Israelite system of land tenure, and *its primary function was economic*. It existed to protect and preserve the viability of its own extended families through such mechanisms as *the redemption of both land and persons* that were in danger of passing – or had already passed – out of the hands of the kinship group . . . [I]t was *a restorative and protective organism* – a "protective association" . . . (Wright 1990: 52–53 [emphasis added])[8]

8 See Ruth 2:20; 4:1–11.

The repeated stress on retrieving ancestral land and the social mechanisms instituted for such a purpose are suggestive of both the prevalence and the severity of the economic burdens of that era.

In summary, the onerous socioeconomic conditions experienced by the people provide the larger backdrop for why there is need for social safety nets in the first place. Indeed, the restorative value of Hebrew debt legislation, slave manumission, and land return is directly proportional to the severity of the economic hardships endured by the beneficiaries of these economic ordinances. These safeguards are systemic responses to the harmful unintended consequences of the marketplace. The whole notion of release – the release of debt, land, and slaves – is in effect a call for the reestablishment of those who have been impaired by economic contingencies or by negative pecuniary externalities.

The Hebrew economic ordinances reveal a people wrestling to understand what God expected of them in their election of responsibility in the face of disruptive socioeconomic changes. Israel, after all, was moving through a series of radical transformations: from being wandering tribes, to becoming a more settled agrarian community, and finally to evolving as a monarchial, centralized, and urbanized nation with a more extensive and vibrant commerce with its neighboring countries. Amidst such profound changes can be found both the beneficial and the hurtful repercussions of pecuniary externalities. Such unintended consequences are in effect market-driven redistributions of burdens and benefits that are dispersed both in a systemic and in a random fashion in the wake of the chance and contingency that are intrinsic to economic life. Through all these shifts, one consistent pattern can be clearly discerned: The harms inflicted by pecuniary externalities and economic exigencies cannot be left unattended and unaddressed. Israel took responsibility for ensuring that hardships experienced within the market were rectified outside the marketplace. Those who found themselves in economic distress, whether from the workings of the market or not, would ultimately see themselves restored to their stature as full and equal members of the common life.[9]

9 For a more detailed discussion of Old Testament economic precepts, see Barrera 2005: chapters 4 and 5.

FORMAL CHARACTERISTICS OF THE PRINCIPLE
OF RESTORATION

There are key features in the nation Israel's economic statutes that must be highlighted, especially in relation to their relevance for our own day and age.

Overarching themes

An economy of hope

There is an obvious rehabilitative undercurrent that ties Hebrew economic ordinances together: recovery of essential resources (freedom, land, and liquidity), reestablishment as a full participant in society, and respite from dependency. The goal is not the attainment of equality in distribution but the provision of a safety net of second chances. These recuperative mechanisms convey an even deeper value at stake – the affirmation of hope in the midst of and despite the vicissitudes of a marketplace that is often unpredictable and unforgiving. After all, the ultimate goal is to restore distressed economic agents to their full and respectable standing in society. These economic tenets essentially provide an assurance that there will always be the possibility of new beginnings. It is fundamentally the promise of reconstituting those who have fallen on hard times in the midst of the chance and contingency of economic life. Indeed, not only is the nation an economy of equality (Birch 1991: 172–82), it is in fact an economy of brimming hope – a confidence stemming from the mutual assistance and the shared sacrifices borne for the sake of each other, a firm assurance that flows from the knowledge that there will always be a ready helping hand to lift up the burdened in the face of the marketplace's uncertainties. As we see in the next section on theological warrants and precedents, this vision of an economy of second chances is part of the woof and warp of the much larger tapestry of salvation history's gift of hope.

Mutual aid as constitutive of Covenant election

Another consistent pattern that can be gleaned across time and across biblical writers pertains to how these Hebrew economic norms, far from being peripheral, are in fact central to the tradition. We can infer this (1) from the extended treatment accorded them in all three law codes and (2) from the manner in which such economic statutes emerge, develop, and are reiterated through all the stages of the formation and development of the nation Israel. These remedial duties are repeatedly stressed as a common concern of the lawmakers, prophets, and reformers. Despite differences and changes in the particulars of norms across the three law codes, there is continuity in the Hebrew ethos and its core vision of the ideal economic life under the Covenant. Furthermore, besides being perennial staples in the law codes, these economic mores are understood to be at the heart of the nation Israel's election as the Chosen People of God.

Lohfink (1987) has been emphatic about this essential feature of God's intervention in human history: There is a necessary economic dimension to God's in-breaking. The challenge posed to Hebrew economic structures and the attempts to reform them are not mere afterthoughts but are in fact *incarnational* of YHWH's saving act. Thus it is that YHWH liberates an oppressed people, gifts them with a "land flowing with milk and honey,"[10] and then gives them charge to care for the indigent in their midst as their way of continuing divine work and as their testimony to God's gracious favors extended to them as a people who were once down and hard up themselves. These economic precepts permeate the very fabric of Israel's relationship with YHWH. An egalitarian ethos of mutual aid is ingrained in their national self-identity because of what God had done for them.

Desired outcomes

Social mechanisms parallel to the market

As part of the aforementioned need to situate economic life within a broader overarching moral framework, social safeguards are deliberately institutionalized parallel to the marketplace. Market outcomes and processes are not held to be inviolable but are viewed as subject to change and correction. The market is not the final arbiter in the disposition of social goods and services; individual and collective moral agency is. Not only is there a willingness to "second-guess" the marketplace, there is in fact a deeply felt obligation to ensure, through extra-market means, that the disadvantaged are able to share in the benefits of market exchange. In other words, these economic precepts serve as shadow mechanisms complementing the marketplace as it allocates scarce resources within the

10 Exod. 3:8, 17; 13:5; Lev. 20:24; Num. 14:8; Deut. 6:3; 11:9; 26:9, 15; 27:3; 31:20; Josh. 5:6; Jer. 11:5; 32:22; Ezra 20:6, 15.

community.[11] There should be non-market corrective-rehabilitative processes to redress deleterious unintended consequences in the marketplace. The Hebrew Scripture provides excellent examples of such initiatives, as seen in the restoration of key wealth-producing assets (land return in the Jubilee Law), of freedom (slave manumission), of solvency (debt forgiveness), and of liquidity (mandatory interest-free loans).

A modern analog would be helpful in appreciating the significance of the nation Israel's economic activism. In the post-World War II era, governments actively fine-tuned their economies following John Maynard Keynes's (1936) path-breaking *General Theory of Employment.* This was in sharp contrast to the prevailing school of economic thought at that time – the Classical School – which frowned on interfering with economic life because markets were deemed to be self-healing. The depth and persistence of unemployment during the Great Depression disproved this thinking and paved the way for Keynes's thesis that markets need to be assisted through extra-market means to attain even distinctly economic goals such as full employment. Thus, governments utilized fiscal and monetary instruments to bring economies into an ideal position of simultaneous low inflation and low unemployment (Yergin and Stanislaw 1998). The nation Israel was likewise "interventionist" in her ancient economy and could be similarly described as "fine-tuning" market processes and outcomes, not for economic goals but to conform to YHWH's vision of an economy of caring and compassion in which no one was left in want, in accordance with the Covenant. In both cases, parallel public structures were in place to assist the marketplace, which, left on its own, was simply unable to secure larger, much less noneconomic, societal goals.

Progressive burden-bearing
There is an evident preferential option for the poor in these economic ordinances. Most of the debts incurred are believed to have been consumption-distress loans rather than commercial credits for trade or

---

11 This is an excellent illustration of the primacy of labor principle proposed by John Paul II (1981) in *Laborem Exercens.* In this encyclical commemorating the ninetieth anniversary of *Rerum Novarum,* John Paul II argues that the value of work output and effort must ultimately be founded on the fact that it is a human person that is responsible for such economic outcomes. He refers to this as the subjective dimension of work in contrast to its objective dimension (such as the cost of production). In other words, work effort and output must be accorded an economic value that affords a gainful livelihood to workers. In providing moral compass and shape to market outcomes and processes, the nation Israel is in effect according primacy to the subjective rather than the objective dimension of work.

production (Gnuse 1985: 19; Lang 1985: 99; de Vaux 1965: 170–73). Thus, it was the poor who were compelled to incur the most liabilities, subsequently lose their patrimonial land, and ultimately end up in debt slavery. In other words, *the more severe the plight of the economic agent, the greater is the concessional grant afforded that person in these corrective-restorative measures.* The mirror image of this burden-bearing, of course, is that it was most likely the well-to-do who paid the requisite outlays for these positive communal obligations. In other words, there is a progressive[12] feature to paying for the cost of rectifying the pernicious consequences of pecuniary externalities and economic contingencies; those who have done well in the marketplace are the ones who bear a larger share of the cost of these concessional grants.

In a study of the economics of the Hebrew Scripture, Soss (1973: 340–42) argues that the provisions of Leviticus 25 on land valuation and transfers are so anti-buyer that it would have been surprising to find any buyer at all willing to agree to such unfavorable terms. The sacrificial demands of these corrective-restorative economic statutes can also be indirectly inferred from the numerous reported violations and from the invention of legal loopholes such as the *prosbul* designed to escape the obligations of debt reprieve.[13] Some scholars would even go so far as to suggest that the Jubilee land return and slave release statutes are in fact pro-wealthy concessions (Ginzberg 1932; de Vaux 1965: 83). These measures are believed to have been enacted as second-best compromises in the face of the widespread violation of the slave manumission laws. Masters promise better treatment for debt slaves in exchange for being allowed to hold on to their indentured labor for a longer period of time: fifty years under the Jubilee provisions in contrast to the six-year period found in Exodus 21:2–6 and Deuteronomy 15:12–18. At any rate, regardless of whether the Jubilee Law is for the benefit of the poor or the wealthy, scholars are in agreement that there is no evidence to suggest that it was ever practiced at all (Fager 1993: 34–36; Lowery 2000; North 1954). This, too, reflects how

12 In contrast, a regressive structure is where the poor pay a disproportionately larger share of the burdens of the community. For example, income taxes in the United States are progressive because wealthier people pay a larger proportion of their income as taxes relative to the poor who pay, if at all, a smaller percentage of their earnings in taxes. In contrast, sales (or value-added consumption) taxes are regressive because these fiscal levies take a proportionately larger bite out of the poor's resources compared with their wealthier counterparts.

13 The *prosbul* was a legal artifice in which the borrower promised to pay back the loan to the lender via the court regardless of the seventh-year debt forgiveness called for under Deut. 15:1–2. Since this law was interpreted to apply only to individuals and not to courts, the debt was turned over to the court, which then collected the debt on behalf of the lender even with the onset of the period for remission (Lowery 2000: 41).

the burdensome impositions of these economic directives discouraged compliance.

This is not the place to debate the finer points of which interpretation of the Jubilee Law is correct. It is sufficient for this study to note that the deliberate efforts to get around the legislation suggest that the Hebrews found these economic statutes to be troublesome in their demands. In other words, there is a large, unavoidable, sacrificial element involved in implementing the principle of restoration. Unlike civil and political liberties that can be easily satisfied with mere noninterference in others' freedom of action, these corrective-restorative measures carry positive obligations that are exacting in the concessions they require from those who have benefited from the marketplace on behalf of those who have been harmed by pecuniary externalities. Embedded within the nation Israel's legislation is a progressive sharing of the cost of injurious market ripple effects. The burden of having to provide interest-free loans, write off debt, emancipate debt slaves, and return land falls disproportionately on the people who have the necessary surplus to buy land from distressed sellers and to lend to the impoverished. The outlays for tithing for the poor, sabbatical fallows, almsgiving, the gleaning laws, and the shared feasts of the sabbatical rests are borne by those who are able to pay for them. This is an attractive feature of the principle of restoration in Hebrew Law, especially in the face of the skewed incidence of some of the market's subsidiary effects, as described earlier in chapter 2. This progressive dynamic provides an ideal counterpoint to the regressive distribution of the cost of participating in the market.

There is yet another feature of these laws that must be highlighted. An ancient "limited goods" economy (Foster 1967) of precarious existence provided enticing opportunities for building patron–client dependencies (Eisenstadt and Roniger 1980, 1984). As will be discussed shortly, the design of these precepts and the motive clauses undergirding them precluded using these releases as occasions for putting the disadvantaged in further subservience to the powerful and the well-to-do. In releasing debts, slaves, and land without any strings attached, those who had prospered were in effect being asked to relinquish the means (land, slaves, and money) for amassing even greater economic and political power for themselves. Recall that this was an agrarian economy in which wealth was created through tangible resources such as land and labor; for commercial traders, capital is the key controlling resource. Thus, what was being given up under these economic ordinances were no ordinary goods but the very productive assets that create wealth. It was not merely the quantity of what was being given up that would hurt; what was even more significant was the quality of the resources foregone.[14] In many ways, this was even more sacrificial because what was ceded here was control over an entire steady stream of potential future earnings.

On top of this, the enormity of the selflessness required can be better appreciated if we keep in mind that all this transpired in a "limited goods" society, that is, in a zero-sum environment. In restoring one's neighbor as a self-sustaining landholding household, it was entirely possible that one was also restoring (or creating) competition for oneself. Once restored to farming, for example, the neighbor would also be competing to hire the same labor or sell the same type of crops in the course of the agricultural cycle. Once reinstated to independence, the neighbor would be competing as a buyer or seller in the same commercial markets.

There is a distinctive cluster of releases called for in Hebrew economic statutes: release of debt, release of slaves, release of land, release of the fruits of the earth (gleaning, sabbatical fallow, and tithing for the poor), and release from work (Sabbath and sabbatical fallow). These releases reflect a deeper call to let go of whatever rightful claims we may have on scarce, highly valued resources – to forego these in favor of the distressed and the needy. As noted earlier, the concessionary element to these corrective-restorative mechanisms is the mirror image of the opportunity loss for those who are invited to enter into this process of "letting go."

Only God has necessary existence; human beings merely participate in the existence of God. Theirs is but a contingent existence. In living up to these economic standards, people in effect partake together in all the dimensions of their common contingency. Not only do they collectively experience the contingency of their existence, they also voluntarily share in the contingencies of each other's life outcomes. The proffered act of rehabilitating afflicted neighbors, at great personal sacrifice, conveys profound meaning: (1) to the people restored – of how valued they are; (2) to God – of how we embrace sacrifice out of love of God; (3) and to ourselves – of how we desire to emulate God.

Not merely basic-needs provision

The economic precepts on almsgiving, tithing for the poor, shared festivals, and gleaning ensure that the basic needs of the marginalized in

---

14 Using modern terminology, people were in effect being asked to voluntarily divest themselves of some of their dominant (Walzer 1983) and positional (Hirsch 1976) goods.

the community are met. However, note that the Law further imposes the obligations of debt remission, slave emancipation, and the return of ancestral land. In other words, Hebrew moral thinking goes beyond merely providing relief to restoring the ability of economic agents to participate fully in the socioeconomic life of the community as free landholding households. Such participation is possible for the economically distressed only with the reconstitution of their freedom, land, and solvency. Walter Brueggemann (1994: 18) observes that the debt and the slave release laws of Deuteronomy reflect the responsibility Israel took upon herself to reinstate those who had fallen by the wayside in the normal course of economic life.

The goal is not merely relief, but rehabilitation as full and equal members of the community; it is about their reestablishment to the point of being able to bear their share of community burdens. The larger aim is the restoration of status – to be able to participate in the community as equals. Property ownership confers this social standing (Porter 1990: 102–103). An excellent measure of such equality and an important goal for the distressed is that of being restored to the point where they are able to contribute back to the community, and perhaps even rehabilitate others in their own turn.

An ancillary benefit of these corrective-restorative economic tenets is that in reconstituting distressed members to their rightful place as free landholding families, not only are they able to provide for themselves without depending on the community, they are also able to bear their share of the obligations of living together as a community. Wright (1990: 97) argues for the central importance of protecting the household's economic viability because it was through the family that Hebrews were able to discharge their military, juridic, and cultic obligations. The family, after all, was the basic social unit of the nation Israel. Indeed, part of the dignity and self-respect that come with being propertied and free is the thought that one is able to contribute to the common good. Thus, even from a strictly fiscal point of view, there are strong pecuniary arguments for corrective-restorative mechanisms and processes in the marketplace. Cast in the language of economics, human resources have a functional utility besides their intrinsic value that stems from personhood. There are rational economic reasons for building up and restoring economic agents' "functionings and capabilities" (Sen 1999) because they are the key building blocks to a more secure and vibrant long-term growth and development.

Underlying processes

Systemic and ongoing rather than ad hoc or reactive
These economic teachings are not merely one-time, ad hoc responses to particular crises or events but flow from an ongoing collective moral introspection that weighs what YHWH expected of the nation Israel. Moreover, they are not left merely to the discretion or the charitable sentiments of people but are embedded within the system itself. In other words, these economic ordinances are a systemic response and gradually emerge and develop from a continuing critical reflection on whether the outcomes and processes of their evolving, growing economy are consistent with their election as God's Chosen People. *There is a ceaseless process of re-centering the economy on those values that truly matter within the larger milieu delineated by the Covenant.*

Bruce Birch's (1991: 145–97) tripartite Covenant model is a good example of this phenomenon. This ideal model of social life consists of an economy of equality, a politics of justice and service, and a religion of God's radical freedom and fidelity. Religion is not separated from economics or politics; rather, it is religion that shapes and defines the character of the community's economic and political life. It is their consciousness of God at work in their midst that leads them to constantly measure their personal and collective choices against the standards defined by their election to responsibility. In their own turn, economics and politics either strengthen or weaken people's understanding, appreciation, and practice of their faith. The prophets forcefully describe this dynamic when they emphatically remind Israel that genuine worship of God comes from the heart and unmistakably manifests itself in the manner in which people treat one another rather than in their holocausts and burnt offerings (e.g., Amos 5:21–22a, 24). Religion, economics, and politics mutually feed off and reinforce each other, with religion serving as the foundational bedrock on which all facets of personal and common life find their ultimate reference point.

All these should not be taken as an apology for modern-day theocracies or be viewed as a call for breaching the walls that separate Church and State. Neither should it be read as an argument for turning the clock back on the enormous strides we have achieved in our understanding of religious freedom (Vatican Council II 1965a). Rather, the experience of the nation Israel should serve as a reminder that one cannot compartmentalize a person's spiritual, political, professional, family, and social life as if they were independent of each other. These different spheres of human life are inseparable and can either mutually nurture or weaken each other. Furthermore, religious traditions are often criticized whenever they speak out on matters that are deemed to be entirely secular and outside the realm of their professional competence. Birch's tripartite description of the nation Israel is an affirmation that not only do societal religious institutions have a right to speak and teach on socioeconomic matters, they in fact have an obligation to do so. For the Christian faith, anything that impinges on human dignity is a matter of concern. This is eloquently and succinctly expressed in the opening lines of *Gaudium et Spes* as it declares that anything genuinely human cannot but raise an echo in the hearts of the followers of Christ. There is the adage that economics is too important to be left exclusively in the hands of economists. Religion should vigorously involve itself in the debates on the shape and direction of the common life not merely because economics is too important to be left to secular experts alone, but because religion has the charge to articulate its distinctive vision of the ideal economic life in the public square of ideas.

Taking responsibility

The imperative of fine-tuning the economy in pursuit of larger societal goals implies taking both personal and collective responsibility for market outcomes and processes. Much can be learned from the example of Hebrew Law in this regard. Unlike other Ancient Near Eastern countries that relied on royal decrees to effect corrective-restorative measures in economic life, the nation Israel not only regularized such practices but also made their implementation the shared duty of the entire population rather than depending on civil or religious leadership alone. Furthermore, note that there are no judicial sanctions specified for noncompliance with these economic precepts. There is reliance only on the moral suasion of wanting to remain faithful to YHWH's expectations. Thus, in lieu of menacing civil penalties, we find the motive clauses that appeal to the human heart and mind in reminding people of the favors God had extended to them in their own lives, favors that in their own turn ought now to be extended to others who are just as hard-pressed as they once were. The enforcement of these economic teachings is in the internal rather than in the external forum. For example, recall how King Zedekiah could not simply compel the population by decree to free those held in bondage; he had to plead, coax, and then strike an agreement with the people to voluntarily release their slaves in accordance with the Law, which they should have been observing in the first place (Jer. 34:8–22).

Positive obligations

Hebrew extra-market mechanisms serve a dual function of both rectifying the detrimental consequences of pecuniary externalities and reestablishing distressed economic agents. The latter are restored not necessarily to their original state but, at least, to a position that affords them the opportunity of participating once again in the economic life of the community as free landholding households.

Isaiah Berlin's (1958) differentiation between negative and positive freedoms (rights or obligations) provides a useful conceptual distinction to better appreciate this dual function of Hebrew economic precepts. Negative rights or freedoms are aptly described as passive because they merely call for noninterference in others' exercise of their freedoms and rights. In other words, the only action that is required of third parties to satisfy these kinds of claims is for them to refrain from doing anything that prevents others from acting. Examples of these would be civil and political liberties such as the right to assembly and free speech. They are relatively inexpensive to satisfy in the sense of not requiring any direct expenditure of resources on the part of anybody else in the community; all that is needed is passive noninterference in others' exercise of their rights.[15] In contrast, positive freedoms or rights require the transfer of real resources between moral agents if such claims are to be satisfied at all. Economic rights provide an apt illustration. The poor's right to food, clothing, and shelter can only be fulfilled through private gifts or social transfers funded by fiscal revenues. In other words, positive freedoms or rights require deliberate third-party action if their claims are to be met. They impose positive obligations that are often expensive to carry out.

Using Berlin's positive/negative distinction, we can see that the ameliorative social mechanisms of Hebrew economic precepts are not merely negative (passive) in the sense of just setting boundaries that cannot be breached, such as prohibiting interest on debt or restricting the kinds of assets that may be used as debt security. More significantly, these community safeguards call for positive, deliberate action that not only attends to the immediate needs of those who are unable to cope with economic contingencies (e.g., almsgiving, gleaning laws, and mandatory loans) but also restores them to a position of independently fending for themselves in the marketplace (e.g., debt reprieve, slave manumission, and land return). In other words, they call for a release from any and all outstanding

---

15 The satisfaction of civil and political freedoms is not entirely costless since there is need for law enforcement, a functioning judiciary, and other social infrastructure to protect such freedoms.

obligations in order to give those who have fallen on hard times a chance to start anew without being burdened by past claims.

No patron–client relationships

Observe that in all these economic ordinances, there are no lingering patron–client indebtedness or dependencies. These releases of debt, labor, and land are completely unconditional. The beneficiaries are restored as *full equals*. There is no expectation of a patron–client relationship after rehabilitation. The restoration is absolute and irrevocable, and without any strings attached or favors owed. People provide such sacrificial releases not to amass prestige, honors, or economic and political power for themselves. Neither do they do it out of the goodness of their hearts alone. Rather, they do all these because it is God who has asked them to do for others what God had done for them. They are merely sharing with others the same favors given to them by God in their own moment of need. The motive clauses that are often appended to the statutes serve to remind people of why God has every right to ask them to live up to these demanding divine economic precepts (Doron 1978; Gemser 1953). In articulating the rationale for these norms, these motive clauses preempt people's using such restorative mechanisms as occasions for personal aggrandizement or for fashioning patron–client subservience. People who are indebted themselves (to God) have no reason to boast or to hold others in perpetual debt. Power over the disposition of freedom, treasure, and land cannot be used as a means of holding people in servility.

THEOLOGICAL PRECEDENTS AND WARRANTS

How does this proposed principle of restoration fit in within the larger witness of revelation beyond the Hebrew law codes? The corrective-restorative nature of the Hebrew economic statutes is founded on theological precedents and warrants. First, these flow from the much larger characteristic divine action of renewing, re-creating, and transforming wounded humanity in salvation history. It is YHWH who restores freedom to an enslaved Israel held in captivity in Egypt and forms them as God's own people. In the depths of the nation's sinfulness and stubbornness, the pre-exilic prophets, even while scathing and severe in their condemnation of the Chosen People, already speak of their vision of a reconstituted Israel. Indeed, an important feature of the prophetic literature is the insight into YHWH's initiative in reestablishing a rejuvenated community and providing all the necessary succor to start anew

(Brueggemann 1994: 19–22). The prophetic writings are not merely harsh indictments of Israel's infidelity but are also about hope – a firm reassurance of the certainty of restoration. And indeed, it is God who reconstitutes the remnants of a chastened Israel in the Promised Land from their Babylonian exile. It is God who revives sinful and fallen humanity with dignity and grace through the incarnation, passion, death, and resurrection of Jesus Christ. In all these cases, the restoration is more than just the provision of liberty, it is also about supplying the necessary means to have a meaningful chance of making something out of this new-found freedom. Thus, YHWH gives Israel the Law; Christ gives the new Chosen People the Gospel. God not only restores but also provides all the requisite assistance to flourish in the genuine freedom that comes with being children of God. New creations invariably follow in the wake of God's initiatives on behalf of humanity.

Second, scriptural teachings on economic life can be roughly divided into at least three categories:

1 As reflective of God's envisioned due order: We find the articulation of such a divine vision in the Covenant model (Birch 1991: 172–82) and in the repeated calls to let our unity as a family be manifested in the mutual help we provide each other in economic life.

2 As a resistance to temptations to corrupt the due order of God's creation: We see this, for example, in the numerous warnings against letting economic life turn into an idolatry of wanton consumption and avaricious accumulation.

3 As corrective of the ills inflicted against the due order envisioned by God: The aforementioned Hebrew economic statutes fall into this last category. YHWH liberates Israel from Egyptian slavery and grants them a "land flowing with milk and honey" so that they may no longer live in want. Thus, YHWH's economic precepts, including the aforementioned corrective-restorative measures, could be viewed as God making provisions for ameliorating the consequences of human sinfulness and for building an economy of equality where no one is left in want. God not only provides for us through each other, but also corrects and makes up for our misdeeds through one another.[16]

---

16 The parable of the vineyard owner (Matt. 20:1–16) is an excellent illustration of how economic life can be used in the service of God's unfolding providence for creatures. Lebacqz (1983: 39–42) uses this parable as a lesson in the gift of restoration.

Stephen Mott (1982: 67–70, 220) observes that the "principle of redress" is constitutive of God's justice; it is a principle that is usually applied indirectly through human instruments, or directly if the latter should fail. Norman Snaith (1964: 70) describes God's justice as securing rights for those who are unable to do so themselves. Birch (1991: 156) echoes and summarizes these positions by noting that God does not merely care for the poor, but in fact aggressively rectifies the root causes and inequities that bring about such economic hardships. In other words, tending to the symptoms of impoverishment is not good enough; redressing their sources is a necessary task, indeed, a divine mandate.

Third, the Hebrew economic precepts are demanding in the sacrifices they exact from people. This should not be surprising at all considering that upright economic behavior is nothing but a continuation of God's in-breaking into human history to provide relief, comfort, dignity, and self-respect to the poor and the oppressed (Lohfink 1987). Thus, it is important to situate these corrective-rehabilitative economic measures as a participation in God's ongoing work and presence in the human community, a participation in divine righteousness. God's righteousness is always saving and restorative. It is empowering and uses secondary, instrumental causes to revitalize others. Through such economic statutes, God restores due order in the world. Lohfink observes that the Law's economic ordinances require not merely the relief of the poor, but systemic change, one of whose constitutive elements, as we have already seen, is the regeneration of those who have fallen on hard times. Such a call for societal transformation is a qualitative step-up in human participation in God's righteousness compared to the mere relief of the poor. It is a more profound commission as a secondary cause in the service of divine providence.

Fourth, the sacrificial nature of these corrective-rehabilitative economic directives finds its ultimate model in the New Testament where sinful humanity is justified, but at the expense of the passion and death of Jesus Christ. It is the paradigmatic self-giving so that others may live and be renewed and re-created.

Finally, the principle of restoration can be situated within the larger context and theology of the first installment of the eschaton breaking into the here and now. Patrick Miller (1985) argues that the Deuteronomic and Levitical releases (debt, slaves, and land) are at a deeper level an appropriation of the sabbatical principle. The Sabbath goes beyond merely prescribing a day of rest; it is at its core about a "much larger principle of social justice, what one might call 'the sabbatical principle'" (ibid.: 93) because it provides surcease to the slaves and the servants who would have otherwise not been able to secure rest from their toilsome work on their own. It affords the occasion for like treatment that bespeaks an equality between master and servant.

Six days you shall labor and do all your work, but the seventh day is a Sabbath to the LORD your God. On it you shall not do any work, neither you, nor your son or daughter, nor your manservant or maidservant . . . nor the alien within your gates, *so that your manservant and maidservant may rest, as you do.* Remember that you were slaves in Egypt and that the LORD your God brought you out of there with a mighty hand and an outstretched arm. Therefore the LORD your God has commanded you to observe the Sabbath day.

(Deut. 5:13–15 [emphasis added])[17]

This mandated Sabbath of rest is expanded further to incorporate a sabbath of releases. Thus, Deuteronomy 15:1–6 calls for a reprieve of debts, while Deuteronomy 15:12–18 calls for the emancipation of those in bondage. Miller concludes that the Sabbath rest and these two release ordinances find their commonality in the motive clause that gives these strictures their force: "You shall remember that you were a slave in the land of Egypt" (15:5). Miller (1985: 93–94) argues that this particular motive clause is distinctive in that it is used solely[18] in conjunction with precepts that protect the weak and the oppressed, and, as such, these ordinances that are protective of the poor are directly tied to the Sabbath commandment.

The sabbatical principle, therefore, is a building into the relentless movement of human existence regular times for release and recouping, for freeing from the chains and burdens that bind members of the community and for ensuring the provision of good for each member of the community, especially to provide equity and opportunity for those members of the community who in varying degrees do not have it. (Miller 1985: 94)

But there is more to these tenets than just rectifying the ills of the human condition. Leviticus 25 completes these sabbatical releases by highlighting the need to restore the original condition, the original gift of the Creator. Schenker describes this dynamic well:

Influenced perhaps by the Deuteronomic year of release which is parallel to the fallow year of the Covenant Code, Leviticus 25 belongs to the same endeavour,

---

17 New International Version translation.
18 See Deut. 16:9–12; 24:18, 22.

placing it in the religious framework of the periodical *restitutio in integrum* where all things come back to the original creation and to the original founding order. It is a periodical eschatology and a periodical purification of human society from the distortions of life and bad luck. The world is close to creation and to the Creator, [w]hen it is close to being a humane world. (Schenker 1998: 37)

Miller (1985: 94) echoes this point of returning to the original condition by noting further that the human experience of time as linear is interrupted by the sabbatical releases that bring us back to the way it was in the beginning.

The association of the Sabbath and the sabbatical principle with God's creative and resting activity is a signal of its deepest meaning. *The sabbatical principle means a restoration of the world and human relationships to their created character and intention.* The sabbatical principle says "no!" to the relentless movement of events that seems unchangeable, "no!" to the assumption that . . . there is no release, and the chain of cause and effect must keep going on . . . "no!" to the relentless cycle of poverty that we assume cannot be broken.

(Miller 1985: 95 [emphasis added])

Albrecht Alt (1967: 165) makes a similar observation when he concludes that the sabbatical fallow is not economic in nature, but religious. It is a de facto abrogation of the right to possess the land that the Israelites have enjoyed in the preceding years but which is now being suspended in humble acknowledgment of the way it was in the beginning, and the way it still is – God as the true and sole owner of land. Moreover, Alt observes that the Feast of the Tabernacles during this sabbatical year is in fact the time set aside to rededicating every member of the Chosen People to the Covenant that had been struck with YHWH in the beginning (ibid.: 165–67).

Von Waldow agrees with the aforementioned view of the sabbatical year not merely as a periodic time for renewal but also as a time for retrieving and restoring the core structure that defines the nation Israel as what it is: "Everything that had happened in the past seven-year period is crossed out. Israel is given a new starting point, the covenant is renewed, she receives anew the land out of the hand of Yahweh, and the social order is reestablished" (von Waldow 1970: 195). This regular readjustment ensures that Israel does not stray too far from the blueprint of the ideal nation characterized by an economy of equality, a politics of justice, and a religion of God's radical freedom and fidelity (Birch 1991: 172–82).

The Jubilee Law has a messianic typology because "it points to a coming era of peace and prosperity" (North 1954: 230). Within the radical economic reform called for by Leviticus 25, these corrective-rehabilitative precepts can be described as eschatological for they prefigure (albeit in an admittedly poor and imperfect fashion) the eschaton in which people are reconstituted to what had been lost, relieved of their burdens, and set free to feast and live together in abundance as equals in mutual caring and regard. The Law is about longing for the inauguration of the New Jerusalem where no one will be left in want. Indeed, these regularly scheduled releases and restoration can be viewed as bringing about a first installment of the eschaton in the here and now.

SUMMARY AND CONCLUSIONS

Commenting on the virtues and limits of the marketplace, Kuttner (1997: 54) observes that the Church "is the longest-running counterweight to the dogmas of a pure market."[19] Indeed, the Christian social tradition has a long-standing track record of situating economic life within a much larger moral milieu. It has always been a strong advocate of social mechanisms and processes that act in concert with and parallel to the marketplace, much to the discomfort, even irritation, of many (e.g., Bauer 1984). We see such teachings in the patristic literature on economic life (Phan 1984; Walsh and Langan 1977). The same pattern is repeated for the medieval doctors. The scholastic doctrine of the just price, for example, is at its root an extra-market response to ensuring that workers reap a gainful livelihood for themselves. Such a moral consideration in effect sets limits to how far pecuniary externalities are allowed to operate unfettered. In other words, custom, law, and usage in the market (e.g., the just price) set boundaries to prevent unintended consequences from unduly harming the medieval economic agent.

An even more remarkable and comprehensive response to pecuniary externalities and economic chance and contingency, however, can be found in an even earlier age – the formation of twelve disparate tribes into the nation Israel. They too experienced an expansion in the scope of their markets and in the kinds of goods and services available to them. Such developments in the marketplace generated profound ripple effects across the rest of their society, for good or for ill. And they reacted accordingly, aspiring to be true to their self-understanding of who they were as the Chosen People of God.

19 Trade unions come in second place.

The writing, subsequent redaction, and further development of the economic statutes of the Hebrew law codes were the fruits of the people's moral introspection as they sought to adapt and respond appropriately to their changing circumstances. The Covenant Code mirrors a desire to institutionalize the egalitarian ethos of an erstwhile nomadic era that experienced firsthand the value of mutual assistance as key to their joint survival. The precepts in Exodus are an attempt to codify such a spirit of reciprocal dependence as their former itinerant way of life increasingly gave way to a more settled agrarian lifestyle. The Deuteronomic Code embodies the earnest priestly and prophetic reaction to the deteriorating socioeconomic conditions precipitated by monarchial abuses and fiscal impositions. Note, for example, the further refinement and development of the economic ordinances that make them even more humane and responsive to the needs of those who have been marginalized by social change. The Holiness Code is believed by most scholars to have been animated by a post-exilic fervor to reconstitute the remnant nation along the lines of the original gift of a Covenant economy of mutual regard where no one is left in want. Thus, the return of ancestral land reflects this desire to bring the nation back to what it was and to what YHWH had intended it to be, in which every family enjoyed economic security. Indeed, we see in the development of these law codes a refinement in Hebrew economic practices in response to, or out of the ashes of, their mistakes. This chapter has argued that a distinctive contribution of that earlier period can be succinctly and aptly described as the principle of restoration – a model for how we in our own turn in postindustrial times can choose to deal with the damaging, unintended, consequences of a rapidly changing, and often disruptive, economic life.

The requisite tasks in resolving seemingly intractable problems in the wake of globalization are overwhelming. The challenges are particularly acute when it comes to reinstating the means that enable the marginalized to participate fully, as equals, in the marketplace, especially when it comes to the question of who has the obligation of paying the cost for such corrective-restorative initiatives. This is not even to mention the need to come to an agreement on the contentious issue of the content of the requisite assistance and the extent to which it is to be furnished. Nevertheless, Christians do not shy away from that which is difficult or from that which has never been tried before. After all, one must remember that this tradition is at its core prophetic and revolutionary.

The sabbatical principle motivated by the Exodus experience is surely the most revolutionary force for the creating and ordering of human community that the Lord's way with Israel set loose, because it didn't simply stop with the seventh day, but began to set all kinds of ways in which the human situation is stopped and changed. It is revolutionary because it cuts against the grain, and it is meant to do so. (Miller 1985: 94)

As Christians, we are willing to sacrifice and to do that which is difficult, indeed well-nigh impossible, because, just like the Hebrews, we too have been witness to the Exodus of our own lives. Having been on the receiving end of God's favor, we now want to extend to others the same favors we have enjoyed, and, in so doing, to participate in the providential work of God itself.

PART 3

Contemporary appropriation

Economic rights-obligations as diagnostic framework

INTRODUCTION

The first two chapters described the nature and dynamics of economic compulsion. The notion of economic security as a divine gift in the Old Testament (chapter 3) provides scriptural warrants for why such negative pecuniary externalities ought to be redressed. The restorative ethos of the Hebrew precepts (chapter 4) exemplifies the spirit with which such adverse unintended consequences ought to be ameliorated. Harmful market ripple effects are still very much with us today, and with even greater severity given the increasing "marketization" of modern society. It now remains for us to examine two issues: (1) how to adapt the biblical vision of economic security in a postindustrial economy, and (2) how to define the threshold that must be crossed before negative pecuniary externalities are considered to be cases of economic compulsion deserving correction and rehabilitative assistance.

The Hebrews had a strong sense of "belonging," given their appreciation for their distinctive corporate identity as the Chosen People of God. It was relatively easier to discern what was expected of them as individuals and as a community since their economics and politics were informed and shaped by a shared religious conviction. Thus, they were able to promulgate laws and statutes with clear specificity in dealing with economic distress (chapters 3 and 4). In the case of the scholastic era, the just price was set by custom, law, and usage. Entitlements were based on what people might demand of each other given the roles and responsibilities they discharged in the community.

While presenting its own set of problems, rights language arguably provides the best means with which to define mutual obligations and claims in ameliorating economic compulsion in our contemporary age of humanism and pluralism. Wertheimer's (1987) path-breaking work outlines a philosophical theory of coercion using courts' adjudication of legal cases as a starting point, and his conclusion on setting the all-important baseline is particularly noteworthy:

I have argued that B's [the coerced party] moral baseline does most of the important work in distinguishing between coercive and noncoercive proposals in cases which involve the ascription of responsibility. But how do we *set* B's moral baseline? In my view, a full answer to this question would require nothing less than a complete moral and political theory . . .

[T]he moral baseline approach rests on a theory of *rights*. To set B's moral baselines, we need to know what A is morally *required* to do for B (or not to do to B). Whether these moral requirements are *ultimately* grounded in a deontological or consequentialist theory, the structure of coercion discourse presupposes that A and B have certain obligations and rights which establish a background against which A's proposals are understood. (Wertheimer 1987: 217 [original emphasis])

As seen in chapter 1, there are key differences between *coercion* and *compulsion* in the way I use the latter in this study. Moreover, just like legal scholars and other philosophers, Wertheimer is interested in the notion of coercion primarily for the ascription of responsibility: To what extent are the coerced bound by the terms of contracts accepted under duress? In contrast, this study seeks to understand economic compulsion for purposes of weighing duties of mutual assistance in alleviating such distress. Nevertheless, despite these differences, the philosophical litera- ture's notion of *coercion* and my exposition on *economic compulsion* overlap in their concern over the "very hard choices" to which people are driven; both accord central importance to setting and defining the moral baseline. For philosophers and legal scholars, such a baseline is essential for distinguishing threats from offers. For this study, this baseline is pivotal in differentiating significant from negligible pecuniary external- ities and in arguing why adverse unintended consequences of the market are morally significant. All dimensions of economic compulsion (why they are important, when they are profound, to what degree they are to be corrected, and how) can be evaluated or measured with reference to the extent to which human rights or obligations are violated.

Correcting injurious market ripple effects takes on greater urgency and becomes more compelling to the modern mind if they can be shown to infringe on human rights. This, however, is not a straightforward exercise. In the first place, the concept of rights leaves many unanswered questions pertaining to its foundations, its addressees, and its correlative obligations (Winston 1989). Second, the existence of economic rights is not uniformly accepted and is still heavily contested terrain (Paul, Miller, and Paul 1992;

Trimiew 1997). Third, even if economic rights were to be accepted as binding, there is the further problem of specifying the content, scope, and force of their claims. Indeed, much preparatory theoretical work is required before the notion of rights can be used effectively. Herein lies another strength of Christian ethics in dealing with the issue of economic compulsion. It already has a well-developed conceptual framework that can fill in much of the lacunae in rights language, even as it provides at the same time a model for assessing deleterious economic outcomes and processes.

The notion of economic compulsion will remain a purely academic exercise unless we are able to delineate at what point the unintended consequences of market transactions become clearly unacceptable and deserving of extra-market correction. This chapter proposes just such an analytical framework that specifies the formal conditions of economic compulsion more concretely and distinguishes trivial from consequential pecuniary externalities. Theological social ethics can be brought to bear on the issue of economic compulsion. To make this exposition manageable, I limit myself to the Old Testament and modern Catholic social thought.[1] In what follows, I advance a rights-based model for assessing economic compulsion. First, I use the biblical notion of economic security as a foundation for modern economic rights. As seen in part II, these scriptural warrants provide reasons why economic distress ought to be the subject of moral discourse; moreover, they also illustrate how adverse unintended consequences ought to be rectified. Second, I present Henry Shue's (1980) formulation of subsistence rights and a schematic synthesis[2] of *Pacem in Terris* as contemporary expressions of the Hebrew vision of economic security for all. Third, I appeal to the notion of the common good as due order and to the modern Catholic social principles as mediating concepts in transposing biblical economic security to contemporary ethical practice. From these, I derive a set of core economic rights, the infringement of which reflects varying degrees of economic compulsion. Fourth, I examine different lexical rules for resolving competing claims.

---

1 I use "modern Catholic social thought" to refer to the major papal, conciliar, synodal, and pontifical commission social documents, namely: *Rerum Novarum, Quadragesimo Anno, Pentecost Address 1941, 1942 Christmas Message, Mater et Magistra, Pacem in Terris, Gaudium et Spes, Populorum Progressio, Octogesima Adveniens, Justice in the World, Laborem Exercens, Sollicitudo Rei Socialis,* and *Centesimus Annus.*
2 Yale Task Force on Population Ethics (1974).

BIBLICAL ECONOMIC SECURITY AS A WARRANT FOR HUMAN RIGHTS

Within Catholic circles, human rights are believed to flow from the dignity that is peculiar to human beings (Henle 1980; Hollenbach 1979; John XXIII 1963; Kasper 1990).[3] However, Alan Gewirth (1981a and b; 1982) and John Coleman (1984: 351) criticize human dignity as a weak and unconvincing justification for human rights. The linkage between human dignity and human rights cannot be presumed to be self-evident and requires a clear articulation of the specific channels by which the dignity of one person translates into particular obligations that someone else must fill. Darryl Trimiew (1997: 250) describes this as the circularity in the use of human dignity as a justification of human rights.

The twofold divine gift of economic security in the Old Testament provides an alternative, scriptural basis for economic rights. In what follows, I briefly summarize the key scriptural insights from the preceding chapter that can be used as arguments for modern economic rights. The Hebrew economic statutes cover a broad range of activities ranging from almsgiving, tithing, gleaning privileges, sabbatical rests, and mandatory lending, to a manifold set of releases of debts, slaves, and land. A common thread running through these ordinances is the distinct obligation to attend to the marginalized. In other words, those who had fallen into economic distress as a result of pecuniary externalities or economic chance and contingency held strong moral claims for assistance from their fellow Hebrews.

The proximate source of such imperatives lay in the bonds and ties they shared with one another. Different theories have been proposed regarding the formation of the nation Israel: as liberated slaves from Egypt, as uprooted people fleeing to the highlands to escape the oppressive yoke of the city-states, or as a combination of both.[4] Regardless of which hypothesis is correct, they all point to the same conclusion: The Hebrews were held together by a deeply ingrained experience of struggle and liberation. This was the provenance of an ethos in which mutual aid was understood and appreciated to be their best chance of personal and collective survival in the face of their common precarious existence. Thus, the Chosen People enjoyed a strong moral claim to succor from each

---

3 This, of course, is in addition to the doctrine of creation and its concomitant gifts and obligations.
4 Albright (1946); Gottwald (1979); Noth (1960).

other; it was an expectation, indeed a birthright, that came by virtue of being a Hebrew.

The case for mutual economic assistance, strong as it already is, stands on the even deeper foundation of God's righteousness. God broke into human history to liberate an oppressed people and restore due order in human affairs. This divine in-breaking gives rise to four critical warrants for economic moral claims and, by extension, modern economic rights. In the first place, God is keenly interested in providing material plenitude in the here and now. The abundance envisioned by God is not reserved merely for the spiritual life or for some future eschaton; rather, the bounty of divine providence overflows into the material conditions of temporal human existence and experience (Lohfink 1987: 5–15). God did not create human beings only to leave them to wallow in Malthusian destitution. The latter is a corruption of God's envisioned order.

Second, Lohfink's description (ibid.) of the providential interest in providing material abundance in the here and now finds concrete expression in the divine gift of a "land flowing with milk and honey." Liberation from oppression was only the first of many divine benefactions; YHWH granted this newly liberated people a land of their own. As discussed in chapters 3 and 4, such a gift of land had practical value beyond its theological import. In an agrarian setting, the Promised Land represented both the grant of a steady livelihood and the much larger values of economic security and a self-respect that came from being able to provide for oneself and one's dependents. The reconstitution of such a divinely envisioned economic sufficiency and independence served as the goal of all subsequent requisite assistance among the Hebrews.

Third, the task of restoring due order in human affairs begun by God's in-breaking was an ongoing endeavor. Israel had been mandated to continue such an undertaking by virtue of its election to responsibility as the Chosen People of God. Thus, the Law provides the blueprint for forming Israel to be a nation different from all the other nations. Imbued with their distinctive religious self-identity, the Hebrews are to maintain an economy of equality where no one is left in want, and a politics of justice where power is used for service (Birch 1991: 172–81). They become each other's keeper; they are entrusted to each other for mutual care and attention. The plight of the economically distressed cannot be a matter of indifference. Such would be an affront to the Covenant election received from YHWH.

Fourth, those who provide assistance to the dispossessed do so not merely out of the goodness of their hearts, but because they are merely extending to others the very same favors they had received from YHWH in their own moment of need. Mutual economic aid is not supererogatory; rather, it is an act of justice. This is clearly evident from the motive clauses (Gemser 1953; Doron 1978) in which the Chosen People are repeatedly reminded that YHWH can demand much from them in the economic ordinances because of what God had accomplished for them in their own turn. These motive clauses provide the most forthright justification for the strong moral claims that the poor can make on the rest of the community.

In summary, there is a necessary economic dimension to the divine inbreaking in history because the due order in human affairs that God has come to inaugurate encompasses even the socioeconomic realm. Economics is not peripheral to salvation history; it is in fact a central venue through which God's providential care unfolds, is revealed, and is appropriated by the Chosen People. The primary obligation they owe to YHWH gives rise to the derivative duties they owe each other, including many of an economic nature as seen in the Law. These, in turn, provide the grounds for the economic moral claims that the weak and the defenseless can make on the strong and the powerful. Indeed, the Hebrew community is held tightly together within a series of interlocking claims and obligations. The biblical notion of economic security discussed at length in chapters 3 and 4 provides an excellent foundation upon which to build the superstructure of a theological economic ethics.

FROM BIBLICAL ECONOMIC SECURITY TO MODERN ECONOMIC RIGHTS

Shue's (1980) formulation of economic rights as an institutional means of protecting human subsistence from standard threats provides an ideal framework for dovetailing the biblical vision of economic security with modern rights language. After all, both the Old Testament economic ordinances and contemporary economic rights share the same proximate goal of setting extra-market protective barriers around people against the hazards posed by negative pecuniary externalities and life's contingencies. Shue's formulation provides a ready-made theoretical platform from which one can use economic rights to address economic compulsion. There are three significant points of intersection between Shue's economic rights, the biblical notion of economic security, and this study's thesis:

1 All three acknowledge that economic outcomes and processes can inflict harm on innocent third parties.
2 All three call for the protection of people, particularly the helpless, from such ruinous economic disruptions.
3 All three assert that it is contingent on the rest of the community to provide redress for such damaging pecuniary externalities.

The following excerpt captures the essence of Shue's (1980) understanding of economic rights in relation to threats:

[O]ne of the chief purposes of morality in general, and certainly of conceptions of rights, and of basic rights above all, is indeed to provide some minimal protection against utter helplessness to those too weak to protect themselves. Basic rights are a shield for the defenseless against at least some of the more devastating and more common of life's threats, which include . . . loss of security and loss of subsistence. *Basic rights are a restraint upon economic and political forces that would otherwise be too strong to be resisted.* They are social guarantees against actual and threatened deprivations of at least some basic needs. *Basic rights are an attempt to give to the powerless a veto over some of the forces that would otherwise harm them the most.* (Shue 1980: 18 [emphasis added])

Recall how the numerous Old Testament economic ordinances in chapters 3 and 4 were principally geared toward ensuring that Hebrews were not left to fend for themselves in the face of economic distress. Thus, we have the admonition on mandatory lending (Deut. 15:7–10; Lev. 25:35–37) at no interest (Exod. 22:25; Deut. 23:19–20; Lev. 25: 36–37) and the employment as hired hands, rather than as indentured servants, of fellow Hebrews who have fallen on hard times (Lev. 25).

Shue (1980: 18) describes the nature of economic rights well as he writes: "Basic rights are the morality of the depths. They specify the line beneath which no one is allowed to sink." Old Testament economic statutes are likewise a "morality of the depths" for they are the safeguards for ensuring that the special solicitude for the poor in God's in-breaking continued to unfold unabated among the Chosen People.

For Shue, finding the addressees of such moral claims is not a problem as the burden of relief and rehabilitation falls on the entire community: "Basic rights, then, are everyone's minimum reasonable demands upon the rest of humanity. They are the rational basis for justified demands the denial of which no self-respecting person can reasonably be expected to accept" (Shue 1980: 19). As seen in chapters 3 and 4, Old Testament legislation on economic life is descriptive of the obligations Hebrews owed each other.

Given these significant points of convergence, Shue's definition of human rights can be easily adapted to the biblical understanding of economic security: "A moral right provides (1) the rational basis for a justified demand (2) that the actual enjoyment of a substance be (3) socially guaranteed against standard threats" (Shue 1980: 13). Of course, the "rational" basis to which Shue refers is expanded within the Old Testament to include the due order envisioned in divine providence. Shue's subsistence rights are entirely consistent with *Pacem in Terris* and its articulation of both a specific set of rights and their provenance in human dignity.

The Yale Task Force on Population Ethics (1974: 102) and David Hollenbach (1979: 98) take John XXIII's peace encyclical a step further by providing a convenient and useful schematic synthesis. Given its importance and utility for this chapter's model, their diagram is reprinted here as Figure 5.1. Their synthesis improves John XXIII's simple enumeration of rights in a number of ways. First, rights are grouped together according to the various facets of life served. These include the bodily, political, associational, economic, religious, sexual, and familial. To these are added the freedoms to communicate and move about freely.

Second, there is an explicit acknowledgment of a hierarchy of rights. Three categories are outlined in a descending order of importance: personal, social, and institutional. Personal rights are essential claims whose satisfaction is a necessary condition if the human person is to physically survive, enjoy freedom of action, and form interpersonal relationships. These are constitutive of human dignity, the most basic rights that must be respected, namely: the right to life and bodily integrity, to self-determination, to freedom of movement, to social intercourse, to work, to the choice of a state of life, to religious belief, and to freedom of communication.

Social rights provide the medium within which personal rights are safeguarded and in fact nurtured. Hollenbach (1979: 96) describes these as the "*conditions* for the preservation of the well-being of the person" and the "expressions of the forms of human interdependence which are indispensable for the realization of human dignity" (original emphasis). In other words, social rights are the tangible outcomes of the community's commitment and efforts to ensure that personal rights are satisfied. These social rights are not merely negative[5] in the sense of only calling for noninterference and delineating the boundaries that must not be crossed.

---

5 Recall Berlin's (1958) distinction between positive and negative freedoms.

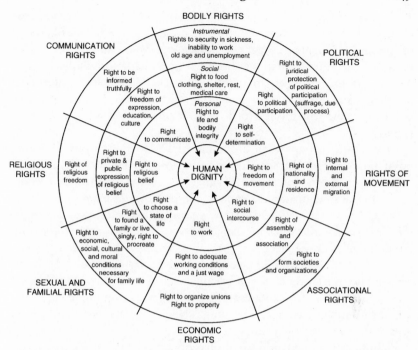

Figure 5.1. Adapted from the Yale Task Force on Population Ethics (D. Christiansen, R. Garet, D. Hollenbach and C. Powers), "Moral Claims, Human Rights and Population Policies," *Theological Studies* 35 (1974): 102 (with permission).
Source: Hollenbach, David. 1979. *Claims in Conflict* (New York: Paulist Press): 98.

They also require positive action in which society commits itself to providing the necessary resources that empower individuals to truly enjoy their personal rights in a meaningful way.

Finally, instrumental rights pertain to the necessary institutional arrangements that facilitate the satisfaction of both personal and social rights. Social rights are important because personal welfare is actualized only within the community, especially given the phenomenon John XXIII (1961) describes as "socialization" in which people are ever more dependent on each other as civilization progresses. However, such social interdependence is in turn mediated through the community's institutions. Human beings interact with each other through a thick network of interlocking human partnerships of differing sizes ranging from the nuclear family, immediate neighborhood, village, church, professional groups, and unions, all the way to the state, the nation, and the community of nations.

These human associations have their own distinctive conventions that, for good or ill, shape the "conditions for the preservation of the well-being of the person" (Hollenbach 1979: 96). In fact, it is these institutions that give particular, definite shape to the abstract conceptualization of social rights. Thus, instrumental rights are listed with greater specificity compared to social rights in Figure 5.1. Instrumental rights could be described as the point where the "tire hits the road" when it comes to implementing rights language.

This schematic exposition on human rights provides a useful starting point for our study because its set of personal rights provides a moral baseline for ascertaining when negative pecuniary externalities become cases of economic distress. Economic compulsion is a matter of concern because it puts the well-being of the person in jeopardy; personal rights serve as tangible measures for gauging severe deprivation resulting from the unintended consequences of market operations. This schema of rights also enjoys the added advantage of differentiating core from derivative rights. The concentric circles of personal, social, and instrumental rights are important both for appraising the severity of economic compulsion and for prioritizing competing claims. These advantages are examined in greater detail in the following sections.

Despite the aforementioned utility of the schema of human rights presented in Figure 5.1, economic rights alone do not provide an adequate framework with which to address economic compulsion, for three reasons. In the first place, the Catholic use of human rights cannot be taken out of the larger setting of the common good tradition in which it is anchored. Cahill (1980) notes that for all its liberal rights language, Catholic social thought is at its heart and core about the "primary obligation" of seeking God. In other words, rights discourse in this tradition is rooted in the grammar not of claims and entitlements but of obligations. Hollenbach (1979: 97; 1994) is keenly aware of this and goes so far as to point out that Catholic human rights are personalist, not individualist. The human person flourishes only within community. Maritain (1947) stressed the same point three decades earlier. There is a marked difference and a significant qualification in the modern Catholic social tradition's appropriation of liberal rights language. Consequently, there is a clear need for an extension of the schema of human rights in Figure 5.1 in which the personalist character of Catholic human rights theory is more explicitly laid out as part of the model.

Second, skeptics criticize the indeterminacy of economic rights. Where does one draw the line between essential and nonessential economic claims and why? Who bears responsibility for satisfying these claim-rights? Coleman (1984) and Trimiew (1997: 246) are critical of Hollenbach (1979) for not following the example of Shue (1980) and Gewirth (1982) in reducing and simplifying John XXIII's extended list of economic rights to a few core rights. This is necessary if the whole notion of economic rights is not to be trivialized or dismissed in the face of its seemingly boundless and ever-creeping claims.

Third, a clash of competing claims is inevitable in dealing with economic rights. After all, the goods of the earth are finite, and these economic entitlements are subject to rival consumption. Not all of them can be simultaneously satisfied to the same degree. There are limits to the community's ability to fulfill all economic claims. Consequently, it is not sufficient simply to list a core set of economic rights; it is equally important to understand the spirit and the warrants that gave rise to these rights in the first place as these are the very criteria that would most likely be used in any triage of competing claims.

All three deficiencies point to the same conclusion: Satisfying the demands of human rights is a highly contextual exercise. Moreover, as already mentioned, social and instrumental rights are rooted in the specific needs of the community and its institutions. Thus, interpretative schemas of human rights, such as the synthesis of the Yale Task Force on Population Ethics (1974), require much further work before they can be applied to resolving social issues. Such abstract statements of human rights are among the "principles of reflection, norms of judgment and directives for action" (Paul VI 1971: #4) that need to be further particularized with reference to local conditions. In fact, these generalized pronouncements may cause even greater harm if uncritically adopted without paying attention to the setting in which they are to be administered. Thus, while *Rerum Novarum* (Leo XIII 1891) and *Quadragesimo Anno* (Pius XI 1931) are emphatic in asserting employers' obligations to satisfy workers' rights to a living wage, both encyclicals are nevertheless modest when it comes to implementation by deferring to people's judgment regarding applicability to their particular circumstances.

Does all this mean that rights discourse is merely an ad hoc exercise? How do we avoid falling into relativism as we tailor the enforcement of human rights to suit local conditions? How do we preserve the objective claims of these rights while giving them the requisite pliability to deal with the particularities of time and place? Thus, the key problem is how to specify the content and the strength of the claims of personal, social, and instrumental rights within an ever-changing set of conditions. As it stands, the interpretative schema in Figure 5.1 requires further implementing guidelines.

It is unlikely that we will ever be able to draw up a method and framework that can specify social and instrumental rights with the measured precision of a cookbook or a mathematical formula. Judicious discretion will most likely always play a large role in actualizing rights. The framework of the common good helps in the exercise of this unavoidable prudential judgment.

MEDIATING CONCEPTS

The use of the notion of the common good is, unfortunately, not without its own set of problems as well.[6] Not only is it difficult to gain a consensus on what it formally means, but it is virtually impossible to win agreement over what it entails in actual practice. Nonetheless, we can still profitably use the notion of the common good for our study by side-stepping the issue of its formal definition and simply limiting ourselves to a statement of the minimum conditions that any reasonable account of the common good must have. I submit that there are three of these minimum conditions. First, the requirements of the long-standing threefold division of justice (legal, commutative, and distributive) must be observed. Second, key interpersonal relationships within the community are nurtured. Third, there is a conscious effort to work toward an equitable division of shared resources. The common good can neither be good nor common unless it satisfies these three necessary conditions in socioeconomic life, at a minimum.

Legal justice pertains to the obligation of individuals to do their share in promoting the good of the entire community. Commutative justice calls for equivalence and reciprocity in exchange between individuals. Distributive justice refers to the community's duties toward safeguarding and nurturing the welfare of every member within its ranks.[7] These three dimensions of justice are unavoidable in dealing with economic compulsion as they provide clarity, language, and precision in weighing competing claims. The moral imperative of ameliorating economic distress flows from the obligation of justice owed to God and to each other. Legal, commutative, and distributive justice add to our working vocabulary in

---

6 See, for example, Hollenbach (2002).
7 See Aquinas (1947/8: II-II, q. 58, art. 2 and 5; q. 61, art. 1, 2, and 3).

grappling with the disposition and satisfaction of economic rights. They also have the advantage of being readily familiar concepts.

Nevertheless, adding these three dimensions of justice to our model is still not sufficient. We need a more definite specification of the manner in which such justice and economic rights are to be fulfilled. In this regard, I propose that the key lies in articulating the relationships that are essential to any community in whatever circumstance it may find itself. After all, justice pertains to giving people their due, and it is fundamentally about relationships; economic rights are about making a claim on others and are, therefore, ultimately relational. Justice and economic rights make sense only in reference to relationships. Thus, any reasonable account of the common good must ensure the satisfaction of (1) legal, commutative, and distributive justice (2) in all the constitutive relationships that define a community.

There are at least five relationships that must be considered in any reasonable Christian account of the community, to wit:

1 the person's love for God;
2 people's solicitude for each other;
3 the community's care for the marginalized in its midst;
4 the community's nurturing of every member within its ranks;
5 people's stewardship of the earth.

This is not an exhaustive listing but is merely an enumeration of what is key (or minimum) in any plausible Christian understanding of what constitutes community.[8]

There are attendant principles and norms that clarify the bonds and ties undergirding these relationships and their corresponding obligations. These social principles are the mediating concepts that bring together economic rights, the threefold dimension of justice, and the common good. They complement the schematic synthesis of *Pacem in Terris* in Figure 5.1 by furnishing the conceptual linkage between personal, social, and institutional rights. In particular, these principles specify the derivative social and instrumental rights that necessarily flow from the core personal rights. This is especially important when it comes to formulating new social and instrumental rights and obligations in response to future problems in political economy. It is these principles that form the

---

8 For example, I have not included the person's relation to self that finds expression in manifold ways, such as self-respect and the commitment to work toward one's integral human development. My thanks to Dan Finn for pointing this out.

growing edges of this living social tradition.[9] To make it easier to follow the arguments of the next sections, readers are advised to refer periodically to the model's summary in Table 5.1 (p. 155) in addition to the schema of human rights in Figure 5.1 (p. 149).

The first relationship is that of the person's orientation to the Final End, God. The first-order principles of human dignity and integral human development highlight the transcendent end (*telos*) of the person. They articulate the need for human beings to have the freedom and the necessary means to requite God's initiatives and pursue the proffered divine friendship. Personal growth and development are not merely about material progress; they are ultimately about spiritual advancement. Thus, both of these principles, in conjunction with the first relationship (God and the human person), provide a theological backdrop for the section on religious rights in Figure 5.1.

The second relationship pertains to people's orientation toward each other. This is enlivened by the principle of solidarity that calls for a genuine and active concern for the welfare of others because we see in each of them a child of God; we see ourselves in them.

The third relationship is the community's interaction with the marginalized in its midst. We have an entire series of principles that sheds light on this relationship since it is a perennial element in most social questions. I use *community* to refer to the entire spectrum of human associations of varying degrees of aggregation and size; it does not necessarily or exclusively refer only to the state or to society in general.

The preferential option for the poor calls for a greater measure of solicitude for those who are unable to fend for themselves in the community. The level and degree of assistance provided to individuals are directly proportional to the severity of their plight. This is founded on YHWH's self-revelation of a special love reserved for the marginalized. The principle of socialization asserts that higher bodies have an obligation to assist lower bodies that are no longer able to function for the sake of the common good. Thus, those who are in a position to provide assistance to the distressed have the duty to do so by virtue of their ability to furnish such aid. The principle of participation argues for an equitable distribution of burdens and benefits across the community. Human beings are social; they must be afforded the opportunity and the means to interact

---

9 For an illustration of the utility of these social principles in meeting new problems with fresh approaches, see Barrera's (2001: 193–226) exposition on the necessary evolution of the universal destination principle in response to globalization and knowledge-based economies.

Table 5.1. *Diagnostic-prescriptive framework for attending to economic compulsion*

I Overarching structure: common good as due order	
Relationship	Concomitant social principles
1 relationship of person to God	integral human development
2 relationship of person to others	solidarity
3 relationship of the community to the marginalized	preferential option for the poor, socialization, participation, restoration
4 relationship of the community to individual members within its ranks	subsidiarity, universal destination of goods, participation, primacy of labor, relative equality
5 relationship of the person to the goods of the earth	stewardship

II Economic rights*

A Core personal economic rights
   1 Bodily rights: right to life and bodily integrity
   2 Livelihood rights: right to work
   3 *Participatory rights*: right to procure the means to contribute to and draw benefits from the common good (individual's right to instantiate the common good)
   4 *Developmental rights*: right to the means necessary for personal growth
B Social economic rights
   1 right to food, clothing, shelter, and medical care
   2 right to adequate working conditions and a just wage
   3 *right to assistance for socioeconomic mobility*
   4 *right to access key regulative goods*
   5 *right to restorative-rehabilitative assistance*
C Instrumental economic rights
   1 right to security in sickness, inability to work, old age, and unemployment
   2 right to organize unions and to private property ownership
   3 *right to trade adjustment assistance*

III Lexical rules for competing claims

1 Hollenbach's (1979: 203–207) three strategic priorities
2 Barrera's (2001: 227–46) three degrees of unmet needs
3 lexical ordering of the four core personal economic rights
4 priority of social and instrumental rights of an ameliorative nature

* *Additions I have made to the original synthesis of human rights by the Yale Task Force on Population Ethics (1974: 102) and Hollenbach (1979: 98) are in italics.*

with others and to share in both the gains and costs of sustaining the common life. However, they can do so only if they are able to participate meaningfully and actively in the various human partnerships constituting society. Finally, we have the principle of restoration described in the preceding chapter. Animated by the spirit of solidarity, obligated by the principle of socialization, and moved by the special love that comes from a preferential option for the poor, the community re-embraces those who have been relegated to the fringes and nurses them back to a condition in which they are able to partake in common life once again as equals. All these principles are descriptive of the requisite tasks embedded in this third relationship if the common good is to be achieved. The whole object of these principles is to move the marginalized from this third relationship to the next level, the fourth relationship.

This fourth relationship pertains to the obligations owed by the community to every individual in its ranks. As seen earlier, the community has a duty to provide the most promising conditions that are conducive for every person to truly flourish. The principle of subsidiarity calls for higher bodies not to arrogate to themselves functions that lower bodies (or individuals) are able to discharge effectively by themselves (Pius XI 1931: #79). Private initiative is nurtured, and people are given the assistance and the encouragement to do what they are able to do by themselves without imposing unnecessary burdens on them. Related to this is the principle of participation, which again calls for every member, as part of the exercise of subsidiarity, to be actively engaged in the affairs of the community. However, not just any kind of societal interaction is good enough. It has to be quality participation – as an equal to others. Thus, the principle of relative equality calls for limits to the disparities legitimately incurred in societal outcomes and processes, especially in those areas that are truly consequential for human flourishing. An important venue for participation is the primacy of labor principle that highlights the need for worthwhile and gainful employment opportunities for people. Again, it is not sufficient to provide people with just any kind of livelihood. It is important that such jobs provide not only a living wage but also the self-respect and the satisfaction that contribute toward a meaningful life.[10] With such a gainful employment, all are afforded access to the goods of the earth to meet their basic needs. These five principles that vivify the community's relationship to every member in its ranks are geared toward serving the primary obligation and the ultimate end: eventual union with God.

10 For a different position on the provision of the living wage, see Klay and Lunn (2003).

The fifth relationship pertains to the care of the goods of the earth. In this regard, we have the principle of stewardship that calls for the proper use of the fruits of creation in accordance with God's vision of providing for the needs of all through their own labors, in cooperation with each other.

For felicity and economy of expression in the following sections, I refer to these five relationships and their auxiliary social principles as the notion of the "common good as due order."[11] Again, it must be emphasized that this does not pretend to be a formal definition or a complete specification of the common good. Rather, it is merely an articulation of some of the minimum conditions that must be part of any reasonable Christian account of the common good.

Note how the notion of due order provides a clear-cut connection between rights language and the common good tradition. It explicitly embeds economic rights within their concomitant web of obligations. All the aforementioned relationships constitutive of the common good find expression in the language of responsibilities rather than claims. For example, relationship 1 (between the person and God) implies not a claim of the person against God, but a human obligation owed to God. The principle of solidarity that animates relationship 2 speaks of mutual duties owed to each other. The same is true for the other relationships: Obligations are the primary phenomena undergirding the community's inter-action with the marginalized and with each member numbered in its ranks. The principle of stewardship that describes the last relationship entails duties in caring for the goods of the earth. Thus, unlike liberal rights discourse that speaks of "correlative obligations" stemming from rights-claims, modern Catholic social thought reverses the order. The primary phenomenon consists of duties owed to God and each other; rights-claims are merely derivative from these responsibilities, as necessary means toward fulfilling our obligations.

In all this, the notion of the common good as due order provides an explicit framework for linking all social phenomena to the "primary obligation" of seeking God. After all, the last four relationships in the common good as due order are rooted in and shaped by the first relationship – that of the person to God. Interpersonal relationships flow from this fundamental obligation owed to God. Nevertheless, despite the preeminent nature of the principal duty owed to God, none of the other four relationships is dispensable. In fact, the latter four relationships and

11 See Barrera (2001: 287–304) for a more extended exposition of this model.

the "primary obligation" mutually reinforce and feed off each other. In other words, the divine–human relationship is distinct but inseparable from human interpersonal relationships; the quality of one's relationship to God is an inescapable function of how well one treats one's neighbors.

A DIAGNOSTIC MODEL OF ECONOMIC COMPULSION

The human rights schema in Figure 5.1, the threefold dimension of justice, and the notion of the common good as due order are useful building blocks for a rights-based assessment of economic compulsion. These conceptual tools allow for both flexibility (to adapt) and fidelity (to the *epikeia* of the rights). They afford better clarity and serve as key guiding reference points while we grapple with specifying the concrete manner in which social and instrumental rights can best serve and promote personal rights within a particular setting. The Yale's Task Force's interpretative synthesis of human rights can be further improved and made more effective by embedding it within an overarching framework in which personal, social, and instrumental rights can be examined further in relation to each other and to the social conflicts they are meant to resolve.

In what follows, I propose a conceptual structure for attending to economic compulsion, and I have summarized its salient features in Table 5.1. This model (1) is focused principally on economic rights and obligations, (2) is situated within the larger backdrop of the common good tradition, (3) is delineated by legal, commutative, and distributive justice, and (4) is self-contained in the sense of bearing within itself the necessary implementing principles and norms at the point of application.

Defining personal rights

In Figure 5.1 (p. 149), the Yale Task Force on Population Ethics (1974: 102) and Hollenbach (1979: 98) identify two specific areas in which economic claims are directly relevant for human development: the right to bodily integrity and the right to work. The former is called bodily rights; the latter economic rights. To avoid confusion in taxonomy, I call the latter "livelihood rights" and use "economic rights" to refer to the entire cluster of claims of an economic nature associated with integral human development. To my mind, these two realms are incomplete. Hollenbach (1979: 99) himself is quick to qualify his exposition of Figure 5.1 by noting that the requirements of the eight spheres of life identified in the schema overflow into each other. They are not hermetically separated from one another. In fact, in many cases, they are necessary conditions for each other. This is clearly true of bodily rights. Physical survival and the enjoyment of basic health are clearly prerequisites to all other activities of personal life. There is a necessary minimum bundle of material goods that must be provided to enable people to develop and enjoy fully the innate powers related to all the other realms described in Figure 5.1.

As already mentioned, the person's fundamental orientation to God as Final End gives rise to the primary obligation of seeking God. Put in another way, this is the duty of working toward one's integral human development, that is, advancement and growth in body, mind, and spirit aimed at eventual union with God. Thus, human beings enjoy inalienable personal rights. These are natural powers (to be everything one can be and is) that no one and nothing can take away from them since they come with personhood. These are natural powers that human beings must be allowed to exercise if they are to reach the fullness of the transcendent destiny that has already been divinely proffered and is theirs for the taking. However, exercising these natural powers often entails the necessary use of scarce material goods.

Genuine integral development is nothing less than actualizing human beings' physical, intellectual, emotional, and spiritual possibilities. Each of these areas of human life has a necessary economic dimension. For example, physical survival requires the satisfaction of the basic needs of food, clothing, shelter, and medical care. Intellectual growth requires the expenditure of enormous resources of time and money for a proper education. Cultivating the emotions and the spirit involves the use of scarce social resources that open opportunities for formative social interaction and afford the luxury of personal space and time for reflection and growth. In other words, there is an unavoidable economic facet to human flourishing stemming from the materiality and sociality of human nature. Moreover, given the finitude of the fruits of the earth, there is invariably a need to economize and allocate. Thus, the whole point of clearly articulating a core set of economic rights is to ensure that the material aspects of human flourishing in the different facets of life are not left wanting. To be deprived of such economic prerequisites to integral human development is to make the self-actualization of one's possibilities much more difficult than would otherwise have been the case; such privation can in some cases even put human dignity itself at risk. Hence, there is much at stake in having society come to a consensus on unresolved issues such as the basis, scope, and degree to which people may legitimately present economic claims against each other and the rest of the community.

In order to account for the necessary material dimension in the other facets of human existence besides bodily integrity and work experience, it is important to go beyond the two core economic rights proposed in Figure 5.1. Hollenbach (1979: 203–207) collapses Figure 5.1 into three categories that are essential for human dignity: those that pertain to basic needs, to one's association with others, and to the exercise of one's liberty. His first category of basic needs obviously encompasses the two afore-mentioned economic rights of bodily and livelihood rights. Both the last two categories, comprising the ability to interact with others and the capacity to exercise one's liberty, clearly require economic inputs as well. These should also be made part of the core set of economic rights. Furthermore, in order to better mirror the personalist character of Cath-olic human rights theory, it is best to express these last two categories in a manner that highlights the importance of human flourishing within the community. Thus, I propose the following two additional core economic rights: those that are essential for the person to contribute toward build-ing the common good (*participatory economic rights*)[12] and those that are indispensable for the person's growth in character and creativity (*develop-mental economic rights*). These two proposed additional core economic rights incorporate the economic-material inputs required by all the other facets of human life reported in Figure 5.1 beyond bodily integrity and work experience.

In summary, building on Figure 5.1 and based on the necessary economic dimension of integral human development, I propose a minimum set of four core personal economic rights: bodily rights, livelihood rights, par-ticipatory economic rights, and developmental economic rights.[13] Three points ought to be underscored. First, these core personal economic rights are derived from the first relationship (person to God) in the notion of the common good as due order and its principle of integral human develop-ment. Second, the primary phenomenon is not the individual's claim, but the person's obligation to God to work assiduously for his or her integral human development in cooperation with grace. It is because of the need to fulfill this primary obligation that the person has claims (rights) to the economic means already afforded by God (relationship 5 on the gifts of the earth) for the attainment of such human flourishing. Thus, neither the rights nor the interests promoted by the person can be made ends in

---

12 This is the personal right to instantiate the common good in one's life, to the extent possible.
13 I reserve the discussion of the lexical ordering of these core economic rights to a later section on resolving competing claims.

themselves because the justification and strength of such claims are both oriented toward serving the larger end of human perfection in community and in God. Third, the justification and the strength of these economic rights are ultimately grounded in the understanding that when God as Creator willed everything into existence, God as the Lord of nature also furnished creatures with all the necessary economic-material means to flourish in life. The division and disposition of these resources, however, have been left to the human community and serve as critical channels for human beings' participation in divine work and providence. It is this appreciation for the earth as a common heritage from God that becomes the basis both for the personal economic right to partake of these gifts and for the communal duties to ensure that all are able truly to enjoy such divine benefaction.

Defining social and instrumental rights

The second, third, and fourth relationships in the notion of the common good as due order provide both the remote and proximate justification for social and instrumental rights. The second relationship pertains to people's orientation toward each other and finds expression in the principle of solidarity, defined as an active and genuine concern for the welfare of others (John Paul II 1987: #38f.). People see themselves in others in addition to acknowledging their common filial relationship to God. This is the remote foundation for both social and instrumental rights. There is a perfect correlativity of rights and obligations. This principle dispels the putative indeterminancy of economic rights because of the difficulty of identifying the addressees of their corresponding duties.

Skeptics argue against economic rights because of the imperfect nature of their obligations. After all, it is not clear who bears responsibility for satisfying the claims presented by such economic rights. For example, person A's rights to free speech and free assembly are perfect obligations because everyone is unambiguously an addressee of the obligation of noninterference in person A's exercise of his/her freedom of speech and assembly. Not so for the economic right to food, clothing, shelter, health care, and employment. These rights-claims require a substantial amount of tangible resources that must be provided by yet unidentified addressees of these economic rights. Of course, the difference in the ease of locating addressees in these two cases lies in the negative nature of political and civil rights versus the positive character of economic rights (Berlin 1958). Rex Martin (1989) and Maurice Cranston (1967) argue that human rights exist only if their claims can indeed be enforced against clearly identified obligation holders. Otherwise, there is no point at all even in having rights if they have no binding force. Critics argue against the existence of economic rights because it is not always clear who holds the corresponding obligations.

Even if this were a valid criterion for the existence of rights, the principle of solidarity solves the indeterminacy of economic rights' addressees since people become each other's keepers. People are accountable for the well-being of others in the measure they are capable of extending such requisite assistance. The principle of solidarity turns economic rights into perfect obligations. Of course, we are talking of moral, not legal, obligations. The former are enforced in the internal forum of the heart, while the latter require exact standards for delineating duties because they are enforced in the external forum of the law, which by its nature requires precise measures of accountability and dues.

The third and fourth relationships of the common good as due order pertain to the community's relationship with the marginalized and with each member in its ranks. These are the immediate, proximate bases for both social and instrumental rights. People require an enormous amount of assistance and nurturing to reach the fullness of their potential because of the finite make-up of human nature; they have requisite needs that must be satisfied first before they can reach their ends. These needs can be fully met only within the community. Thus, genuine integral human development is also about affording each other the means for reaching the fullness of human potency – mind, body, and spirit. Actualizing personal rights and powers is possible only in cooperation with others, who are likewise engaged in the same endeavor. As already mentioned, social and instrumental rights provide the milieu within which personal rights can be protected and advanced.

Since the end of the community is understood to be the perfection of the individual, there is a need for society to supply every person in its ranks with the means of fulfilling the primary obligation of seeking God and attaining integral human development. Thus, social and instrumental rights are at the service of personal rights, which in their own turn are for the sake of discharging the primary obligation of aspiring for union with God. Social and instrumental rights are embedded within a web of primary and derivative obligations. In speaking of the outer two concentric rings of Figure 5.1 (p. 149), it is more accurate to refer to them as social and instrumental "rights-obligations." After all, these social and instrumental rights are meant solely to serve the proximate, intermediate end of satisfying personal rights.

Two points must be considered in specifying the content of these rights-obligations. First, these derivative rights-obligations are highly dependent on context. Thus, unlike the four core personal economic rights that are rooted in and derived from human nature itself, these social and instrumental rights-obligations cannot be fully itemized in abstraction. We can infer and outline some of their necessary content given the nature of markets, but we cannot enumerate a complete a priori specification separate from the concrete particularities in which personal rights are to be satisfied. The most that we can do is to list the general social and instrumental rights-obligations that we expect to be common across all settings.

A second qualification pertains to the differing objects of relationships 4 (members of the community) and 3 (the marginalized). Since the needs of these disparate segments of the community are different, we expect their resultant claims to be likewise dissimilar. In other words, there are two sets of social and instrumental rights-obligations, one for the ordinary members of the community and another for the hardship cases.

For community members
Since the end of the community is the perfection of every individual member within its ranks, economic social rights-obligations are meant to provide the most favorable economic conditions for human flourishing (relationship 4). As mentioned earlier, the principles of relative equality, subsidiarity, participation, universal destination, and primacy of labor spell out with greater specificity some of the community's obligations toward its membership. Common to these principles is the people's right to the means not only for surviving but for productive engagement within the larger community. Thus, Figure 5.1 lists the right to food, clothing, shelter, rest, and medical care as social rights put at the service of the personal economic right to life and bodily integrity; the right to adequate working conditions and a just wage is a social right that serves the personal economic right to work. Of course, both sets of social rights-obligations also serve the other core personal economic rights of being able to participate in the common good and of personal growth in creativity and character. To these I propose two additional social rights-obligations pertaining to (1) socioeconomic mobility and (2) access to regulative goods.

I believe it is important to highlight the community's obligation to provide assistance in building and enhancing its members' capacity for socioeconomic mobility given the nature of the marketplace. There are two mutually reinforcing reasons for this new social right-obligation I would like to add to Figure 5.1. In the first place, as we have seen in part I, market operations inflict unintended consequences on unsuspecting third parties. This is unavoidable and derives chiefly from the intricate interdependency that binds all market participants together. In other words, economic agents are relentlessly besieged by fluid market conditions that require constant readjustments in their personal economic behavior and decisions. Some of these pecuniary externalities are extremely disruptive, precipitating radical and even damaging alterations in personal lives.

Second, as we have also already seen in part I, the personal ability of people to respond appropriately to these harmful pecuniary externalities is a function of the widely unequal entry costs that community members pay in order to partake in market exchange. These entry prices vary according to the economic agents' personal characteristics and their sociohistorical location. An important facet of market participants' ability to reap benefits from exchange is their mobility. In sharp contrast to neoclassical economists' assumption of a frictionless economy, there are significant costs (monetary, psychological, temporal, and emotional) incurred in moving around goods, labor, and factors of production to their most valued uses. The lower these costs, the greater the agility to respond to a changing market environment. The faster and the greater ease with which one can adapt to rapidly evolving economic conditions, the greater the benefits one can reap from market participation. Moreover, the greater the capacity to move about the economy with minimum cost, the greater the economic agent's ability to survive and perhaps even profit from negative market ripple effects. Thus, there is a great premium accorded to socioeconomic mobility in the marketplace, particularly in the even more frenetic pace of the globalized knowledge economy.

Given the dynamic and often detrimental impact of market transactions and given the real costs incurred in responding to and perhaps protecting oneself from such changes, the community has an obligation to develop within its membership what I would call the capacity for socioeconomic mobility.[14] The better developed such capabilities, the easier it will be for people to weather and perhaps even gain from the

---

14 In economic terminology, market participants – as factors of production – ought to have the necessary assistance to develop their capacity for factor mobility.

unavoidable vagaries of the marketplace, and the better it will be for the whole economy.

The second additional social right-obligation I propose is the provision of community assistance in developing people's ability to access regulative goods. The latter is distinctive for its ability to shape or "regulate" the life prospects of people. Education is an excellent example. It is a regulative good in the way it can open doors for improving one's economic status.

Such regulative goods are important for market participation. In fact, the disparity in the entry costs faced by people is largely a function of their access to such goods. After all, recall from part I that the ease or difficulty with which economic agents are able to benefit from the market is largely determined by their personal capabilities and sociohistorical location. These are in turn shaped by regulative goods such as the opportunities for education and skills training. The precise content of these regulative goods depends on actual local conditions. Nevertheless, we can generalize one thing about them: It would seem reasonable to expect the community to ensure an equitable distribution of such regulative goods as part of the common good.

For the marginalized
The marginalized are members of the community too and, thus, all the aforementioned claims and obligations pertinent to relationship 4 (community to every member in its ranks) are also applicable to those at the fringes of society. Nevertheless, there is a need to go beyond what is offered to the general membership and specify an additional set of duties for the benefit of a distinct group of people – those who are unable to avail themselves of the general assistance afforded by the community to all its members, to the point of being marginalized from societal outcomes and processes. After all, people are relegated to the edges of society because they are unable, on their own, to utilize effectively the communal means made available to everyone. Thus, there is a supplementary set of shared responsibilities to provide an extra measure of assistance to this segment of society.

The object of such auxiliary communal duties is to bring the hardship cases back to the point where they are able independently and effectively to benefit from the resources made available to everybody else, as described in the preceding section. In other words, the goal of the social and instrumental rights-obligations of the third relationship (the community caring for the marginalized) is not to breed dependency but to nurture the helpless back to a condition in which they are able to fend for themselves, to the extent possible, within the bounds of the regular assistance afforded by the community to its members. Chapters 3 and 4 vividly illustrate this social right to recover from economic distress. In other words, the community has the duty to provide a safety net and the possibilities of a fresh start to those who have fallen on hard times. Put in another way, this could be described as the *social economic right to "second chances" and restorative assistance* (cf. chapter 4).[15] Again, such a social right-obligation is consistent with the attendant social principles of a preferential option for the poor, socialization, and participation called for by the third relationship of the common good as due order.

Specifying the precise content of instrumental rights-obligations is even more context dependent than in the case of social rights-obligations. This should not come as a surprise since such instrumental rights-obligations are geared toward setting up the appropriate societal institutions responsible for satisfying the social and personal rights. Thus, it is not possible to completely specify a priori instrumental rights separate from the particular circumstances in which they are to operate. Nevertheless, besides the instrumental rights in Figure 5.1, there are some actual examples that ought to be cited and generalized. Government assistance to those adversely affected by trade is an excellent illustration of an instrumental duty of the community to foster a capacity for socioeconomic mobility. In other words, trade adjustment assistance programs (Schoepfle 2000; Trebilcock et al. 1990) are a de facto institutional implementation of a social economic right to assistance in securing factor mobility in response to negative pecuniary externalities from the global market. Bankruptcy laws are good examples of an instrumental right that promotes the larger social right of "second chances" in the face of economic contingencies. These laws are in effect an acknowledgment of the community's duty to provide relief and assistance to those who are unable to bear their liabilities by themselves. Other members of the community (e.g., lenders) furnish succor to the distressed through concessions and perhaps even partial debt forgiveness or generous deferred repayment plans. The court serves as a venue for facilitating such interpersonal aid.

In summary, there are two sets of social and instrumental rights-obligations corresponding to the two objects of the community's concerns:

---

15 Of course, the claims of this right are even stronger and more urgent for those who never get a "first chance" to begin with, such as children trapped in a poverty cycle who grow up as adults still helplessly mired in destitution.

the general membership and the marginalized (relationships 4 and 3 of the common good as due order, respectively). This differentiation and the special attention given to the latter are consistent with the tradition's preferential option for the poor.

Revisiting Old Testament economic security as economic rights

We can gain a better appreciation for just how closely the Old Testament vision of economic security corresponds to our modern language of economic rights through a retrospective application of this chapter's proposed model. Bodily integrity is certainly a key goal of the Old Testament economic ordinances. Physical survival and basic health are the proximate ends of the statutes on gleaning (Deut. 24:19–21; Lev. 19:9–10; 23:22; Ruth 2), tithing for the poor (Deut. 14:22–29), mandatory lending (Deut. 15: 7–10; Lev. 25:35–37), and interest-free loans (Exod. 22:25; Deut. 23:19–20; Lev. 25:36–37), since these provisions are geared toward ensuring that those who have fallen on hard times will always be able to satisfy their basic needs. The importance accorded to bodily integrity is also evident in the prohibitions on the kind of collateral that may be used to secure loans. Exodus 22:26 and Deuteronomy 24:6, 10–13 bar certain items as surety: possessions that are important for health (such as a cloak) or are sources of a livelihood (such as a millstone for grinding grain). It was on account of this goal of ensuring the physical survival and basic health of the Hebrews that YHWH settled them in a "land flowing with milk and honey." Better yet, it was because of the need to keep a material body alive, nourished, and sheltered that God entrusted the earth to humans for their safekeeping and sustenance (Gen. 1:27–30; 2:15–16).

The personal economic right to a livelihood is likewise affirmed in the Old Testament vision of the ideal economic life. The Promised Land was divided with great care in which the allotment took into account the soil's fertility and family size. As already noted, besides its theological significance, such ancestral land served the practical value of enabling every household to maintain its freedom and independence by providing for itself. Thus, the Jubilee Law (Lev. 25) and the numerous admonitions to redeem family land had their practical utility in ensuring that households supported and sustained themselves through their own efforts.

The personal economic right of having the necessary material means to partake of and contribute to the common good (participatory economic right) is likewise affirmed in chapter 4's exposition on the principle of restoration. As Wright (1990: 97) observes, landholding families were the backbone and the basic unit of Hebrew society because it was through them that people discharged their juridic, cultic, and military obligations to the nation. However, observe the qualifier Wright adds – they had to own land. After all, it was only landed households that were able to produce the necessary surplus that allowed them to fulfill their obligations to the rest of the community.[16] Thus, note the importance of Leviticus 25 and the sense of urgency in the Law's repeated exhortation to redeem kin and ancestral land.

Finally, the personal economic right to have access to the material means necessary for one's growth in character and creativity (developmental economic rights) can be indirectly inferred from YHWH's providential gift of the Promised Land. The Lord of history takes away a "land flowing with milk and honey" from another people and gives it to the Hebrews so that the latter may establish a community different from its neighbors and be a beacon and example for all the other nations. The Hebrews will be able to keep the land only if they live in righteousness (von Waldow 1974: 503–506). YHWH provides all the necessary material means of life to enable the Hebrews to live in personal and collective righteousness. Such instrumental value to economic goods can also be seen, for example, in the confident expectation that YHWH will furnish a two- or threefold harvest in anticipation of the sabbatical fallow to enable the nation to comply with all that God is asking of it (Lev. 25:18–22). Indeed, YHWH's dual gift of economic security to the nation Israel is for a much larger end – that of participating in the righteousness of God itself. This represents the crown of the Hebrews' moral life, the end for which they are given the means to securing and enjoying economic security. YHWH unfailingly bestows whatever is necessary to accomplish all that God expects of the nation Israel in her journey toward the proffered gift of holiness.

These four core personal economic rights – to bodily integrity, to a livelihood, to a viable participation in the common good, and to personal growth in creativity and character – are served by social and instrumental rights-obligations. Economic security is a divine gift for the benefit of the entire people; it is a gift effected only within community. Joel Feinberg's description of the nature of claim-rights applies appropriately to Old Testament economic statutes:

16 Of course, the modern-day equivalent of land is education.

A world without claim-rights, no matter how full of benevolence and devotion to duty, would suffer an immense moral impoverishment. Persons would no longer hope for decent treatment from others on the ground of desert or rightful claim . . . [W]henever even minimally decent treatment is forthcoming they would think themselves lucky rather than inherently deserving, and their benefactors extraordinarily virtuous and worthy of great gratitude . . .

A claim-right, on the other hand, can be urged, pressed, or rightly demanded against other persons . . . Rights are not mere gifts or favors, motivated by love or pity, for which gratitude is the sole fitting response. A right is something that can be demanded or insisted upon without embarrassment or shame.

(Feinberg 1973: 58–59)

Hebrews had moral claims against each other on account of their shared bond and ties as the Chosen People of God. Moreover, the motive clauses (Gemser 1953; Doron 1978) provided an even more powerful basis for why being a Hebrew meant opening oneself to the moral demands of one's fellow citizens. Such motive clauses served as the biblical warrants for Cahill's (1980) point regarding the "primary obligation of seeking God" that undergirds Catholic rights theories. The Hebrews' rightful moral claims against each other stemmed from the prior duties they owed to YHWH to begin with.

From chapters 3 and 4 we can discern various social rights-obligations: the duty to provide Hebrews with assistance to recover from economic chance and contingency and the communal obligation to reconstitute households that had fallen on hard times as viable independent, landholding entities. These social rights-obligations were in turn served and actualized by a wide array of instrumental rights-obligations, that is, by the various economic ordinances found in the Law. As we have already seen, these included tithing for the poor, almsgiving, gleaning privileges, debt remission, mandatory lending, interest-free loans, slave manumission, land return, and the family-clan's obligation to redeem both kin and ancestral land. These instrumental rights-obligations were dependent on local circumstances; their mandates were largely shaped by the agrarian nature of Hebrew society.

In summary, it is possible to retrospectively fit the biblical vision of economic security within the framework of modern rights language. The Hebrew economic ordinances are instrumental rights-obligations that are in turn undergirded by larger societal goals (the social rights-obligations). These statutes and their corresponding *epikeia*, however, are ultimately geared toward ensuring the economic viability and physical survival of the Chosen People (the core personal rights).

COMMON GOOD AS DUE PROPORTION: RANKING
COMPETING CLAIMS

This chapter's proposed model also provides guidelines for resolving
competing claims. It is to this that we now turn our attention. At its
core, economic compulsion is most likely a clash of competing claims
over scarce societal resources. Are rights equally held by all, and do they
have to be equally held by all?[17] Is there a hierarchy of rights that provides
a method for resolving conflicting interests? Is the strength of the rights-
claims a function of the type of rights or of the holder of the rights, or
both? And if it is indeed agent-relative, are there criteria for ascribing
varying degrees of strength to these claims?

It is widely held that there is indeed a hierarchy of rights. There are *core
rights*, which directly affect the interests to be promoted, and then there
are *derivative rights*, which are a step removed from the principal interests
protected or promoted. *Prima facie rights* are also widely acknowledged.
These are rights that can be overridden by more compelling interests (or
rights). This differentiation complements the personal-social-instrumen-
tal taxonomy in Figure 5.1 (p. 149). However, helpful as they are in
analyzing variations in the strength of rights, these distinctions are
nevertheless merely typologies and do not provide norms for resolving
competing claims.

Due proportion is another quality (in addition to due order) that the
community must have if it is to enjoy the common good.[18] Due proportion acknowledges that there are legitimate inequalities within society
given differences in people's needs, responsibilities, roles, contributions,
and capabilities. For example, justice itself demands that people be
remunerated differently to reflect disparities in the aforementioned criteria. However, due proportion requires that these legitimate inequalities
be kept within bounds for the sake of harmony and due order. Beyond a
certain limit, even legitimate inequalities erode the bonds that tie people
together in solidarity.

Of course, the difficulty in actualizing due proportion lies in identifying what the proper thresholds are for tolerable inequality. At its root, the
question of legitimate inequalities is essentially about resolving competing

---

17 Much has been written on this debate. See Finnis (1980: 221–23), Gewirth (1982: 3–4, 19–20),
Huber (1979: 7–8), and Pennock (1981: 15).
18 Barrera (2001: 297–301). I am not claiming that due order and due proportion fully exhaust all the
features of the common good. I am simply claiming that these are necessary minimum qualities in
any reasonable account of the common good.

rights. I propose that Hollenbach's (1979: 203–207) three strategic priorities, Barrera's (2001: 227–46) three levels of unmet needs, and this model's ranking of personal and social rights provide useful guidelines for the unavoidable triage in sorting through conflicting claims in socioeconomic life. Each of these is briefly discussed in the following sections.

Hollenbach's strategic moral priorities

In tracing the development and role of human rights in the Catholic social tradition, Hollenbach ultimately acknowledges the formidable challenge posed by reconciling clashing claims. He proposes three strategic moral imperatives:

[T]he societal effort to implement and institutionalize rights should adopt the following three strategic moral priorities:

1 The needs of the poor take priority over the wants of the rich.
2 The freedom of the dominated takes priority over the liberty of the powerful.
3 The participation of marginalized groups takes priority over the preservation of an order which excludes them. (Hollenbach 1979: 204)

As mentioned earlier, Hollenbach distills the rights in *Pacem in Terris* into three major areas of concern: the satisfaction of basic human needs, the freedom to interact with others, and the opportunity to form and sustain relationships. Thus, he focuses his decision rules on needs, freedom, and participation.

Hollenbach's three strategic imperatives still leave many unanswered questions such as how to distinguish needs from wants, how to measure and compare the freedoms enjoyed by people, and how to gauge the quality and scope of participation.[19] Nevertheless, these are not insurmountable hurdles; the value of these priorities lies in the moral decision rules they propose.

Degrees of unmet needs

These moral imperatives can be supplemented by Barrera's (2001: 227–46) model for distinguishing varying degrees of unmet needs. It is particularly relevant to the question of what qualifies as a genuine need. Rival consumption is a feature of human nature, and there is need to allocate the finite supplies of goods to their competing uses. The problem is how

---

19 See the Heritage Foundation's (2002) initiative of quantifying and comparing freedom across different nations in its *Index of Economic Freedom*.

to resolve clashing claims for economic goods. What criteria do we use in prioritizing these competing claims?

The use and consumption of goods or services are either functional or dysfunctional for purposes of attaining integral human development. Thus, chemical compounds provide the medication necessary for restoring people to good health. Such is a functional use of these goods and of the labor that went into producing these medicines. On the other hand, the abuse of the same chemical compounds for recreation is a dysfunctional use as evidenced in the ravages wrought by drug addiction. Dysfunctional uses of goods have no claims at all.

Within the functional use of goods, we can make a further distinction as to the urgency of these commodities for people's integral human development. Some goods are "constitutive" in their use when they are essential for survival and basic health. Thus, we have the basic needs of food, clothing, shelter, and medical care. This class of goods has the strongest possible claims and takes precedence over other claims. A step below this are commodities that are "regulative" in use because they are key to gaining access to the many other goods needed for human flourishing. Thus, in our contemporary era, education and the means to acquire, process, and interpret information are regulative in their use because they open new horizons and opportunities for gain and advancement in the postindustrial knowledge economy. During the Industrial Revolution, capital was regulative in use because of its key role in procuring and melding together the technologies, equipment, raw materials, and products that led to market leadership. At the level of the individual person, these "regulative" commodities shape people's life prospects, at least in the economic realm. Finally, the third category of uses pertains to all other functional uses that are neither constitutive nor regulative in their use; these could be described as merely enhancing one's enjoyment of these goods and services.

A quick exercise in applying these lexical rules:

1 A starving person's consumption of a loaf of bread is constitutive as it pertains to basic health and survival. The same loaf of bread when consumed by a well-fed person merely enhances his/her enjoyment of life. A glutton eating that same loaf illustrates a dysfunctional use of the good. Thus, the starving person has the strongest claim to the loaf of bread.

2 The resources devoted to educating children in sub-Saharan Africa are at least regulative in use because such schooling breaks the poverty cycle and opens possibilities of future upward mobility. Thus, uneducated children have a strong claim over these resources compared to devoting such scarce capital to setting up expensive, cutting-edge Ph.D. programs to enhance the academic reputation of their indigenous national universities.

A strength of this typology is that it can be used to distinguish trivial from consequential adverse pecuniary externalities. After all, it is only the latter that genuinely constitute economic compulsion. The three levels of unmet needs help to define varying degrees of economic compulsion.[20]

Ranking core personal economic rights

In addition to Hollenbach's (1979: 203–207) three strategic moral imperatives and Barrera's (2001: 227–46) distinction between varying degrees of unmet needs, we can add the lexical ordering of this chapter's proposed model. The four core personal economic rights are all indispensable for integral human development. Nevertheless, the urgency of the claims presented by each of these four core rights varies and is largely dictated by human nature. The strength of their claims can be presented in the following descending order of priority:

1 right of bodily integrity;
2 right to livelihood;
3 right to participate in and contribute to the common good;
4 right to personal growth in character and creativity.

The satisfaction of these rights is sequential, that is, the preceding rights on the list are necessary conditions, indeed the very grounds, for the satisfaction of the later rights.

The lexical ordering of social rights

As seen earlier, there are two sets of social economic rights-obligations corresponding to the two disparate objects of relationships 3 and 4 of the common good as due order. Recall that relationship 4 pertains to the

---

20 Gewirth (1985: 28) resolves competing claims according to his "criterion of degree of necessity for action." There is a hierarchy of goods in a decreasing order of necessity, to wit: basic, nonsubtractive, and additive goods.

community's obligation to furnish the most favorable conditions for every member in its ranks to flourish in life. Relationship 3 refers to the additional assistance the community is obligated to provide to those who are unable to fend for themselves. Thus, we have the additional social right-obligation of rehabilitative-restorative support for the marginalized.

These two sets of social rights reflect two different sets of communal obligations and their correlative claims. Given the array of social principles concomitant to relationships 3 and 4 of the common good as due order, one can only conclude that the needs of the marginalized carry greater urgency and enjoy prior claims relative to other members of the community who are able to avail themselves of social goods and benefits by their own effort. In other words, *the obligations and claims associated with the social right to restorative aid enjoy priority relative to other claims over the community's scarce resources; social rights-obligations of an ameliorative nature require immediate attention.* This is consistent with all the other preceding criteria (strategic moral imperatives, degrees of unmet needs, and differing grades of core personal economic rights) because the marginalized are most likely the ones with the most severe, perhaps even life-threatening, unmet needs. Moreover, it reflects the spirit of the Old Testament economic statutes that revolve principally around those who are in great distress. Besides, such priority is consistent with the long-standing preferential option for the poor within this tradition.

THE DIAGNOSTIC FRAMEWORK RECAPITULATED

Chapters 1 and 2 described the nature and dynamics of pecuniary externalities. Chapter 3 presented the case for why the resulting economic compulsion from such negative unintended consequences ought to be a matter for moral discourse, and chapter 4 examined how they ought to be rectified. Drawing from the theological and philosophical resources[21] afforded by Catholic social thought, this chapter has outlined a proposed model whose three constitutive elements (economic rights, overarching conceptual framework, and lexical rules) are summarized in Table 5.1

---

21 The preceding sections have been drawn from: (a) the Hebrew Scripture's economic statutes and ordinances; (b) the human rights framework of *Pacem in Terris* together with the Yale Task Force on Population Ethics (1974: 102) and Hollenbach's (1979: 98) diagrammatic schema of personal, social, and instrumental rights; (c) the notion of the common good as due order and due proportion with its supporting array of mediating social principles (Barrera 2001: 251–303); (d) Hollenbach's (1979: 203–207) three strategic moral priorities and Barrera's (2001: 227–46) varying degrees of unmet needs.

(p. 155). The utility of this model is best appreciated by referring back to the original questions that motivated this entire exercise.

How do we adapt the biblical vision of economic security to our own postindustrial era of global economic integration?

The underlying relationships constituting the notion of the common good as due order correspond to the distinctive formal characteristics and dynamics undergirding the biblical vision of economic security. After all, the Hebrews' relationship with each other, with the poor in their midst, and with the goods of the earth were ultimately formed and shaped by their filial relationship to YHWH. Thus, the five relationships described in the notion of the common good as due order provide a structure for generalizing the Old Testament response to economic distress, thereby facilitating its adaptation and use in our own day and age. A collateral benefit of all this, of course, is the provision of scriptural warrants for modern economic rights. The notion of the common good as due order serves as the conceptual bridge that links the *epikeia* of Old Testament economic statutes to modern economic rights.

How do we separate trivial from consequential pecuniary externalities? How do we recognize and measure when negative market ripple effects are so severe as to constitute economic compulsion?

I have defined economic compulsion in chapter 1 as a state of severe economic distress in which people are compelled to give up vital interests in order to procure or protect their other nontrivial claims that are in jeopardy. The above-mentioned four core personal economic rights define these critical interests and claims. Moreover, the severity of economic compulsion corresponds to the lexical ordering of these four core personal economic rights. We are in a condition of economic distress whenever any of these four core personal economic rights are in peril or the subject of compelled trade-offs. The more profound the opportunity cost and the more important the core personal economic right at stake, the more severe is the economic compulsion experienced. Furthermore, the gravity of such detrimental unintended consequences can be partly and indirectly measured by the degree to which the community fails to discharge the social and instrumental rights-obligations that correspond to the core personal economic rights at risk.

How do we mitigate the severity of economic compulsion?

This proposed model can be utilized as a framework for designing and packaging ameliorative action. Policymaking and providing rehabilitative assistance are both highly dependent on the particular problems to be addressed. Having a theoretical structure with which to think through the whole process is essential if we are going to be rigorous and comprehensive, to the extent possible, in our approach to redressing instances of economic compulsion. This chapter proposes "principles of reflection, norms of judgment and directives for action" (Paul VI 1971: #4) that apply abstract concepts to concrete local particularities. Using modern Catholic social thought, I have embedded rights language within the minimum features one would expect of any reasonable account of the common good: due order, due proportion, and justice in the key relationships that constitute a community.

This chapter's model combines disparate elements of the Catholic social tradition into a mutually reinforcing synergy. In particular, the notion of the common good as due order (Table 5.1, p. 155) and human rights (Figure 5.1, p. 149) both serve to address each other's limitations and deficiencies. The schema of human rights provides nonexhaustive[22] benchmarks that partly define the particular requirements of the relationships described in the common good as due order. Moreover, these human rights conveniently lend themselves as specific proximate goals that are helpful when it comes to implementing social principles in actual practice. The social principles, for their part, provide the "language" for articulating the constitutive elements and dynamics of the relationships intrinsic to the common good. On the other hand, the common good ties the disparate social principles together within a single overarching framework. Coleman (1984) is critical of *Pacem in Terris* and Hollenbach (1979) for their failure to establish definitively the link between human dignity and human rights. I believe that such a perceived deficiency lies in the failure to specify further the larger milieu in which human rights flow from human dignity – the notion of the common good.

SUMMARY

Modern Catholic social thought and the notion of economic security as a divine benefaction dovetail each other well. As Cahill (1980) observes, despite its use of rights language, Catholic social thought is at its core still about duties and obligations. This deep underlying social dimension and the tradition's personalism lend themselves well to analyzing economic security in its three constitutive elements: (1) basic needs access for all,

---

22 As already mentioned, social and instrumental rights are heavily context-dependent and cannot be enumerated comprehensively, separately from the concrete particularities in which they are to be applied.

(2) through people's own exertions (to the extent possible), (3) but always with the help of others in the community. Catholic social ethics and the biblical notion of economic security converge in their assertion that the human person can flourish only within the community.

This chapter has sketched a model for dealing with economic compulsion. Modern Catholic social teachings provide critical mediating concepts that translate the biblical vision of economic security into modern rights language. Taken together, the Hebrew economic statutes, Catholic social norms, and modern economic rights language provide a useful diagnostic-prescriptive framework for appraising the point at which negative pecuniary externalities turn into economic compulsion and for assessing the gravity of such adverse unintended consequences. Unfortunately, despite the range and specificity of the rights, norms, and rules enumerated in Table 5.1, these are still at the level of general guidelines, at best. Many gray areas remain unresolved and require further work. For example, how do we separate a genuine need from a mere want? How do we specify the precise content of the four core personal rights without being relativistic while at the same time taking context into account? After all, the all-important moral baseline of chapter 1 – the yardstick for what constitutes economic compulsion – evolves over time. Nonetheless, the proposed model is a first step in ethical reflection. The next chapter applies it to an actual, pressing case of economic compulsion: agricultural protectionism.

CHAPTER 6

Application: the case of agricultural protectionism

INTRODUCTION

At first glance, it would seem that agricultural support is the wrong case to pick for this application. After all, its resolution calls for lifting governmental farm controls and letting markets operate freely, quite the opposite of what the preceding chapters have been saying all along on the need for extra-market interventions to rectify unintended consequences. On the contrary, agricultural protectionism is an ideal case with which to illustrate the utility of this study's conceptual framework, for three reasons.[1] In the first place, such farm support is fundamentally about coping with adverse pecuniary externalities and averting their resultant economic compulsion – indeed, much along the lines of this book's point on the need for collective moral agency to take responsibility for ameliorating economic distress. Second, such public assistance is not a simple matter of dealing with a single episode of harmful market ripple effects. It turns out to be a more complicated case of multiple but related instances of economic compulsion in both wealthy and poor nations, and of having to sift through their competing claims against each other. One could argue, for example, that states have a primary moral obligation to the economic rights to life and subsistence of their own citizens compared to noncitizens both at home and abroad (Raphael 1967: 65–66). Thus, there is an additional ethical issue of whether countries are morally justified in protecting their own farmer-citizens from economic compulsion in the marketplace even at the expense of inflicting economic distress on other nations' farmers. Third, within theological ethics, very little has been done to assess the moral dimensions of interventions in the global

---

1 This chapter is neither a survey nor a synthesis of public policy on agricultural markets. My primary interest lies in using the preceding chapter's model in assessing the social ethics of governmental assistance to beleaguered farmers.

agricultural marketplace.[2] Given these manifold advantages, the following sections focus on farm support programs in applying the preceding chapter's proposed model.

THE CASE FOR ASSISTANCE

Let us begin by reviewing the reasons given in support of farming assistance programs. A well-known and well-documented empirical regularity in the economic growth of nations is the continued decline of agriculture relative to industry and services in terms of contribution to national income and employment (Kuznets 1966).[3] After all, technological change and product innovation are more promising and virtually unlimited in manufacturing and services compared to farming. This is not even to mention the relative difficulty of farm work and its intrinsic uncertainties due to weather shifts and animal diseases. Moreover, the share of food in consumer expenditures declines as incomes rise.[4] Furthermore, international trade has made it much more difficult for developed country farmers to compete in the marketplace. The abundance of labor and land relative to capital in less developed nations gives them a natural comparative advantage in the production of many agricultural products. Thus, the decline in advanced countries' agricultural sectors can be attributed to three adverse pecuniary externalities: (1) the greater relative dynamism of industry and services in the domestic economy, (2) the relative decline of food shares in budget expenditures, and (3) the overwhelming competition from overseas farmers. This is reflected in the exodus of younger generations from agricultural work and the continued precipitous decline in the number of farms in industrialized nations (Fackler 2004).

Public assistance for agriculture and heavy government interference in food markets are not recent phenomena. Such practices date as far back as the fifteenth century.[5] Moreover, recall the British Corn Laws which became such a source of division between farmers, on the one hand,

---

2 Examples of theological reflections on agricultural issues include Finn (1996: 105–46), John XXIII (1961: #123–56), and National Conference of Catholic Bishops (1986: #216–50).

3 Contrast, for example, the share of agriculture to gross domestic product in 2001. It ranges from nearly 60 percent for the poorest nations (Myanmar, Central African Republic) to less than 1 percent for the major industrialized countries. The average for low-income countries is 23 percent compared to 1 percent for countries like the United Kingdom, Germany, and Japan (World Bank 2003: pp. 238–39, Table 3).

4 In technical terms, this means that food is income inelastic. Recall Engel's Law.

5 See Tyers and Anderson (1992: 45) for references on the history of agricultural protectionism.

and industrialists and free traders, on the other. Or take note of the agricultural protectionism in late nineteenth-century Europe in reaction to the large inflow of grains from the United States (Kenwood and Lougheed 1992: 70–72). Continental farmers could not compete even in their own markets against the onslaught of highly productive American farmers and the steep drop in the cost of rail and steamship transportation. In recent history, US public assistance to farms emerged as a defensive measure during the Great Depression in the face of declining agricultural farm prices. Europe rose from the ashes of the Second World War determined never again to endure rationing and to ensure its self-sufficiency when it came to food (Becker 2003; Thurow and Winestock 2002). An important common characteristic in all this is that governments have a long-established track record of intervening to protect their agricultural sectors from both local and international negative pecuniary externalities.[6]

Numerous reasons have been advanced to justify public support for farmers.[7] First, agricultural production is by its nature fraught with great volatility and instability given the vagaries of weather. This variability in supply causes wild price swings that lead to so much uncertainty in the livelihood of rural populations.[8] Public assistance smooths out these erratic cycles. Second, food is a strategic commodity, and national security requires that countries maintain their capacity for self-sufficiency. Third, agriculture is part of a nation's cultural heritage, a way of life that must be preserved and handed down to the next generations. Fourth, there is a long-term secular deterioration in agricultural prices relative to those of manufactures. Fifth, farm work is an important source of employment both for the rural areas and for the ancillary industries supplying the agricultural sector (e.g., fertilizer, farm equipment, and feed). Sixth, such public assistance serves as a venue for encouraging farmers to protect the environment in their land use. Seventh, agriculture needs public help in the face of a very harsh marketplace (infant-industry argument). Eighth, it is a vital source of foreign exchange earnings. Ninth, farmers need

---

6 There is a paradoxical pattern in the history of government agricultural policies. In the early stages of development, nations have generally adopted anti-agricultural policies (e.g., hidden taxes) against their farmers precisely at a time when their economies are heavily dependent on the vibrancy of the sector and their comparative advantage lies in agriculture. The pendulum swings to the other end when, as industrialized countries, they heavily subsidize and protect their farmers at a time when they are less dependent on agriculture and have a strong comparative disadvantage in farming (Tyers and Anderson 1992: 80).

7 See, for example, *The Economist* (2000c, 88) and Piccinini and Loseby (2001: 9–13).

8 Such fluctuations are compounded further by the inelasticity of the demand for food.

governmental assistance as a defensive measure to level the playing field given the protectionist stance of other nations in favor of their own farmers. Tenth, farms are unable to compete for funds in capital markets on their own, thereby requiring extra-market preferential treatment.

A case for public assistance for farmers can also be made by viewing the agricultural sector as a public good. The enormous social benefits of the sector (preserving local culture and heritage, adding diversity to national life, handing down a way of life, national security, and food production) do not filter down to farmers in a tangible way despite their having to bear the full cost of the risks intrinsic to this occupation. As a consequence, there will be an underproduction of this public good because farmers fail to fully capitalize (internalize) these enormous social benefits in their private calculations. Governments can rectify this gap by directly giving farmers some of the social gains they produce but are unable to appropriate for themselves.

It is beyond the scope of this study to go into the details of developed-country farm support, which takes the form of price guarantees, tariffs, quotas, subsidies, income support payments, loans, production restraints, and other environmental and social measures.[9] It is sufficient for our purposes merely to highlight the extent of agricultural protectionism by briefly presenting descriptive data, especially for the European Union (EU), Japan, and the United States, the key players in global agricultural assistance [10]

1 Aid to farmers is sizable. Based on the appraisal of the Organisation for Economic Development Co-operation and Development (OECD), its member nations[11] provided a total of over $320 billion to support agriculture in the year 2000.[12]
2 As a percentage of gross domestic product (GDP), this aid amounts to approximately 1.2 to 1.3 percent for OECD. For the EU, its support has hovered around 1.3 percent of its GDP, down from 2.7 percent in 1986–88; 1.4 percent for Japan, down from 2.3 percent (1986–88); 0.9 percent for the United States, down from 1.4 percent (1986–88).

---

9 See Piccinini and Loseby (2001: 20–31, 48–57) for a brief overview of the European Union's Common Agricultural Policy (CAP) and the United States' agricultural stance. For an analysis of the 2002 U. S. Farm Bill, refer to OECD (2003a).
10 Data are drawn from OECD (2003a).
11 The OECD nations are: Australia, Austria, Belgium, Canada, Czech Republic, Denmark, Finland, France, Germany, Greece, Hungary, Iceland, Ireland, Italy, Japan, Luxembourg, Mexico, Netherlands, New Zealand, Norway, Poland, Portugal, Slovak Republic, South Korea, Spain, Sweden, Switzerland, Turkey, United Kingdom, and the United States.
12 The provisional total for 2002 is placed at $318.3 billion (OECD 2003a: p. 229, Table III.12).

3 A substantial part of farmers' gross farm receipts comes from transfers from consumers (in the form of higher agricultural prices) and taxpayers. For the EU, this amounts to 35 percent of the farmers' total farm income in 2000–2002, down from 40 percent in 1986–88. For Japan, it is 59 percent (2000–2002), comparable to 61 percent for the 1986–88 period. For the United States, it is 21 percent (2000–2002), down from 25 percent (1986–88). For the OECD as a whole, it is 31 percent (2000–2002), down from 38 percent (1986–88). In other words, farmers in developed countries are heavily dependent on government assistance for a substantial part of their farm income.[13]

4 There is great disparity between domestic and international agricultural prices. This reflects governments' efforts to shield their farmers from both damaging price swings and inadequate earnings. Note the ratio of the average protected domestic prices received by producers relative to the border (international) prices. For Japan: 2.37 (2000–2002), down from 2.46 (1986–88); EU: 1.33 (2000–2002), down from 1.76 (1986–88); United States: 1.13 (2000–2002), down from 1.19 (1986–88); OECD 1.32 (2000–2002), down from 1.57 (1986–88).[14] A ratio of one means no protection accorded to farmers since domestic prices are equal to international prices.

Is such considerable public assistance warranted? First, the most compelling case for public intervention in agricultural markets is the need to provide relief to small family farms that are at risk from the adverse pecuniary externalities of the marketplace, both domestic and international. Their core personal economic right to a gainful and meaningful livelihood is in jeopardy given the unfavorable economic conditions stacked against small farming operations. This is an important, though not the only, moral justification for public action on behalf of distressed farmers in industrialized nations.

Second, the precarious condition of these small farming families must also be examined in the light of communal obligations. As noted in the preceding chapter, any reasonable account of the common good must at a minimum ensure integrity in the relationships constitutive of the community. This includes (1) the relationship of the community to every member within its ranks and (2) the relationship of the community to the marginalized in its midst. In the first instance, the community has the

13 Swiss farmers top the list with 73 percent of their 2000–2002 income drawn from transfers from consumers and taxpayers. See OECD (2003a: p. 213, Table III.3).

14 These nominal protection coefficients (NPC) are drawn from OECD (2003a: 213–14, Table III.3).

duty to provide the most favorable conditions for its members to flourish in integral human development. Thus, the social principles of subsidiarity, universal destination of the goods of the earth, participation, primacy of labor, and relative equality all justify the provision of public assistance to imperiled farmers in an effort to preserve their status as full, free, equal, and productive members of the larger community. Public assistance in this case takes the hard edge off an endangered and intrinsically difficult occupation and allows farmers to hold on to their chosen profession without undue burdens. This public support takes on even greater urgency when viewed in light of the community's obligations to the marginalized; many rural families fall below the poverty line. Governmental help for these poor farming families is entirely consistent with the social principles of the preferential option for the poor, socialization, participation, and restoration that call for aggressive public assistance for those at the edges of the community. Nothing less is expected in any reasonable account of the common good.

In summary, a prima facie case can be made in favor of developed countries' public support of their endangered agricultural sectors based on the framework of human rights set within the common good tradition. The extensive public measures pursued on behalf of farmers at risk are consistent with the social and instrumental obligations that flow from the two fundamental core personal economic rights to subsistence and to a livelihood (see Figure 5.1, p. 149). Unfortunately, the case is not as simple as it seems to be. In responding to deleterious market ripple effects, these public measures precipitate their own set of even more extensive and more damaging pecuniary externalities. Thus, a complete ethical appraisal must necessarily take these injurious second-order effects into account.

THE CASE AGAINST AGRICULTURAL SUPPORT

There are strong arguments presented against industrialized nations' agricultural programs.[15] Such heavy interference in markets and in the free trade of nations impedes allocative efficiency and imposes real costs on everybody else in the global economy, especially future generations whose growth prospects are dimmed. Potential dynamic gains from trade are needlessly lost. Particularly hard hit are many developing countries, especially the poorest, whose opportunities for economic development are seriously hampered by wealthier countries' agricultural protectionism.

15 See, for example, the series of *New York Times* editorials (*Harvesting Poverty*) published in 2003. Go to www.nytimes.com/harvestingpoverty. See also Becker (2003) and Thurow and Winestock (2002).

The harmful impact on less developed nations is best appreciated by recalling that agriculture is their predominant economic activity, accounting for 27 percent of their GDP and exports, and providing for as much as 50 percent of their employment (Lankes 2002: 10). These static, snapshot statistics do not even adequately capture the intangible contributions of the agricultural sector to a nation's development. Advanced countries, with very few exceptions, industrialized on account of their vibrant agricultural sectors that provided industry with the necessary savings for capital investment, a labor pool, and a consumer market for its output. In the early stages of development, it is agriculture that pulls the rest of the economy since it is the biggest and the most dominant sector. Farming drives the rest of the national economy through its forward and backward linkages (Lewis 1954; Fei and Ranis 1964). Thus, the detrimental consequences of interventions in global agricultural markets carry significant long-term costs since they directly inhibit the development efforts of poor countries.

World Bank analyses suggest a global welfare loss of \$120 billion (at 1997 prices) due to distortions in agriculture. A fifth of this is borne by the less developed countries (Lankes 2002: 10). Rod Tyers and Kym Anderson (1992: 210) estimate developing countries' net economic welfare losses in 1990 at \$11.2 billion (at 1985 prices). And this is not even to count the much larger losses from the forgone dynamic gains from trade and development, such as technological change. Numerous model simulations reach the same conclusion: Unilateral reduction by the European Community of its agricultural price supports would singlehandedly improve overall welfare not only in Europe but in other countries as well and provide for greater stability in agricultural markets (Tarditi et al. 1989: 21).

Tyers and Anderson (1992: 305) conclude that developed-country agricultural policies are chiefly responsible for a reduction in international food prices by 14 percent and an increase in their volatility by as much as 50 percent. Depressed agricultural prices are expected to worsen further over time without any global reforms in food markets. Except for rice, the European Community is the major cause of depressed prices even after the "combined effect of *all* other industrial countries' policies" (198 [original emphasis]). It is estimated that if developed and developing countries act together to liberalize food markets, they can reduce price volatility by as much as two-thirds, less than most countries' inflation rates. If developed countries were to liberalize unilaterally, they would reduce price volatility by 25 percent (225). Furthermore, there has been a corresponding drop in world trade volume across all commodities except wheat on account of OECD practices. There has been an overproduction of wheat and sugar because of the European Community's practice of disposing of its surpluses through export subsidies (198). Many other scholars, using partial and general equilibrium simulations, uniformly conclude that agricultural trade liberalization would unambiguously improve prices for poor countries' commodities (Goldin and Knudsen 1990: 475–85).

In depressing agricultural food prices and generating greater volatility in global food markets, OECD policies have turned developing countries into food importers by destroying their short- and long-term incentives for technological change and investments in agriculture. As a result, there is a loss of their food self-sufficiency, and their comparative advantage is not properly pursued to its full potential. Emerging nations should have been net food exporters otherwise. Thurow and Winestock (2002) claim that developed-country agricultural policies hurt poor countries by as much as $50 billion in lost annual export revenues, which is just as much as, and essentially negates, the $50 billion in foreign aid extended by industrialized countries. Tyers and Anderson (1992: 201) peg Argentina's loss at $2 billion in potential yearly food export earnings, an amount larger than its total interest payments on its external debt in the 1980s.

MORAL EVALUATION

Critics have long raised a hue and cry over OECD[16] agricultural subsidies. These criticisms often fail to point to specific moral principles undergirding their position. It is not sufficient to say that such subsidies are unfair or unjust. It is equally important to explain why. The diagnostic framework proposed in the preceding chapter helps in this regard. In what follows, I employ human rights and the common good as lenses with which to appraise agricultural protectionism.

The rights framework: locating where the clash occurs

In Figure 5.1, agricultural subsidies directly impinge on the livelihood and bodily rights of all the parties involved. For both OECD and less

---

16 I use "OECD" to refer to developed countries only for felicity and variety of expression. Not all OECD nations are developed (as in the case of Mexico and Turkey), nor are all of them protectionist in their agricultural policies (as in the case of Australia). In fact, farmers in some of the OECD countries themselves suffer from the ill effects of the agricultural protectionism of their fellow OECD members.

developed country (LDC) farmers, what is at stake here is their personal right to work within the larger social right of enjoying working and business conditions that allow for a remunerative livelihood. This is ultimately served by the instrumental rights that effect the aforementioned ideal business and working environment that makes life a little easier for farmers. Part of these instrumental rights is the sovereign right of nations to manage their economies in the interest of their citizens, and this includes trade policy. Thus, agricultural subsidies, tariffs, and other barriers fall under this instrumental right (obligation) of governments to provide the most propitious conditions possible for their constituencies. Observe that the competing claims of OECD and LDC farmers occur across the entire spectrum of the personal, social, and instrumental rights of these two relevant spheres from Figure 5.1: livelihood and bodily rights. LDC governments, after all, enjoy the same rights and owe the same obligations to provide their own citizens (farmers and other workers) with favorable business conditions that furnish a gainful livelihood. The OECD nations' use of protectionist measures (as part of their sovereign instrumental right to provide a livelihood for their farmers) creates negative pecuniary externalities that subject LDC farmers and OECD/ LDC consumers to varying degrees of economic compulsion. However, without agricultural protection, OECD farmers will in their own turn be subjected to economic distress given the expected drop in their revenues from unfettered world agricultural markets. The value of Figure 5.1 and its typology of rights lies in their identification of the setting and source of these two sets of competing claims. Let us now weigh these clashing economic rights using the proposed common good diagnostic framework of the preceding chapter. To better follow the arguments in the rest of the chapter, the reader should refer constantly back to the model's summary in Table 1 (p. 155).

The common good as due order

Commutative and legal justice

The second relationship in the notion of the common good as due order pertains to the obligation of mutual care that people owe each other. By harming farmers worldwide through their agricultural policies, developed countries do not live up to the demand of general justice – that of contributing positively to (or at least not harming) the general welfare of the rest of the global community. Moreover, there is also a violation of commutative justice among sovereign nations. By depressing international food prices and spawning greater volatility in global food trade, industrialized countries fail to give other nations their due by destabilizing markets.

By their nature, markets allocate scarce resources to their most valued uses by changing the behavior and decisions of economic agents (e.g., firms and consumers) through the information conveyed by constantly shifting prices. In other words, price signals serve as important mediating vehicles for bringing demand in line with existing supplies through both price and quantity adjustments. For example, in a freely operating market, a drop in the price of sugar or cotton because of technological advances signals an oversupply and should lead both to a greater quantity demanded of these commodities and to an exodus of high-cost cotton and sugar growers toward other cash crops or nonagricultural activities. Equilibrium is restored after such price and quantity corrections. Such realignments are often painful as they usually require major, uncertain, or disruptive changes in the livelihoods and lifestyles of economic actors.

Most OECD agricultural assistance programs are designed to insulate their farmers from international commodity prices to protect them from having to endure such distressing changes (Tyers and Anderson 1992: 65–74). For example, OECD producer support began to decrease in the late 1980s and reached its lowest level in 1997, only to increase again that same year when agricultural prices dropped (Lankes 2002: 11). In the earlier statistics cited, recall how domestic OECD farm prices were not merely held steady but were also kept much higher than global food prices.[17] Thus, less developed countries were left to bear the full brunt of the adjustments needed to deal with price fluctuations in global food markets. In choosing not to heed such price signals, OECD nations – comprising a large segment of the global food market – have in effect passed on their share of unsettling but necessary domestic changes (in order to equilibrate markets) to less developed countries. Thus, emerging nations have had to absorb even larger and more potent price shocks than would have been the case had OECD countries been more forthcoming in fulfilling their share of troublesome price and quantity adjustments as expected of all participants in the global marketplace, or in any market for that matter. To illustrate the significance of this impact, note the findings

---

17 For the years 2000–2002, the ratios of domestic to border prices of agricultural goods were 2.37 (Japan), 1.33 (EU), 1.13 (US), and 1.32 (OECD). These nominal protection coefficients (NPC) are drawn from OECD (2003a: pp. 213–14, Table III.3). The absence of any protection would mean a ratio of 1.

of Tyers and Anderson (1992: 201–203). The elimination of OECD agricultural support programs would cause disconcerting short-term effects: a sudden drop in food prices for OECD countries and a sudden rise in agricultural prices in less developed countries. In both cases, the amplitude of such price swings (and therefore the cost of short-term alterations) could be minimized if all industrial countries were to liberalize simultaneously. For example, European Community producers would have lost $66 billion in 1990 if they had unilaterally rescinded all forms of protection. However, this adjustment cost would have dropped to only $53 billion (a 20 percent reduction) if all developed countries had followed suit. The potential results for the United States are even more dramatic and reveal the value of collective action. Unilateral farm liberalization would have cost the United States a total of $19 billion, in contrast to a positive gain of $3 billion if all developed countries had dropped their agricultural protectionism (Tyers and Anderson 1992: 212). Ian Goldin and Odin Knudsen (1990: 477) observe that various partial and general equilibrium studies arrive at the same conclusion: A joint liberalization in less developed and OECD countries would "mute price increases." In other words, free-ridership imposes costs on everybody else.[18]

This passive "act of omission" (by failing to absorb their share of price and quantity adjustments), however, is but a small part of an even bigger infraction of the OECD's obligations under general justice. In deliberately failing to make the necessary painful domestic corrections in response to the price signals from the global food markets, OECD nations overproduce and dump these resulting surpluses overseas through export subsidies. This action is a primary cause of major price shifts. In effect, domestically generated volatility (booms or busts in harvests) in the OECD countries is also passed on to the international arena. Thus, far from doing their share of ensuring stability in food markets for the sake of the common good, protectionist OECD nations further aggravate the intrinsically uncertain nature of agriculture. They magnify or even precipitate market cycles in their desire to protect their own farmers from such price fluctuations. By insulating their own farmers from having to make the necessary sacrificial responses to international price signals, OECD nations have instead passed on the burdens to less developed nations, which end up having to endure more than their rightful share of adjustments while at the same time having to deal with an exacerbated

---

18 This is also the classic case of the prisoners' dilemma in which the optimal solution can be reached only with a cooperative rather than an adversarial, self-interested, solution.

price instability due to the OECD's dumping. Such a double burden goes against the legal and commutative justice that is incumbent on industrialized countries by virtue of their participation in and gains from international trade. Economic agents should not pass on their share of requisite market realignments to others, and especially not to those who are poor to begin with. By protecting their own farmers from the discipline of the marketplace, OECD members have spared their agricultural sectors from negative pecuniary externalities to the detriment of other nations; worse, they have aggravated even further the severity of such deleterious market ripple effects given the greater volatility engendered by their protectionism.

There is a second breach of both commutative and legal justice stemming from the uneven and often expedient implementation of trade rules. Developed countries have been largely successful in moving poor countries toward stricter compliance with intellectual property rights and a further liberalization of their (LDCs) markets in goods, services, and capital – areas in which developed countries clearly exhibit a commanding comparative advantage and reap the most benefits. In contrast, these same advanced countries have balked at liberalizing their agricultural markets in which emerging nations stand to gain the most. Furthermore, industrialized countries have selectively restricted trade in certain manufactures such as textiles and shoes – essential foreign exchange earners for poor countries – despite their avowed commitment to and calls for liberalized trade in manufactures.[19] This kind of behavior has led to accusations of hypocrisy on the part of the developed countries that subscribe to free trade only when it is in their own best interest. More important, however, there is a violation of commutative justice on the part of advanced countries that have failed to live up to the obligations of fairness and reciprocity that are supposed to be at the heart of market exchange's goal of mutual advantages for all.

Distributive justice

OECD agricultural farm support is at its core a clash between the right of OECD farmers to a livelihood and the same right on the part of LDC farmers. Without government trade protection, OECD farmers would have been priced out of the market for certain crops. However, OECD agricultural protection directly displaces LDC farmers from international

19 See for example, Lankes (2002), Smith (2002), and essays in Bhagwati and Hirsch (1998).

markets, reduces the real income of OECD consumers, and inflicts hurtful second-order effects on the rest of the LDC populations by retarding their economic development. *Thus, OECD farm support is fundamentally about who gets to bear the brunt of the economic compulsion occasioned by the negative pecuniary externalities of both free trade and agricultural protection regimes.* We examine two sets of demands stemming from distributive justice: the community's obligations to the marginalized in its midst and to every member in its ranks.

The common good as due order: communal duties to the marginalized

A starting point in deciding the propriety of OECD farm support has to be the third relationship of the common good as due order in light of the special circumstances of LDCs. The global community has a distinct obligation to the poor. That such is the case for LDCs is beyond question. Low-income countries have an average per capita income of $430, a life expectancy of 59 years, and an adult illiteracy rate of 37 percent. This is in sharp contrast to the high-income countries' average per capita income of $26,710, life expectancy of 78 years, and negligible adult illiteracy rate (World Bank 2003: pp. 234–35, Table 1).[20] The human development index for high-income OECD countries is more than twice that of the poorest group of nations.[21] Less developed countries are a clearly disadvantaged group.

The preferential option for the poor calls for assistance to be provided in direct proportion to the need of the distressed. Thus, in the case of farm support, OECD countries are twice removed from satisfying their obligations because, far from furnishing any preferential assistance, they are in fact even imposing additional burdens which prevent these poor nations from improving their economic lot. In fact, OECD agricultural trade policies are regressive in their impact because these measures' inimical unintended consequences fall disproportionately on the very people who can least afford to bear them.

This glaring deficiency is also observed in the other social principles that describe the community's duties toward the poor (the third relationship in the common good as due order). By the principle of socialization, OECD countries ought to be helping LDCs in their economic plight.

20 See World Bank (2003: 243) for a listing of these low- and high-income countries. Figures are for 2001.
21 The human development index is a composite of achievements in life and health outcomes, knowledge, and standard of living. See United Nations Development Programme (UNDP) (2001: p. 144, Table 1).

However, far from providing such succor, even more hurdles are added to these impoverished nations' development path. OECD agricultural protection impedes LDC access to both overseas and their own (LDC) domestic food markets. This goes against the principle of participation. To make matters worse, OECD protective measures encumber the very people who have very little participation in global trade to begin with. Contrast, for example, the twenty-four-fold disparity in the total value of merchandise exports in 1998 for the high-income countries ($3.9 trillion) compared to low-income nations ($165 billion) (World Bank 2000: pp. 312–13, Table 20).

Within the framework of the due order that must characterize the relationship of the global community with its marginalized members, and on the basis of the principles of the preferential option for the poor, participation, and socialization, OECD agricultural protection is de facto a double failure of moral obligations. It is a failure of omission in that OECD countries do not live up to their positive duty of assisting the distressed. Furthermore, it is also a failure of commission in which they deliberately ignore the foreseen adverse consequences of their trade policies, which are protective of their own farmers but hurtful to poor agricultural populations. There is both merit and great urgency in affirming LDC claims for immediate relief from the deleterious pecuniary externalities of OECD agricultural protection, based on the global community's obligations to the disadvantaged in its midst.

The common good as due order: collective duties to every member of the community

The preceding discussion pertained to the rightful claims of less developed nations on account of their marginalized status in the global community. There is yet another set of principles that can be brought to bear on this issue simply by virtue of these nations' membership in the global economy. As equals in this international community, both LDC and OECD nations have claims pertinent to the fourth relationship of the common good as due order: the obligation of the entire community to provide each of its member states with the most favorable conditions for human flourishing.

The principle of subsidiarity calls on higher bodies to protect and nurture the private initiative of individuals and lower bodies under their care. Thus, there is an obligation under this principle for the community of nations to ensure that individual countries are furnished with all the assistance and the necessary conditions for them to achieve what they are fully capable of doing for themselves, including self-governance and economic self-sufficiency, to the extent possible. As we have seen earlier, OECD agricultural protectionism undercuts the economic base of those nations that have a comparative advantage in farming: the less developed nations. The benefits afforded OECD farmers at the expense of eroding the productive capacity of LDCs go against the principle of subsidiarity. Enfeebling the LDCs' agricultural sectors impairs their ability to accumulate the much-needed farm surplus that is the primary source of funding for their industrialization and social spending (Fei and Ranis 1964; Lewis 1954). Thus, it has often been argued that OECD nations can provide better and more long-lasting assistance to LDCs by opening their markets (World Bank 2001).

Related to the principle of subsidiarity is the principle of participation. The formal quality of this principle is its call for an equitable distribution of the burdens and benefits of living together as a community so that every member has a meaningful opportunity to be a productive part of the common economic life. This norm also touches on the principle of relative equality, which calls for limits to legitimate inequalities within the community. By precluding LDCs from fully developing their comparative advantage and reaping benefits from the global marketplace, OECD trade policies are in effect widening the global economic gap even further; they also hinder greater LDC (trade) participation which is minimal to begin with.[22] Thus, the principles of both relative equality and participation raise legitimate concerns over the anti-LDC bias of OECD farm support as it exacerbates imbalances in global economic outcomes and processes.

The principles of both participation and relative equality have another important insight to contribute to this issue. A common implication of these two principles is that burdens ought to be borne in proportion to members' ability to bear such costs. Like it or not, in a world of finite resources and rival consumption, there will always be sacrifices to shoulder. It is not a question of whether there will or will not be adverse unintended consequences; it is, rather, a question of who gets to absorb them. With respect to the issue at hand, someone will ultimately have to accept the burden of necessary economic adjustments: the OECD farmers under a free-trade regime or the LDC populations under current OECD protectionist practices.

---

22 See, for example, World Bank (2000: pp. 312–13, Table 20).

OECD farmers and consumers are in a better position to absorb the necessary pain of economic adjustment relative to LDCs. There is no denying that many OECD farmers would have to either shift to other crops or leave farming altogether. OECD nations have a much broader economic base that presents a relatively wider spectrum of alternative economic activities for these displaced farmers and the agricultural sector's ancillary workers and suppliers. They have more developed linkages across their economic sectors that make it relatively easier (compared to LDCs) to find new employment. Moreover, OECD nations have deeper financial reserves that can be tapped to provide transitional aid to their beleaguered farmers. Furthermore, as noted in the next section, OECD nations have a much more robust consumer base, which is larger, has enormous purchasing power, and readily lends itself as a source of financial assistance for their distressed agricultural workers. In addition, the decline of the agricultural sector as part of the process of economic growth and development is not a new phenomenon. It has long been documented and studied (Kuznets 1966), and OECD countries have had a long time to prepare themselves to deal with this problem. Besides, the agricultural sector represents only a small part of their labor force and of their gross domestic product (GDP).

In contrast, LDC populations do not enjoy any of these advantages that could have afforded them the capacity to bear the cost of OECD protectionist pecuniary externalities. LDCs do not have a consumer base that has sufficient purchasing power to absorb the adjustment costs incurred by their farmers. They have neither the depth nor breadth in their socioeconomic infrastructure to furnish alternatives for their distressed farmers, whose only recourse is unemployment, underemployment, or flight to the urban shanty towns where life is just as, and perhaps even more, squalid. Moreover, LDCs have far weaker social security safety nets in the rural areas, if any at all, compared with the OECD nations. Furthermore, the disruption would be far greater in LDCs since agriculture provides a substantial part of employment and income for their nascent economies.

There are enormous transaction costs to moving factors of production around in response to nations' changing comparative advantage. Examined just on the basis of who is in a better position to bear the burdens of the unavoidable economic dislocations and realignments in an evolving and increasingly integrated global marketplace, the principles of participation and relative equality would call on the OECD countries to bear a greater part of these costs. As it is, however, there is a regressive phenomenon in which it is the poor who pay for the cost of preserving the OECD's agricultural sectors.

The principles of participation and relative equality converge in their key requirement: equity in the mutual collaboration of members in the community. This is an important consideration in our current case. OECD countries have firsthand experience of the benefits of free trade, and they have been the most vocal proponents of trade liberalization in manufactures, services, and capital markets. They have also been insistent on the proper enforcement of intellectual property rights in order to improve the workings of the international marketplace. However, it is not a level playing field when it comes to agriculture. LDCs have long complained about the harms done to their economies by farm protectionism. To this day, international agricultural markets have yet to be liberalized. OECD nations should not seek to benefit fully from their comparative advantage (capital, manufactures, and high-skilled services) while preventing LDCs from availing themselves of their own comparative advantage (agriculture, low-end manufactures, and routine services). The global community and its multilateral institutions, such as the World Trade Organization (WTO), the World Bank, and the International Monetary Fund (IMF), have to be even-handed and fair in their policy recommendations. They ought not to be selective in liberalizing markets in capital, manufactures, and high-tech services, but not in agriculture. This goes against equity in market processes and rules. The principles of participation and relative equality are about mutual advantages for all.

Another inequity in market processes highlighted by these principles is the additional burdens borne by global consumers. As noted in the statistics presented earlier, consumers lose out because a distortion-free trade regime in the farming sector would have allowed them to consume more agricultural goods at lower prices. There should otherwise have been an increase in their real incomes. As it is, however, current farm support measures are a de facto massive transfer of resources from OECD consumers and taxpayers and LDC farmers to OECD farmers/landowners and LDC consumers. Again, this goes against the principles of participation and relative equality in market processes. The infraction is actually even worse in light of the regressive distribution of the benefits of such protectionism within the OECD countries themselves, as we find in a later section.

Finally, the primacy of labor principle calls for the provision of meaningful and gainful employment. As already noted, OECD agricultural protection directly hurts LDC incomes and also inflicts second-order effects on the livelihoods of the rest of the LDC populations. Industries and services in an emerging nation are heavily dependent on their most predominant sector (agriculture) for markets, financing, and labor. By hurting the farming sector's prospects, these OECD protective measures in effect also injure the nonagricultural segments of LDC economies. In other words, these OECD policies' pecuniary externalities severely limit the livelihood prospects of agrarian emerging nations and go against the principle of the primacy of labor.

Based on the community's obligations to the marginalized and to every member in its ranks, OECD nations' agricultural support programs in their present form do not satisfy the requirements of distributive justice and in fact preclude the necessary conditions of equity for the attainment of the global common good.

The common good as due order: care for the goods of the earth
The final relationship that must be examined in the framework of the common good as due order pertains to the impact of OECD agricultural subsidies on the principle of stewardship. There is great appeal to incorporating economists' notion of allocative efficiency as part of the requirements of the principle of stewardship. After all, it would seem that allocating the scarce resources of God's creation to their best uses is indeed a reflection of the care and respect we accord the earth's fruits. However, a slight change in the formulation of allocative efficiency is required if it is to be properly adopted as part of this principle.

Allocative efficiency is not identical to engineering efficiency, which refers to getting the most output from given inputs. Allocative efficiency pertains to being able to produce the right goods and services in the right quantities, quality, and style, using the right factors of production and methods, and then bringing them to the right place at the right time. In other words, all markets clear, there are no unsold inventories, and consumers' wants are met. By changing consumer "wants" to consumer "needs," the notion of allocative efficiency can indeed be incorporated into the principle of stewardship and its claim of an obligation to be efficient. At the very least, there is a duty not to waste the fruits of creation as part of the principle of stewardship.

International trade theory has demonstrated the enormous gains that are attendant on unimpeded trade. Of course, the corollary of this claim highlights the correspondingly enormous economic losses that flow from policies that distort or obstruct free trade. The welfare losses suffered by global consumers and LDC populations on account of OECD agricultural protectionism go against the principle of stewardship. And this is not even to mention the losses from the forgone dynamic gains (e.g., technological change) that could have been reaped had OECD nations simply followed their comparative advantage without recourse to trade-distorting measures.

Finally, the principle of stewardship is also violated in the degradation of land and water resources that results from overproduction occasioned by farm support. To its credit, the European Community has taken steps to reform the European Common Agricultural Policy (CAP) by deliberately incorporating environmental conservation as a distinct goal (Piccinini and Loseby 2001: 110–24).

The common good as due proportion

As observed in the preceding chapter, any reasonable account of the common good must necessarily include equity in the division of scarce societal resources as part of distributive justice. OECD agricultural protectionism also fails in this regard because of the regressive allocation of its resulting burdens and benefits.

The regressive distribution of public benefits and burdens

OECD countries

Developed countries themselves are not immune to the regressive adverse pecuniary externalities generated by their pro-agricultural support policies. This is particularly true for both their consumers and their small farmers. First, consumers and taxpayers, many of whom are poor themselves, bear the full cost of pursuing such agricultural assistance programs. Developed-country consumers face higher food prices as a consequence of farm support. A substantial portion of what consumers pay for agricultural products is a pure transfer to farmers. For EU consumers this amounts to as much as 26 percent (2000–2002) of their farm purchases, down from 41 percent (1986–88). For the Japanese, it goes as high as 51 percent (2000–2002), down from 57 percent (1986–88). American consumers are the exception, as they receive a positive net gain of 2 percent (2000–2002) in contrast to their net outward transfer of 7 percent in 1986–88. For OECD consumers, the transfer represents 24 percent

(2000–2002) of their farm purchases, down from 33 percent (1986–88).[23] In other words, OECD citizens overpay by a third, Japanese consumers by half, and EU residents by over a third for their agricultural products because of their governments' support for farmers. And, of course, anything that is not covered by consumers in terms of higher food prices is paid for through taxes. In terms of absolute amounts, Tyers and Anderson (1992: 203) estimate that nonfarm households in Western Europe and Japan pay anywhere from $800 to $1700 (at 1985 prices) in additional taxes and higher food prices every year as a result of aid to farmers. These substantial impositions are troubling, especially when one remembers that the poor are numbered among these consumers. Taxing consumption, whether explicitly or covertly, is always regressive because the poor pay a disproportionately larger share of their resources to such fiscal impositions. Moreover, such food consumption "taxes" are blunt instruments and cannot be targeted to select segments of the population. The poor are forced to provide transfers to farmers, no differently from others in the population who are in a better position to afford and absorb the cost of such consumer subsidies to the farming sector. Thus, Lankes (2002: 10) criticizes the regressive nature of developed-country agricultural policies because low-income OECD consumers are disproportionately affected even as the bulk of such assistance goes to the large farms and the wealthy growers. Furthermore, one must remember that food takes up a much larger proportion of the poor's budget.[24] The poor transfer a much larger share of their income as aid to farmers compared with the rest of the population.

Second, small farmers themselves have in some cases been inadvertently hurt or bypassed by the very policies designed to assist them. Note the conclusion of an OECD study on the market effects of different crop support measures:[25]

Landowners were found to be the major beneficiaries of support regardless of the measure used to provide it. In fact, among the categories of support measures

---

23 These are the consumer subsidy equivalents (CSE), which are defined as the monetary transfers from the consumer as a result of governmental agricultural policies in a given year. A negative value represents a transfer from the consumer. When expressed as a percentage, they are based on the total value of consumption (at farm gate prices). Data cited are drawn from OECD (2003a): Table III.1 (p. 211), Table III.20 (p. 240), Table III.26 (p. 249) and Table III.44 (p. 276).

24 See the entry for "Engel curve" in Eatwell, Milgate, and Newman (1998).

25 The crop support measures studied are market price support and budgetary payments based on output, variable input usage, current area planted, and historical area planted. See OECD (2001: 7).

studied landowners captured the largest share of benefit in all cases except that of payments based on variable inputs. Even in that case, the estimated landowner share was only slightly less than that of the main beneficiary – suppliers of purchased inputs. Although the estimated transfer efficiency of area payments was found to be relatively high, *almost all the associated income gains go to landowners, benefiting farm households only to the extent they own the land they farm.* (OECD 2001: 8 [emphasis added])

What is also disturbing in these OECD findings is the observation that even the agricultural policies that are most efficient in increasing household farm incomes ultimately and invariably benefit landowners. Piccinini and Loseby (2001: 15–16) confirm these findings. Landowners gained the most from the 1992 European reforms designed to make agricultural support more transparent. In addition, production quotas unwittingly create windfall "rents" for the original producers, thereby making it that much more expensive for new and small farmers to enter the field.[26] Because governmental agricultural support payments have been capitalized in property values, land prices have gone up, as have property taxes and land rents. All these impose additional burdens on the poorest farming families who are dependent on renting land to till; moreover, it also makes it that much more difficult for them to eventually purchase their own land.

Despite these distortions and hidden fiscal impositions, a compelling argument for OECD agricultural support programs can arguably still be made if it can be shown that they are largely for the benefit of small family-owned farms. Unfortunately, this is not the case. The bulk of such public assistance is captured by wealthy families and large corporate industrial operators. The bulk of transfers from consumers is believed to go to the wealthiest 20 percent of farmers.[27] Traditional farm support programs in the United States come in the form of crop insurance, direct payments, and environmental conservation programs. In a study of the impact of alternative programs on different-sized farms, Gundersen et al. (2000: 1) conclude that current US government direct payments benefit the most well-off rather than the small, low-income farmers for whom these programs were meant in the first place. For example, in 1997, less than 20 percent of very small farms received such payments, compared

---

26 This additional barrier to ease of entry bodes ill for technological change and innovation and harms long-term prospects for the productivity and growth of OECD agriculture. Their farms will be even more inefficient over time, and continued agricultural support will become even more distortionary. This runs the danger of creating a vicious cycle.

27 Tyers and Anderson (1992: 81), citing United States Government (1987).

with 75 percent of large farms and 60 percent of very large farms (ibid., p. 19, Table 9).[28] According to the OECD, the top 25 percent of farmers have increasingly secured most of the public assistance in the last decade: as much as 70 percent of the subsidies in Europe and even 90 percent in the case of the United States.[29] The predictable consequence is, of course, overproduction, especially on the part of the industrial-sized farms. Surpluses are then dumped in international markets causing both a depression and even greater volatility in food prices. This is not even to mention the increasing concentration of farm operations and damage to the environment through an undue depletion of land and water resources.

Less developed countries
OECD agricultural protectionism does not merely exacerbate the gap between developed and developing countries, it also worsens inequality within emerging nations themselves by imposing additional costs on LDC farmers, who already have to bear heavy burdens. Tyers and Anderson (1992: 214–15) note that the OECD agricultural policies' effect of lowering food prices benefits LDC consumers and taxpayers by as much as $15 to $33 billion annually, but at a loss to LDC farmers of anywhere from $26 to $35 billion a year. Thus, OECD farm policies are a de facto hidden transfer of economic welfare from LDC rural to urban populations. This is a grossly regressive outcome because the poor are generally net sellers of staple foods while the buyers are predominantly the relatively better-off urban dwellers.[30] Inequalities in income and economic welfare are already wide, to begin with, even before we factor in the generally anti-agricultural policies of LDC governments themselves.

The regressive nature of global agricultural policies is also reflected in the widely divergent treatment of agricultural and manufactured products, in which the former are subjected to higher trade barriers. For example, for imports coming from developing countries, the European Union imposes an average ad valorem tariff of 20 percent for agricultural products compared to only 4.5 percent for manufactures. The same

28 Gundersen et al. (2000: 5) define "very small farms" as "limited resource farms" with gross sales of less than $100,000 and a total household income of less than $20,000. Large farms, on the other hand, are defined as operations having sales between a quarter to half a million dollars. Very large farms have sales exceeding half a million US dollars.

29 Becker (2003). Moreover, she notes that according to the Environmental Working Group, a nonprofit environmental research and watchdog organization, the top 10 percent of US farmers captured 65 percent of subsidies in 2002, up from 55 percent in 1995.

30 The urban poor would be hardest hit by agricultural liberalization and its resulting increase in food prices.

pattern is found in Japan (agriculture = 21.9 percent; manufactures = 2.5 percent), the United States (agriculture = 12.7 percent; manufactures = 3.6 percent), and the rest of the OECD (agriculture = 32.5 percent; manufactures = 7.4 percent). Such widespread and consistent bias against agricultural products is a cause for concern, both because it is regressive in the incidence of the burdens it inflicts on farmers (comprising most of the poorest in the world) and because economic history and evidence point to the central role of the agricultural sector as the all-important engine of growth in the early stages of economic development. It is also paradoxical to observe that LDCs for their part impose an average ad valorem tariff of only 14.5 percent on OECD farm products, a rate that is lower than most OECD nations' tariff on LDC agricultural goods (Lankes 2002: p. 9, Table 1).

As noted earlier, agricultural protectionism makes international food prices even more volatile than would otherwise have been the case (Tyers and Anderson 1992: 216, 225–32). This, too, is another source of regressive unintended burdens, as the adjustment costs fall disproportionately on the poor who are less able to deal with wide fluctuations given their limited resources. Moreover, while OECD countries have the necessary fiscal resources and civil infrastructure to protect their farmers and consumers from such unpredictable, wild swings in food prices, emerging nations do not possess such capabilities. Again, note the irony in this particular case. The countries that are least dependent on agriculture and the most capable of weathering instabilities in food prices (OECD) are precisely the ones that are most protective and the ones most responsible for such greater and unwarranted volatility because of their efforts to assist their own farmers. The cost of such policies is shifted to the nations that are the most dependent on agriculture and the ones with the least resources to deal with disruptions in food markets, the LDCs.[31]

It is best to end this necessarily brief sketch of the skewed structure of global agricultural markets with an anecdotal illustration of the disparity in the human costs and benefits that follow in the wake of OECD agricultural programs. Take the case of sugar. Roger Thurow and Geoff Winestock (2002) contrast the lives of Dominique Fièvez in Fontaine-sous-Montdilier, France, and Monica Shandu in Entument, South Africa. Despite the enormous flux in international sugar prices, Mr. Fièvez has

---

31 Many sub-Saharan nations derive more than 50 percent of their national income from agriculture compared to 1.8 percent on average for OECD nations. See *The Economist* (2003d: 44) and OECD (2003b: 24).

received a steady price since 1984 for his sugar crop from his 420-acre farm. Devoting 66 acres to sugar beet, Mr. Fièvez receives a government subsidy of $46,000, making sugar beet 50 percent more profitable than growing either wheat or sweetcorn. "Rich, highly organized and concentrated in a few electorally sensitive regions," farmers such as Mr. Fièvez have succeeded in ensuring that reforms in the European Common Agricultural Reforms (CAP) exempted sugar beet growers. In contrast, Mrs. Shandu of South Africa has to content herself with tilling her four-acre farm of sugar cane by hand as she is too poor to own a tractor. Despite being named South Africa's small-scale Cane Grower of the Year for her "top-quality harvest" in 2001, Mrs. Shandu nevertheless received only two-thirds ($200) of what she would otherwise have earned because of depressed sugar prices. South African farmers are on their own in facing price swings in international sugar prices as their government does not have the resources to insulate them from such volatility. What makes the plight of Mrs. Shandu and the other 3,700 small-scale cane growers in her area (working on ten acres or less) even more dire is the need to expand their joint production further by an additional 50,000 tons if the local sugar mill is to stay open and be economically viable in the long term. This minimum economic size could easily be attained, if only the international sugar market were not distorted. South Africa's forgone export revenues due to OECD sugar subsidies is estimated at $100 million a year. The EU alone accounts for approximately 20 percent of sugar exports worldwide, and a unilateral EU liberalization of its sugar market is expected to improve prices by 20 percent. Thurow and Winestock's (2002) contrast between these two farms vividly illustrates and puts a face to the regressive incidence of OECD agricultural protectionism. Europe is not alone, however, in wreaking so much damage on small sugar cane growers worldwide. While not dumping surplus sugar abroad, the United States nonetheless depresses international sugar prices through its strict quota that nearly triples the price of sugar for American consumers. In an editorial entitled "America's Sugar Daddies," the *New York Times* (11/29/03) calls this corporate welfare and finds it unconscionable to bestow windfall gains in the tens of millions of dollars on wealthy corporate farmers at the expense of small farmers in LDCs.

The heavy protection afforded by the EU to its sugar beet growers as reported by Thurow and Winestock (2002) can easily be confirmed in the OECD's (2003a: p. 241, Table III.21) statistics. In the years 2000–2002, the EU provided an average of 2.4 billion euros per year to support its sugar beet growers. This represented nearly half (48 percent) of the latter's farm income.[32] Moreover, the EU provided its sugar beet growers with domestic sugar prices more than twice (2.24 times) that of international prices.[33] In the case of the United States, total support for sugar amounted to $1.2 billion, constituting 55 percent of sugar growers' income. Producer prices were 2.07 times those of world markets (OECD 2003a: p. 277, Table III.45).

Lexical rules

The foregoing examination of the regressive distribution of burdens and benefits in the wake of OECD agricultural policies can be further reinforced with the lexical rules proposed in the literature. Hollenbach's (1979: 203–207) three strategic imperatives provide insights into resolving the competing claims surrounding OECD agricultural protectionism.

Based on the first moral imperative, both OECD and LDC farmers' claims are about the satisfaction of their basic needs through the preservation of their livelihoods. Thus, with the exception of OECD corporate farmers, we cannot use Hollenbach's first moral imperative since the conflict is not between trivial wants versus life-threatening needs; both are ultimately about meeting the basic needs of farming families, OECD and LDC alike. The case of OECD corporate farmers will be treated shortly using the threefold typology of needs.

With respect to Hollenbach's second moral imperative, we can say that the injurious consequences of agricultural protectionism are, at the very least, restrictive of the economic freedom of those who have to bear such pecuniary externalities. Thus, the issue at hand is about limiting the economic freedom of LDC farmers in order to provide greater liberties to OECD farmers. By Hollenbach's rules, OECD farm support ought to be removed. To this, I would add the earlier observations made under the principles of participation and relative equality. LDC freedoms are affirmed over OECD liberties not because of the latter's wealth, but because of OECD nations' greater capacity to absorb and perhaps even completely mitigate the ill effects of necessary price and income adjustments. In other words, OECD countries are in a better position to provide assistance to their displaced farmers by providing new opportunities and alternatives for the loss of their livelihoods. LDC populations, on the other hand, are in a less robust position to provide anything

---

32 This is the producer subsidy equivalent (PSE).
33 This is the nominal protection coefficient (NPC).

comparable. Hence, in terms of net losses of freedoms, OECD countries are in a clearly superior position to minimize or even make up for such deprivations.

Hollenbach's third moral imperative highlights the importance of ensuring the participation of the marginalized. As argued earlier, OECD agricultural protection impedes impoverished nations' participation in the global food markets. The need to remove such protectionist policies is made even more urgent in the light of empirical evidence suggesting that greater market participation is an important venue for improving the lives of large segments of the population in an efficient, timely, and enduring manner (Dollar and Kraay 2001).

Barrera's (2001: 227–46) threefold typology of unmet needs similarly provides insights for resolving these competing claims. Not all beneficiaries of OECD agricultural policies are small farmers. In fact, a good number of them are large or corporate farmers (Gundersen et al. 2000: p. 19, Table 9). There is a need to distinguish between small-scale farmers and corporate operators. LDC small-scale farmers clearly have the strongest claims as they are fighting for that which is constitutive to their survival: a simple livelihood to provide for their basic needs. OECD small-scale farmers likewise have a claim, though not as strong as their LDC counterparts based on my earlier arguments on the ready availability of OECD safety nets that provide adjustment assistance and economic alternatives. OECD large and corporate farmers have the weakest claim of all, if any, with respect to keeping the current protectionist schemes in place. The resources they would lose from trade liberalization would be regulative at most. It is unclear where the claims of LDC large and corporate farmers lie in relation to the OECD small-scale farmers. This requires further study.

In summary, OECD agricultural policies do not serve the interests of the global common good, if we incorporate equity in the distribution of societal resources as a constitutive consideration in any reasonable account of the good of the community (that is, common good as due proportion). The bulk of agricultural support is captured by farming entities that are neither poor nor small. There is a grossly uneven distribution of the benefits of such protection and aid both in the OECD and in the less developed countries. In fact, the resulting increase in land values and rents has hurt small farmers even further. The severity of this regressive feature completely undercuts the strongest argument for agricultural support: public assistance for small farming families at risk.

This book's proposed conceptual framework can be useful in shaping prospective ameliorative action. It is clear from the preceding sections that there are strong moral warrants for reshaping OECD agricultural support policies. Such reforms would no doubt create adverse pecuniary external-ities themselves and inflict unintended consequences not only on OECD farmers but also on segments of LDC populations that have heretofore benefited from lower food prices. It is thus important to ensure that the requirements of commutative, distributive, and legal justice are observed in the course of reducing OECD agricultural support. The model can be helpful in this regard.

OECD farmers

We run the proverbial risk of throwing the baby out with the bath water in completely abandoning all forms of OECD agricultural assistance. In the United States, 10 percent of farm families are believed to fall below the poverty line. Moreover, "the current farm safety net still provides a measure of support to poor farm families that is not redundant with general social safety net programs such as food stamps and Medicaid" (Gundersen and Offutt 2003: 20).

Once again, the requisite legal, commutative, and distributive justice embedded in the relationships constitutive of any reasonable account of the common good provides guidance. First, obligations to assist the marginalized and the economically distressed stand unchanged regardless of whether they are in the OECD or in less developed countries. The moral justification for assisting *small* OECD household farms cope with and adjust to the negative pecuniary externalities of global food trade remains valid and strong. This is a requirement of the distributive justice integral to the community's obligation to every member in its ranks, especially the marginalized.

The most controversial part of my proposed conceptual framework lies in the principle of restoration as part of the community's obligation to its marginalized. Regular market operations invariably create winners and losers. The principle of restoration calls for a safety net for the latter, paid for by the former. For a market community to move to a better economic position, what is important is no longer merely the potential compen-sation of losers by winners (as is the case in neoclassical economic theory), but the actual compensation of the most severely affected and distressed by those who have gained the most from the economic changes. Liberalizing agricultural trade will uproot many in the OECD agricultural sector. This includes not merely farmers but also the ancillary industries that supply farm services and inputs. Unless assistance is forthcoming, the neediest among these run the danger of forming a new underclass within OECD nations. The principle of restoration calls for assistance from the rest of the OECD communities for the benefit of these displaced groups. The goal is a reconstitution of their means to participate in the economy in some other productive capacity as self-supporting members of the community able to bear their share of the costs of sustaining the common life.

However, as already evident in the preceding sections, current forms of assistance are problematic because of the extensive detrimental pecuniary externalities they spawn in their wake. Thus, other forms of assistance must be devised that are neither as harmful nor as regressive as current protectionist measures. For example, the institution of "geographic indicators" or "specialty labeling" (as in copyright law) for products such as Roquefort cheese and French wines should allow for the production and protection of high-quality wine, olive oil, and meats. The higher prices these products could command in the market would go a long way in preserving the economic viability of local cultures and long-standing ways of life (Becker 2003). Unfortunately, this works only for a small and select group of agricultural crops. Product differentiation for the vast majority of farm goods is unimportant, especially for bulk commodities.

Reforms have been instituted over the years, and there is a palpable decline in the level of protection as seen in the period between 1986–88 and 2000–2002 (OECD 2003a). There are numerous promising alternative OECD programs that have the dual attractive feature of being more efficient in raising household farm incomes even while minimizing distortions in global food markets. There have been serious discussions and preliminary efforts to delink farm subsidies from production levels. However, much further refinement is still needed in these programs to prevent landowners from extracting most of the gains from small farming families (OECD 2001; Piccinini and Loseby 2001). Small-scale OECD farming households, particularly the poor and the helpless, have claims to public assistance just like distressed LDC farmers.

Besides the principle of restoration, there are many other possible forms of assistance. Any reasonable account of the common good requires rectitude in interpersonal relationships between individuals and the larger community. This requires the satisfaction of both commutative and general justice. The latter is of particular interest to us because it highlights the point that social and instrumental rights-obligations (which effect the core personal economic rights in Figure 5.1, p. 149) do not fall exclusively on government. Both individuals and nongovernmental associations of various sizes bear their share of these social-instrumental duties of satisfying basic economic rights. General justice calls for people to contribute to the welfare of their neighbors and the community in the measure they are permitted to do so by their own personal means and well-being.

Take the case of OECD consumers. The second relationship in the framework of the common good as due order pertains to the person's orientation to others and is animated by the spirit of solidarity. This principle provides us with guidance on how to deal with the disruptive effects and costs of economic adjustment. In particular, substantive reform of OECD policies will undoubtedly inflict hardship and suffering on small agricultural families (particularly those that have been farming all along down through the generations) and the auxiliary industries and suppliers dependent on the sector.[34] The question is whether these people have to bear the cost of adjustment by themselves or whether they can rely on the empathetic support of the rest of the nation. The principle of solidarity suggests less harmful alternative measures of assistance compared with existing programs. OECD consumers will benefit from removing such protectionist policies through lower food prices; this represents an increase in their real incomes. Part of such a gain can be tapped as a source of assistance to the displaced. In other words, OECD consumers may, in a spirit of solidarity, choose to share their gains from a liberalized agricultural market with their farmers who have been hurt by free trade. This can be effected through private donations or through income taxes for a period of time until distressed farmers have completed their transition.[35] Of course, the spirit of solidarity may also move OECD consumers to assist their farmers by voluntarily paying a premium – a higher price – for the produce of local farmers.[36] Such conscience-pricing

34 In an examination of alternative crop support measures, the OECD (2001: 8) notes that input suppliers are the biggest beneficiaries of programs that furnish budgetary payments based on variable input use.

35 A consumption tax is not as ideal because it will introduce even greater distortions in the marketplace and affect the efficiency of the economy. Such inefficiencies levy unseen costs on others. Hence, this becomes another case of passing on burdens to other unsuspecting economic agents. Furthermore, as mentioned earlier, consumption taxes are regressive. This is particularly true for food because of Engel's Law.

36 This is similar to apparel and other products that have been prominently labeled "Made in the USA" in an effort to entice consumers to buy domestic products in reaction to the influx of cheap imports and the consequent loss of jobs.

is already widely practiced as in the case of fair-trade coffee, organically grown vegetables and fruits, and garments produced by workers paid a living wage (McLaughlin 2004).[37] Unfortunately, such a market-based approach entails enormous practical and organizational problems.

LDC constituencies

The principle of solidarity and the obligations of general justice take center stage when it comes to dealing with the ill effects of agricultural liberalization on segments of LDC populations. Michael Lind (2003) argues that scrapping subsidies will produce more harm than good because less developed countries are not as efficient in the use of land, and an increase in their agricultural production would lead to the destruction of even more forests and inflict more damage on the environment. Furthermore, small LDC farmers will be crowded out by agribusinesses that are sure to industrialize LDC farming in response to liberalized food markets. Mark Weisbrot and Dean Baer (2002) are also pessimistic and claim that even the broadest possible trade liberalization beyond agriculture would lead to only a minimal increase in LDC incomes. Moreover, emerging nations that have benefited from subsidized food imports from the OECD nations will now have to pay much higher prices, thereby straining their precarious foreign exchange reserves even further. This is not even to mention the inability of many LDCs to absorb drastic shifts in their labor markets. Furthermore, freer trade will lead to a secular decline in the terms of trade against LDCs in which agricultural prices deteriorate relative to those of manufactures.

These concerns over the deleterious effects of OECD agricultural liberalization have long been known and acknowledged. Such reforms in the global food markets will have a differential impact across LDC populations and will in fact hurt some (Goldin and Knudsen 1990: 14). The key difference, however, is the distinction between the short and the long term. The burdens are short-run in duration while the gains accrue in the long term. Tyers and Anderson (1992: 21–22) observe that between the periods 1961–64 and 1983–86, LDCs became even more dependent as food importers. The proportion of OECD food exports in global trade increased during this period. This phenomenon in LDCs can be explained by the increase both in their populations and in their per capita

---

37 This will still have harmful ripple effects on LDC populations since demand for their goods will be weaker. However, it will not be as damaging as the current sweeping protectionist OECD agricultural policies.

food consumption. Thus, there is no doubt that, as a group, LDCs will be hurt in the short term given the expected rise in food prices from agricultural liberalization. Nonetheless, Tyers and Anderson still see great value in reforming current OECD policies because LDCs will be net food exporters in the long run and should benefit from current efforts to liberalize global trade in food. Model simulations predict substantial foreign exchange earnings for less developed countries (ibid.: 222–24).

Technological change and its attendant growth in productivity are responsive to price changes. This means that LDC farmers will adopt better technologies and invest in their farms given the increase in their earnings as a result of OECD liberalization. Thus, while Lind's (2003) characterization of LDC farming as inefficient and wasteful of land resources may be true for now, we cannot assume that LDC technologies will remain static. Farmers are rational in their economic behavior, and they will respond to the incentives of higher earnings in the wake of freer international food markets. Peasants may be poor, but they are efficient in the allocation of what limited resources they own (Schultz 1964).

Lankes (2002: 11) argues similarly; it is true that LDC consumers and farmers will be affected differently by agricultural trade liberalization in the short run. What is important is to implement a staggered liberalization to make adjustment manageable for both LDC and OECD nations. Moreover, one can sequence the necessary reforms (such as removing subsidies and quotas first before eliminating tariffs) to minimize the cost of transition. Goldin and Knudsen (1990: 479) list global cooperation, time, and money as critical factors if those who will be harmed by agricultural reforms (e.g., urban poor in the face of increased cereal prices) are to avoid the short-term pain of requisite structural adjustments. Included as part of this international collaboration are LDCs' elimination of their own anti-agricultural policies and the liberalization of their domestic food markets, which are often as restrictive and distorted as the OECD's agricultural markets, and in some cases even more so (Tyers and Anderson 1992: 216–25).[38] In the absence of a world governing body and in the face of national sovereignty, there is nothing to preclude nations from balking at painful reforms or simply free-riding on the adjustment efforts of other countries. In this regard, the preceding chapter's conceptual framework is useful in articulating nations' obligations to each other and to their own citizens. The social principles should be

---

38 Developing countries on the average impose a 17 percent tariff on each other's agricultural goods, which is nearly as much as the EU's 20 percent and Japan's 21.9 percent rate and much higher than the 12.7 percent tariff levied by the United States (Lankes 2002: p. 9, Table 1).

particularly helpful in specifying the concrete requirements of commutative, general, and distributive justice in attending to the deleterious pecuniary externalities that are sure to follow global agricultural trade liberalization, just as these principles are useful in highlighting deficiencies in current OECD policies.

A final word on reforms. The principle of restoration is perhaps the most problematic of all the social principles in the model, even if we limit our discourse to assistance within the same nation. An even more controversial application of the principle of restoration has to do with those who have been severely affected by OECD agricultural protection over the years. Do OECD countries have an obligation to restore LDC farming communities to the state of affairs that would have prevailed in the absence of OECD trade-distorting policies? Two types of duties must be distinguished in these questions. The first pertains to rehabilitative assistance that seeks to help LDCs fully reap benefits from their comparative advantage as quickly as possible. This is simply the ordinary obligation of restoring a marginalized neighbor even if one had not been the wrongdoer and regardless of who is responsible for the harm. The second and stronger obligation pertains to the duty of restitution, that is, the need to repair the damage inflicted on LDC economies by OECD farm support. This goes beyond merely removing agricultural subsidies to providing extra aid to make up for lost time and opportunities and to speed up LDCs' integration into the global economy after the damage caused by years of OECD protectionism in agriculture. Unfortunately, these moral obligations are easier to assert than apply because of the many practical difficulties surrounding the implementation of compensatory justice (Kershnar 1999). It is beyond the scope of this study to deal with the morality and economics of correcting past wrongdoings. The question of "agricultural compensation" in light of OECD farm subsidies, as some less developed countries have demanded in recent trade negotiations (Hagstrom 2003), is simply too complex a matter to deal with in this chapter.

SUMMARY AND CONCLUSIONS

The object of this chapter has been to illustrate the use of the diagnostic-prescriptive framework proposed in the preceding chapter. The issue of farm supports is ultimately about whose farmers (OECD or LDC) get subjected to the economic compulsion that follows in the wake of unfettered global food trade. OECD agricultural protection produces market ripple effects that hurt the development prospects of less developed nations that are still heavily agrarian. The ill effects of such protectionism have long been known, acknowledged, and studied. Nevertheless, OECD countries have steadfastly refused to liberalize their agricultural markets, choosing instead to shield their farming communities from harsh international competition that is sure to drive them out of their livelihoods. However, these very same policies that protect OECD farmers have wreaked much harm on LDC economies, especially on their rural communities. Thus, it becomes a question of who gets to bear the brunt of the detrimental pecuniary externalities of agricultural markets.

OECD countries cannot justify their agricultural support policies by the claim that their primary responsibility lies with promoting the economic welfare of their citizens. In the first place, less harmful alternatives are available for protecting their own farmers from the damaging consequences of international agricultural trade without inflicting even more extensive and injurious market collateral effects on everybody else, especially the poor. Second, participation in foreign trade implicitly assumes adherence to formal and informal standards that ensure fairness and mutual advantages for all. In availing themselves of the benefits of liberalized trade in product lines in which they enjoy a comparative advantage (capital, high-end manufactures, services, and intellectual property), OECD countries have in effect subscribed to a "social compact" that acknowledges the benefits of free trade and the need to conform to the rules of such a regime. Furthermore, membership in the World Trade Organization (WTO) is in essence an assent to the principles of equity in participation and market processes. Thus, LDCs have a rightful claim in calling for the liberalization of OECD's agricultural sectors.

The interpretative schema of human rights in Figure 5.1 (p. 149) locates this LDC/DC tension in the realms pertaining to livelihood and bodily rights. It is morally appropriate for OECD countries to exercise their sovereign instrumental rights (such as trade policies) in order to create the appropriate business conditions (called for by social rights) that satisfy the personal rights of their farming communities to work and secure a livelihood that supplies their basic needs. However, these are the very same set of instrumental, social, and personal rights that LDC populations possess and which are negatively affected and put at risk by OECD policies. Whose rights-claims take precedence?

There is a prima facie case for assisting OECD farmers whose core personal economic rights to a livelihood are at risk from both (1) the expected decline of the agricultural sector in the course of economic growth and (2) the stiff competition from developing countries that enjoy a comparative advantage in agricultural production. However, OECD public assistance programs in their current form have spawned their own set of even more hurtful pecuniary externalities, this time for less developed countries. This is morally problematic because they go against both the general and commutative justice that is integral to the orientation of people to each other,[39] and the distributive justice called for by the global community's obligations both to the marginalized and to the members within its ranks.[40] Moreover, these policies are regressive in their distribution of burdens and benefits. OECD farm support impedes the global community from discharging its obligation to provide the most promising conditions for growth and development for every member nation in its ranks. Such agricultural protectionism has pecuniary externalities that harm fellow members in the global community. These market distortions preclude dynamic efficiency gains in productivity that are important for the welfare of succeeding generations. To make matters worse, the nations that are hurt by OECD farm policies are precisely the marginalized that should have been receiving assistance in the first place. Thus, far from living up to their duties to assist LDCs, OECD countries have in fact been saddling impoverished nations with additional burdens that make it much more difficult for them to participate as equals in the international marketplace. Consequently, LDC farmers have more compelling claims compared to their OECD counterparts. Industrialized countries have an obligation to reform their agricultural support policies as they currently stand. As part of general justice and their contribution to the global common good, OECD nations should not impose such unnecessary adverse pecuniary externalities on others, especially since there are other ways of delivering public assistance to their distressed farmers. They should not protect their own agricultural sectors from economic compulsion by inflicting the same on the less developed countries' rural populations.

It is ironic that for all the ill effects they have engendered, longstanding OECD agricultural support measures point to the promise and possibilities of systemic assistance for victims of adverse pecuniary externalities. Tyers and Anderson (1992: 80–122) trace distortions in global food markets largely to heavy lobbying by special interests and political expediency. Contemporary OECD agricultural support measures are deliberate choices, not the outcomes of some "invisible hand." Thus, we

---

39 Second relationship of the common good as due order.
40 Third and fourth relationships, respectively, of the common good as due order.

have a wealth of experience when it comes to extra-market measures of assistance for segments of the market that have been hurt by pecuniary externalities (OECD farmers in this case). Of course, with the benefit of hindsight, we now understand the enormous damage that such measures have generated in their own turn. However, such proven national and even transnational (e.g., EU) capabilities to insulate segments of the population from deleterious economic collateral effects can cut both ways: They can cause ill (as current OECD policies have), but they can also be harnessed to produce much good. This book has argued much about our need to ensure that people do not face hard economic choices on their own but to attend to instances of economic compulsion together as a community. The OECD's long experience with agricultural support policies provides valuable insights (1) on how communities can mitigate the market's ruinous unintended consequences if they put their minds to it, (2) provided they do so only with great circumspection and collaboration, lest they engender even more injurious economic disruptions. Indeed, lessons from global agricultural trade policies reveal the need for both respect (for the promising possibilities) and caution (of the dangers) in undertaking collective remedial action for the market's distressful subsidiary effects.

It has long been known that international trade, or any kind of economic exchange for that matter, is always disruptive. By their very nature, market transactions occasion constant readjustments in the disposition of economic resources and factors of production. Global trade moves countries to their comparative advantage; such changes precipitate gains and losses both within and across nations.[41] Losses are properly called negative pecuniary externalities, and the real human suffering they unleash often falls on the poor. Thus, in addition to allocative efficiency and vibrant long-term growth, another essential goal of the common economic life is to ensure that such harmful unintended consequences are not left unaddressed. To leave them unattended and to provide no cushion at all for those who have to bear a disproportionate share of the inescapable harms of market operations is to leave these people to face hard economic choices by themselves. Economic security, after all, is a twofold divine benefaction: the gift of having our needs met and the gift of participating in divine providential work by letting God provide for us through each other.

41 Trade brings about changes in income distribution. This results in winners and losers with respect to relative standing even if there is an absolute increase in economic welfare for all. See, for example, the Stolper-Samuelson theorem of international trade theory.

CHAPTER 7

Summary and conclusions

The preceding chapters analyzed the market's secondary effects and their attendant moral obligations. An externality – technological or pecuniary – is an unintended consequence inflicted on a third party. Technological externalities arise because economic actors neither fully bear the cost nor fully reap the benefits of their decisions. The classic example, of course, is that of a factory discharging effluents into its surroundings without having to pay for restoring a damaged ecology or without the economic incentive to employ cleaner, but more expensive, technologies. There is a disparity between the factory's private cost and the social cost. The general public ultimately pays for this differential (for example, by having to suffer ill health or inconvenience on account of a dirtier environment). In such a situation, unfettered market operations alone will not lead to the much-sought allocative efficiency, and extra-market mechanisms (such as pollution taxes) have to be employed to effect the optimum overall welfare possible. Thus, in mainstream (neoclassical) economics, techno-logical externalities are viewed as market failures deserving of remedial action.

On the other hand, pecuniary externalities are unintended conse-quences that are entirely mediated through the price mechanism of the market. For example, California farmers find themselves having to pay more for their irrigation because the relentless growth of cities has bid up the price for increasingly scarce fresh water supplies. Unlike the preceding case of technological externalities, these unintended consequences of urban development are accepted as a normal part of the workings of a market. Indeed, such price adjustments, regardless of their inadvertent ripple effects, are deemed to be the essential dynamic of market processes. Thus, far from requiring extra-market relief or correctives, neoclassical economics calls for unimpeded markets to take their course. *Technological and pecuniary externalities are treated differently because while the former obstruct allocative efficiency, the latter effect it.*

Following Aristotle's notion of the mixed action, I have defined economic compulsion as a voluntary act, albeit as a second-best choice among disagreeable alternatives on substantive matters. It is an economic decision with profound opportunity costs. Economic agents find themselves in a dilemma of having to make very hard choices in a severely constrained environment of an expansive, but nonetheless restricted, freedom of association; of an atomized economic agency that cannot change market outcomes and processes by itself; and of a bounded rationality that sets institutional rules and conventions for market exchange. Economic life teems with both positive and negative pecuniary externalities since price adjustments are at the heart of market operations. This book has examined the contributions of Christian ethics in addressing why economic compulsion ought to matter and how we should weigh and redress such unusually hard choices.

WHAT IS AT STAKE AND WHY NOW?

People go to the marketplace to sell their produce or services and earn some purchasing power. At the same time, they also use the marketplace to procure the goods and services they are unable to produce themselves. Without the market, the specialization and division of labor that have been chiefly responsible for the stunning technological developments and economic growth of the past two hundred years would not have been possible at all. More important, however, the strength of the market goes beyond merely spawning collaborative work among disparate and widely dispersed economic agents. Of even greater significance is the unique and unparalleled ability of the market to allocate scarce resources to their most valued uses. Unfortunately, this singular capacity to effect allocative efficiency comes with a severe downside to it.

The allocation of scarce resources to their most valued uses is achieved chiefly through a ceaseless process of price adjustments. Price is a powerful vehicle for conveying immense volumes of critical information in a timely, effective, and cost-efficient manner to a large number of people across a vast geographic area. In particular, price communicates the relative value (or scarcity) of particular goods and services. These price adjustments are chiefly responsible for effecting marginal changes in economic agents' behavior and decisions. A secondary effect of these price realignments, however, is the corresponding alteration in the economic valuation of the goods and services that people bring to or purchase from the market. Such changes can have significant ramifications on the economic welfare of people for good or for ill.

If pecuniary externalities are nothing new but are intrinsic to market operations, then why is there a sudden need or even urgency to examine this phenomenon closely in contemporary moral reflection? In a word: globalization. The overall gains from international trade are impressive and formidable. Cheaper imports are in effect an increase in real incomes; shifting the nation's production bundle to what it does best (its comparative advantage) puts its scarce resources to their most valued uses; and specialization opens the door to economies of scale and ever more vibrant technological change. Empirical evidence from earlier periods of free trade – in the late nineteenth century and the post-World War II era – supports these theoretical suppositions (O'Rourke and Williamson 1999; Wee 1986). Global economic integration has improved the lives of many. The modern market economy is not only able to support a larger population base, but is able to do so at a higher per capita income.

Unfortunately, the measured overall benefits frequently mask the costs that are borne, often by the unseen segments of the population. The fallacy of division reminds us that what is true for the whole is not necessarily true for every part of that whole. After all, as students of international economics know well, trade occurs because of differences in the prices faced by economic agents. Pre-trade prices change and converge toward a single post-trade equilibrium price as required by the unfettered market's "law of one price." This shift benefits those who see an increase in the price of their endowments, but at the expense of owners of those resources whose relative prices drop correspondingly. In other words, there will always be winners and losers in the wake of trade-induced price adjustments.[1]

Even as mainstream trade theory provides an elegant analytical proof of the enormous gains from trade, these very same neoclassical economic models themselves show that not everyone necessarily benefits from expanding markets. International trade reapportions *relative* incomes and wealth, even in the most optimistic but unlikely scenario of an *absolute* increase in the welfare of all participants. Thus, it is not surprising

---

1 Or, take note of the Stolper-Samuelson theorem of the Heckscher-Ohlin model that can be found in any international trade textbook: Trade leads to a relative increase in the returns of the abundant factor at the expense of a relative decline in the returns of the scarce factor. In other words, international trade effects unintended changes in income distribution. Even as the pie grows larger, there are attendant changes in the relative sizes of the slices of that pie.

that greater market openness has been a hotly contested and divisive issue not only for contemporary globalization, but for other periods in economic history in which markets expanded across traditional borders.[2] Livelihoods are at stake because international trade, by its nature, requires changes in a nation's production mix[3] and a corresponding repositioning of its factors of production. Such concomitant shifts are often substantial and disruptive. International trade effects income and wealth redistributions both *across* and *within* nations. There are accompanying changes in market participants' real incomes through either a drop in the prices of their consumption basket or an increase in their nominal incomes (factor returns).

The combined effects of society's increasing "marketization" and pecuniary externalities merit immediate attention. Postindustrial globalization is vastly and qualitatively different from earlier similar periods of expanding markets because of the speed, scope, and depth of the changes it unleashes. Such dynamics are due largely to information technologies, enormous capital movements, and the increasing consolidation of geographically scattered industries into a single global manufacturing network. In other words, (1) the unavoidable pecuniary externalities that come as part of market exchange, (2) the attendant market-generated income redistributions of international trade, and (3) the technologically and information-driven global economic integration can all result in a malevolent synergy that inflicts harmful collateral effects on unsuspecting third parties. Given the swiftness of these changes, affected third parties are often ill equipped to deal with these unsettling disequilibria in the marketplace. They are also often the ones who do not have much to begin with. Hence, observe the precipitous decline in employment in the US textile and furniture industries (26 percent and 28 percent, respectively[4]) within a very short period of time, thereby providing little warning for people to prepare for a transition. And it is the lower paid workers (textile and furniture) who are affected first, before the higher paid industries (information technologies), suggesting a regressive incidence in the distribution of globalization's costs. All this only goes to highlight further the need to deal with negative pecuniary externalities.

2 The wage premium of master weavers in eighteenth-century England was erased overnight with the onset of mechanization in the Industrial Revolution, just as numerous contemporary manufacturing workers have seen their livelihoods upended in the last two decades of liberalization in goods and capital markets.
3 A movement along the nation's production possibilities frontier.
4 Data are from the US Department of Labor as reported in the *Wall Street Journal*: textile-apparel manufacturing [6/24/03] and wood-furniture making industry [10/31/03].

The increasingly central role played by markets in contemporary society has to be reflected in our moral discourse. I propose four questions, at the very least.

1 Are negative pecuniary externalities morally significant? Why?
2 To what degree should they be corrected?
3 How should they be rectified?
4 Who bears responsibility for such ameliorative action?

Even as it gives rise to problems that are daunting and expensive to address, globalization nonetheless also provides the economic means to mitigate its ill effects. It turns out that *the more difficult and urgent task that lies ahead is the matter of changing the ethos with which we operate our markets and with which we treat one another.* In this regard, Christian ethics has much to teach us.

WHY SHOULD ADVERSE PECUNIARY EXTERNALITIES MATTER?

The most cited article in mainstream economic literature is Ronald Coase's (1960) "Problem of Social Cost." The key insight of the Coase theorem is that externalities can be corrected and pareto optimality[5] achieved if we simply leave people to negotiate and exchange with each other regardless of the initial distribution of entitlements. Unfortunately, it does not go further than this to examine the final disposition of the benefits and burdens involved in eliminating the externality. Thus, in commenting on the Coase theorem, Carl Dahlman notes a particularly revealing mindset with regard to dealing with negative externalities:

Perhaps the real significance of the court cases cited by Coase is that the distinction between emittor and recipient of an externality is irrelevant: what matters is whether we achieve a higher-valued output by putting the liability on one or the other of the parties involved, and not who is the "source" of the externality. (Dahlman 1988: 230)

The concern is only about reaching allocative efficiency regardless of the dispersion of the gains and the losses.

Such a disposition finds a significant parallel shortcoming in mainstream economic thought and policy: its preoccupation with creating value and attaining that much-desired point of pareto optimality. There is little concern, if any at all, for distributional ramifications. Thus, note

---

5 Pareto optimality is a state of affairs in which no one could be made better off without making somebody else worse off.

the asymmetric treatment of technological externalities (like pollution), which are subjected to policy correction because they are considered to be market failures, compared with pecuniary externalities, which are left on their own. The latter are seen as the core, indeed, the very mechanism that enables the market to accomplish what it does best – allocating scarce resources to their most valued uses through the price signals and the corresponding adjustments they elicit from economic agents. The incidence of the market's positive and negative unintended consequences is not examined, much less evaluated for corrective action. The preoccupation is with creating value.

To my mind, Wertheimer states it well when he asks whether people should be left alone to face "(very) hard choices" by themselves.

Suppose B must choose between death and an expensive and potentially debilitating medical procedure. He has two hard choices: whether to undergo the procedure on medical grounds, and whether to jeopardize his family's financial security. Although we can do nothing to remove B's hard medical choice, it may be thought that a just society should mitigate such financial dilemmas by socializing the monetary burdens of medical care. By referring to such choices as coercive, we may signify that there is a strong, if rebuttable, case for their amelioration. (Wertheimer 1987: 234)

Note that all the other cases of economic compulsion mentioned throughout the book (from displaced workers to migrant workers, to child labor, to the elderly hard-pressed to pay for their medication) are variants of Wertheimer's hypothetical example. All are desperate choices precipitated by the unintended consequences of market exchange, both past and present. These pecuniary externalities are cumulative in their impact given the evolutionary nature of economic life. After all, economic agents' social and historical location determines the burdens they bear and the benefits they reap whenever they participate in the marketplace. How we respond to the question of whether or not we allow people to face very hard choices all by themselves says much about ourselves both as individuals and as a community.

This study is unequivocal on this issue. There are strong mutual obligations for people to face each other's hard choices together. There are at least two reasons for this position. First, it is the collective agency of individual market participants that sets and sustains economic customs, practices, and institutions in place. Thus, market outcomes and processes are not amoral either in their provenance or in their impact. Economic agents, both as individuals and as a community, are ultimately responsible for the conduct and shape of the marketplace because the repercussions of their individual economic choices reinforce existing conventions and rules as part of the process of bounded rationality discussed in chapter 1.[6]

Second, people ought not to be left alone to deal with economic compulsion by themselves because of the biblical affirmation that economic security is a divine gift for all (chapters 3 and 4). Moreover, this is a twofold benefaction: (1) the gift of material provisioning for all that we need to flourish in life as part of creation and (2) the added gift of serving as the very instruments by which God effects this material sufficiency in divine providence. We are each other's keepers.

Economic distress can arise from one or all of the following three sources: (1) from the chance and contingency that are inherent in economic life, (2) from acts of commission in which market participants' economic behavior directly inflicts harm on others (as in the case of conspicuous consumption or inordinate accumulation), or (3) from acts of omission in which community members fail to live up to their responsibilities of mutual assistance. Given the biblical claim of divine security as a dual gift, there is no excuse for leaving the ravaging effects of the chance and contingencies of economic life unaddressed and unattended. Thus, chronic economic compulsion reveals the failure of collective and individual moral agency. Wertheimer (1987: 234) too goes so far as to claim that even if hard choices are occasioned by the unavoidable "sad facts of life" (such as illnesses or accidents), rather than by the social injustice of others, there is nonetheless moral force to the claim of a social obligation to mitigate the coerced's "background conditions."[7] Observe how these positions are in sharp contrast to opponents of systemic poor relief. For example, Thomas Malthus (1798), William Paley (1802) and John Sumner (1816) ascribe an instrumental value to the evil of scarcity as the essential venue for the formation of the mind. Left on their own, people are prone to languor and indolence; it is the economic compulsion of necessity that animates people into activity and creativity.

What is also worth noting is that these duties of reciprocal assistance and rehabilitation are binding even before we determine who is to blame for the condition of economic compulsion to begin with.[8] Whether or not

---

6 Besides this roundabout effect, there is also the cost they inflict on the rest of the community through the pecuniary externalities resulting from their individual economic choices. These can sometimes inflict much distress on unsuspecting third parties.

7 Wertheimer does not go so far as to examine what happens to such a community obligation in cases of economic hardship brought about by one's own fault or negligence.

8 Recall that we cannot conclude a priori that the market per se is chiefly or solely accountable for economic circumstances because the person's opportunity set is not exclusively shaped by exogenous factors. As I note in chapter 1, personal striving and initiatives, together with past

such a state of economic duress is self-inflicted, people are ultimately responsible for each other. Blameworthiness neither absolves nor changes people's fundamental obligation of mutual solicitude for each other. This is one contribution of Christian ethics to the issue of economic compulsion.

One can use economic theory itself as an argument for mitigating economic distress. Using Becker's (1965) and Lancaster's (1966) household production model, briefly described in chapter 2, we can view market participants in a different light – as individual "microfirms" that combine manifold inputs (such as purchased goods and services from the market, personal time, and skills) to produce and consume much-sought qualities such as nutrition, rest, recreation, knowledge, and so forth. In other words, people do not buy and consume merchandise or services as ends in themselves but for the characteristics they provide. Recall, too, the central importance of human capital and sociohistorical location in the efficiency with which individuals are able to "produce" these commodities. The time and effort expended in such a process are part of the *full transaction costs* of market exchange. And, as I argue in chapter 2, these associated "entry" costs to participating in the marketplace can be truly uneven. In many cases the market can be regressive in its pricing structure, given the higher transaction costs paid by the marginalized in view of their poor human capital and their disadvantaged position within the community.

Using Becker's and Lancaster's reformulation of consumer theory, one can argue that the total productive capacity of the economy is nothing but the sum, indeed the synergy, of all these individual household production functions. Consequently, it is in the community's own long-term economic interest to care for the proper development of the human capital that undergirds the efficient functioning of these individual "microfirms." Viewed in a dynamic setting over the long run, the community is rational in its economic behavior if it attends to economic distress within its ranks and restores individual agents' ability to participate fully and freely in the market.[9] In other words, a strong case can be made for rectifying both economic compulsion and its regressive incidence in the language of neoclassical economics itself: Long-term allocative efficiency and dynamic

---

investments in human capital, are important determinants of what economic agents bring to the market. Under ordinary conditions, these are well within the realm of personal responsibility.

9 This is not to say that one has to be utilitarian in attending to economic compulsion. As repeatedly observed in this study, ameliorating economic distress has intrinsic value on the basis of human dignity alone, regardless of its other corollary benefits such as further strengthening the long-term economic performance of the community.

growth are functions of the viability and strength of the community's human capital undergirding its individual Beckerian-Lancasterian household production functions.

SHAPING EXPECTATIONS

How do we go about evaluating and redressing economic compulsion? If we are to assist and relieve each other in severe economic distress, it is important to establish first the threshold for what constitutes "very hard choices." While a consumer's inability to get the latest in fashionable shoes or the hottest new video game qualifies as an adverse pecuniary externality stemming from intense market demand, most people would consider this economic ripple effect to be trivial compared to a poor family's inability to pay for winter heating oil because of a surge in fuel prices. The problem here, of course, is that not all cases are as unambiguous. For example, it is not all that clear whether the unemployed who "volunteer" to join the military for want of a better alternative or to take advantage of its training and educational opportunities are a case of economic compulsion.[10] The same question can be posed for recent college graduates who spend a year in unpaid public service for want of a job offer. Likewise, is it economic duress if children from poor families are stuck in failing state-funded schools because their parents do not have the financial resources to matriculate them in better, private, schools like children from families of means? The crux of the matter here is the ability to separate the trivial from the truly substantive trade-offs.

This is exactly the same dilemma bedeviling traditional economic analysis – how to distinguish wants from needs.[11] Every economic decision is a constrained choice. After all, economics is fundamentally about allocating in the face of scarcity. The problem is twofold: How do we arrive at a consensus on what constitutes a need, and how do we deal with the shifting boundaries between needs and wants? Defining the precise content of the four core personal economic rights is time- and culturally conditioned. In other words, establishing the moral baseline is all-important and an ongoing endeavor when dealing with the issue of economic compulsion.

---

10 See, for example, Holmes (2003).
11 And in the case of neoclassical economics, there is the added problem of how to make such a distinction without becoming normative.

Wertheimer (1987: 217) suggests that such a moral theory must ultimately be based on a theory of rights because it is essential to have a clear and precise understanding of what people may expect of each other. Rights language is effective in identifying the moral floor below which no one will be allowed to sink. Not only does it signal when a condition of economic compulsion exists, it is also useful in separating insignificant from consequential negative economic ripple effects. In defining a basket of core economic rights that will be protected, to the extent possible, we have a ready guideline for knowing how and to what degree we intervene in market outcomes and processes to provide extra-market relief.

Unfortunately, the use of rights language is itself also controversial because of the well-known disagreements over its nature, justification, content, correlative obligations, and addressees. The skepticism becomes even worse when we talk of economic rights (Trimiew 1997). However, far from viewing these contentious debates as liabilities, we should value these disagreements for the opportunities they present. Trimiew (ibid.: 281–315) notes that Nancy Fraser's (1989) "politics of needs interpretation" applies just as well to rights discourse. These debates unleash political discourse that forces the community to deal with core issues such as needs and rights. In grappling with the moral justification and foundations of our fundamental collective choices, we gain a better understanding of who we are as individuals and as a community. In other words, such political conversations, painful as they are, may occasion community-building.

> The existence of certain defined groups with certain shared beliefs may give rise to rights claims. But it may sometimes work the other way around: advancing rights claims may help define certain groups and/or create shared beliefs.
>
> (Speak 1988: 36)[12]

I submit that Christian ethics ought to take its place in such a community-defining exercise.

There are two alternatives in establishing the basis for what constitutes coercion: a statistical-empirical approach and a moralized account. The former depends on the usual expectations of the community while the latter relies on a moral theory (Wertheimer 1987; 2001). Recall the Ambulance Case examined in chapter 1. Person A comes across severely injured person B who has been in a bad car accident. A tells B that he would call an ambulance only in exchange for a $100 payment. Under a

---

12 Quoted in Trimiew (1997: 291–92).

moralized account, A is coercing B because there is a moral obligation to provide assistance in such cases. However, under an empirical-statistical approach, A may not be coercing B at all if such payments are standard practice in the community.[13] This latter perspective does not seem far-fetched when we deal with real political economy. For example, is it coercive of public officials to ask for a "commission" from private contractors of public works projects? Under a moralized account, such kickbacks are coercive, illegal, and immoral because they are thefts from the public coffers, go against transparency, and ruin civic trust. However, under an empirical-statistical approach, such "grease" payments may be standard business practice, particularly in many less developed countries where bribes are the norm if one is to get anything done at all. In fact, such payoffs may even be accepted in the larger culture as a necessary form of occult compensation for civil servants who are grossly underpaid. They may be viewed as an unspoken but understood perquisite of public office. In other words, "expectations formation," or arriving at what is considered to be normal and acceptable in society, is just as important as articulating a moral theory that undergirds the all-important baseline. There is much at stake in forming societal conventions.

Whether we use an empirical-statistical or a moralized account of coercion, Christian ethics has much to contribute to this transformative political-moral discourse because of its relatively well-developed understanding of rights-obligations within the larger overarching framework of the common good (see chapter 5). Such "expectations formation" is even more important when it comes to dealing with adverse pecuniary externalities. For example, some authors would say that the negative collateral effects of higher prices are not coercive threats but are merely "less attractive offers" (Wertheimer 1987: 209–11). Others, however, may disagree and view such higher prices as unacceptable threats deserving of extra-market communal action and relief. These dissimilar positions are partly driven by the prevailing conventions within the community. Is it commonplace, for example, to provide adjustment assistance to those who have been hurt by trade? In many less developed countries, governments do not have the necessary fiscal resources, and displaced workers are consequently expected to bear the cost of transition to a new job on their own as part of the typical course of events.

13 See Wertheimer (1987: 207–209) for other examples that highlight the divergence of standard expectations from moral theories in determining what constitutes coercion.

Expectations of what is made part of custom, law, and usage are important because they spell the difference between aggressively redressing or simply acquiescing to the harmful unintended consequences of market exchange. What is at stake here is nothing less than what is going to be accepted as "customary" at the baseline, or what people may ordinarily expect of each other. As a community, we may choose to be either callous or compassionate when it comes to deciding what we ought to do in the face of our neighbors' very hard choices. The boundaries of what is considered to be standard practice are subject to change and development, especially as people's moral sensibilities evolve in response to particularly reprehensible experiences. We have witnessed this in the numerous grassroots actions to force changes in Third World infant formula marketing, in child labor, in the pricing of coffee, in the employment practices of overseas subcontractors, and, most recently, in the rules of international trade. Observe how these cases are all directly or indirectly instances of negative pecuniary externalities. Christian ethics has an essential duty to address harmful ripple effects of the marketplace as part of Trimiew's (1997: 283–90) characterization of the process and "politics of needs and rights interpretation." What is at stake here is whether or not we, as a community, will take the easy route of simply viewing and accepting unattended harmful pecuniary externalities as a normal part of market operations.

THE MORAL FOUNDATIONS OF CAPITALISM

Grappling with the notion of economic compulsion is not merely a dry analytical exercise in language and its meaning. After all, the moral foundations of capitalism are eroded to the extent that market transactions are indeed intrinsically coercive.

My own position in this book is that economic exchange is not inherently coercive, but it can be under certain circumstances. In particular, we enter the realm of economic duress once economic agents are forced to give up vital claims in order to protect or satisfy their other nontrivial interests that are at even greater risk. People ought not to be compelled to trade off constitutive elements of their dignity and personhood. Market exchange turns out to be a case of economic compulsion rather than a welfare improvement when it inflicts detrimental unintended consequences, such as when:

1 Parents are compelled to make their children forgo their education and go to work in order to supplement meager family incomes.

2 People are driven into prostitution as a ready source of livelihood.
3 The elderly are forced to choose between going without food or medicine given the unrestrained price increases in medical care and drugs.
4 Families go without health insurance because of unaffordable premiums and inadequate incomes.

There are varying degrees of economic compulsion, each pointing to correspondingly different degrees of responsibility for corrective action on the part of the community. Many of these ameliorative measures will entail imposing limits to market operations. However, these extra-market interventions should neither be uncritically nor be automatically viewed as unequivocal losses of individual autonomy.

We also set limits on markets to enhance human freedom. The loss of liberty that results from a sudden unmerited termination of one's job, capricious eviction from one's home, inability to pay the doctor, absence of decent schools for one's children, is every bit as real and often more serious than the loss of the liberty to pollute or to choose among a hundred brands of breakfast cereals.

(Kuttner 1997: 54)

Pecuniary externalities are at their very core about expanding opportunities for some economic agents at the expense of contracting others'. Attending to economic compulsion is about ensuring fairness in the market-driven redistributions of such freedom of action.

In conclusion, mutual advantage is a key guiding principle undergirding the ideal economic exchange. A completed transaction cannot be viewed as prima facie evidence of fairness and mutual benefits since outcomes must ultimately be weighed against the extra-market standard of economic security for all members of the community. The institutions and conventions that make the market what it is are the creations of our collective economic agency. The end (*telos*) of the market is the economic security of every member in the community; it is an obligation-bearing institution. Such a lofty goal, however, is not automatically satisfied by market operations, for two reasons. First, chance and contingency are intrinsic to economic life. Second, the necessary and unceasing price adjustments that are at the heart of market processes inflict both positive and negative unintended consequences across all participants. Thus, market outcomes will always have a mix of winners and losers. Many of the latter will find themselves in deep economic distress; they are also often the ones who are least able to weather such disruptive changes. What the market is unable to achieve on its own (economic security for every member), the community ought to provide through extra-market mechanisms. As individuals or as a collective, we are to fill in the lacunae of the marketplace since we are bound to each other by mutual obligations of assistance and care. Thus, chronic conditions of economic compulsion that remain unredressed are reflective of our failure to live up to the second half of the divine gift of economic security – that of having a role, indeed, a central unmerited part, in effecting divine generosity by letting God provide for us through each other. We cannot leave people to have to face very hard economic choices alone; we are, after all, privileged vessels of God's unfolding providence.

References

Albright, William. 1946 [1948]. *From the Stone Age to Christianity: Monotheism and the Historical Process.* Second edition. Baltimore, MD: Johns Hopkins Press.

Alt, Albrecht. 1967. "The Origins of Israelite Law," in *Essays on Old Testament History and Religion.* Translated by R. A. Wilson. Garden City, NY: Doubleday.

Aquinas, Thomas. 1947/8. *Summa Theologica.* Translated by the Fathers of the English Dominican Province. Three volumes. New York: Benzinger Brothers.

Aristotle. 1951. *Nicomachean Ethics.* New York: Odyssey Press.

Avila, Charles. 1983. *Ownership: Early Church Teachings.* Maryknoll, NY: Orbis.

Baldwin, John W. 1959. *The Medieval Theories of the Just Price: Romanists, Canonists, and Theologians in the Twelfth and Thirteenth Centuries.* Transactions of the American Philosophical Society, Vol. 49, Part 4. Philadelphia: American Philosophical Society (series paper).

Barrera, Albino. 1991. "The Interactive Effects of Mother's Schooling and Unsupplemented Breastfeeding on Child Health," *Journal of Development Economics,* 34:81–98.

2001. *Modern Catholic Social Documents and Political Economy.* Washington, DC: Georgetown University Press.

2005. *God and the Evil of Scarcity: Moral Foundations of Economic Agency.* Notre Dame, IN: University of Notre Dame Press.

Barta, Patrick. 2003. "Lending Patterns Remain Unequal," *Wall Street Journal,* December 10.

Bartlett, Randall. 1989. *Economics and Power: An Inquiry into Human Relations and Markets.* Cambridge and New York: Cambridge University Press.

Bator, Francis. 1958. "The Anatomy of Market Failure," *Quarterly Journal of Economics,* 72 (285):351–79.

Bauer, P. T. 1984. "Ecclesiastical Economics: Envy Legitimized," in *Reality and Rhetoric.* Cambridge, MA: Harvard University Press.

Becker, Elizabeth. 2003. "Western Farmers Fear Third-World Challenge to Subsidies," *New York Times,* September 9.

Becker, Gary. 1965. "A Theory of the Allocation of Time," *Economic Journal,* 75:493–515.

Beckerman, Wilfred. 1997. "The Sinner and the Saint." Book review of *Betrayal of Science and Reason* by Paul and Anne Ehrlich, *Regulation*, 20.

Benjamin, Medea. 2000. "Toil and Trouble: Student Activism in the Fight against Sweatshops," in Geoffry White with Flannery C. Hauck (eds.), *Campus, Inc.: Corporate Power in the Ivory Tower.* Amherst, NY: Prometheus Books.

Berlin, Isaiah. 1958. *Two Concepts of Liberty.* Oxford: Clarendon Press.

Bernstein, Nina. 2004. "Immigrant Businesses (From Gallbladder Importers to T-Shirt Vendors) Are Called Vital," *New York Times*, March 12.

Bhagwati, Jagdish and Mathias Hirsch (eds.). 1998. *The Uruguay Round and Beyond: Essays in Honor of Arthur Dunkel.* Ann Arbor, MI: University of Michigan Press.

Birch, Bruce. 1991. *Let Justice Roll Down: The Old Testament, Ethics, and Christian Life.* Louisville, KY: Westminster/John Knox Press.

Blank, Rebecca. 2003. "Selecting Among Anti-Poverty Policies: Can an Economist be Both Critical and Caring?" *Review of Social Economy*, 61:447–69.

Blaug, Mark. 1985. *Economic Theory in Retrospect.* Fourth edition. Cambridge: Cambridge University Press.

Boettke, Peter and David Prychitko (eds.). 1998. *Market Process Theories.* Vol. I. *Classical and Neoclassical.* Vol. II. *Heterodox Approaches.* Elgar Reference Collection. International Library of Critical Writings in Economics, Vol. 91. Cheltenham, UK and Northampton, MA: Elgar.

Bowles, Samuel and Herbert Gintis. 2002. "Social Capital and Community Governance," *Economic Journal*, 112:F419–F436.

Brown, Raymond, Joseph Fitzmyer, and Roland Murphy (eds.). 1990. *The New Jerome Biblical Commentary.* Englewood Cliffs, NJ: Prentice-Hall.

Brueggemann, Walter. 1994. "Justice: The Earthly Form of God's Holiness," *Reformed World*, 44:13–27.

Buchanan, James and Viktor Vanberg. 1991. "The Market as a Creative Process," *Economics and Philosophy*, 7:167–86. Reprinted in Boettke and Prychitko (1998, II).

Burstein, Paul (ed.). 1994. *Equal Employment Opportunity: Labor Market Discrimination and Public Policy.* New York: Aldine de Gruyter.

Cahill, Lisa Sowle. 1980. "Toward a Christian Theory of Human Rights." *Journal of Religious Ethics*, 8 (Fall):277–301.

Chase, Marilyn. 2003. "Gates Foundation Targets Malaria in Project Grants," *Wall Street Journal*, August 22.

Chirichigno, Gregory. 1993. *Debt-Slavery in Israel and the Ancient Near East.* Sheffield: JSOT Press.

Christiansen, Drew. 1984. "On Relative Equality: Catholic Egalitarianism after Vatican II," *Theological Studies*, 45:651–75.

Clark, J. B. 1899. *The Distribution of Wealth.* New York: Kelley and Millman. 1956 reprint.

Clarke, Thomas. 1958. "St. Augustine and Cosmic Redemption," *Theological Studies*, 19:133–64.

Coase, Ronald. 1960. "The Problem of Social Cost," *Journal of Law and Economics*, 3:1–44.

Cohen, Bernice. 1997. *The Edge of Chaos: Financial Booms, Bubbles, Crashes, and Chaos.* New York: John Wiley & Sons.

Coleman, John A. 1984. "Catholic Human Rights Theory: Four Challenges to an Intellectual Tradition," *Journal of Law and Religion*, 2:343–66.

Coleman, Mary. 1993. "Movements in the Earnings–Schooling Relationship, 1940–88," *Journal of Human Resources*, 28:660–80.

Conlin, Michelle and Doug Robson. 2001. "California Here I Go." *Business Week*, May 28:95.

Cooke-Taylor, Richard Whately. 1891. *The Modern Factory System.* London: K. Paul, Trench, & Trübner.

Cornia, G., R. Jolly, and F. Stewart. 1987. *Adjustment with a Human Face.* Vol. I. *Protecting the Vulnerable and Promoting Growth.* Oxford: Clarendon Press.

Cranston, Maurice. 1967. "Human Rights, Real and Supposed," in D. D. Raphael (ed.), *Political Theory and the Rights of Man.* London: Macmillan.

Curran, Charles. 2002. *Catholic Social Teaching, 1891–Present: A Historical, Theological, and Ethical Analysis.* Washington, DC: Georgetown University Press.

Dahl, Nils Alstrup. 1977. *Studies in Paul: Theology for the Early Christian Mission.* Minneapolis, MN: Augsburg Publishing.

Dahlman, Carl. 1988. "The Problem of Externality," in Tyler Cowen (ed.), *The Theory of Market Failure: A Critical Examination.* Fairfax, VA: George Mason University Press. Reprinted from the *Journal of Law and Economics*, 22 (1979):141–62.

Dobson, Wendy and Gary Clyde Hufbauer. 2001. *World Capital Markets: Challenge to the G-10.* Washington, DC: Institute for International Economics.

Dollar, David and Aart Kraay. 2001. "Trade, Growth, and Poverty," *Finance and Development*, 38:16–19.

Doron, Pinchas. 1978. "Motive Clauses in the Laws of Deuteronomy: Their Forms, Functions and Contents," *Hebrew Annual Review*, 2:61–77.

Dorr, Donal. 1983. *Option for the Poor: A Hundred Years of Vatican Social Teaching.* New York: Orbis.

Downey, Liam. 1998. "Environmental Injustice: Is Race or Income a Better Predictor?" *Social Science Quarterly* 79:766–78.

Eatwell, John, Murray Milgate, and Peter Newman (eds.). 1998. *The New Palgrave Dictionary of Economics.* London: Macmillan Reference.

The Economist. 2000a. "Out of Anarchy," *The Economist,* February 19:74.

2000b. "Nor Any Drop To Drink," *The Economist,* May 25:69–70.

2000c. "Going Too Far in Support of Trade," *The Economist,* December 16:88.

2003a. "Raise a Glass," *The Economist*, May 3:68.

2003b. "A Cruel Sea of Capital: A Survey of Global Finance," *The Economist*, May 3.

2003c. "A Place for Capital Controls," *The Economist*, May 3:15.

2003d. *World In Figures 2003*. London: The Economist Newspaper Ltd.

Eichrodt, Walther. 1961. *Theology of the Old Testament*. Vol. I. Translated by J. A. Baker. Philadelphia, PA: Westminster Press.

Eisenstadt, S. N. and L. Roniger. 1980. "Patron–Client Relations as a Model of Structuring Social Exchange," *Comparative Studies in Society and History*, 22:42–77.

1984. *Patrons, Clients, and Friends: Interpersonal Relations and the Structure of Trust in Society*. Cambridge, UK and New York: Cambridge University Press.

Fackler, Martin. 2004. "Japanese Farmers Lose Clout," *Wall Street Journal*, February 20.

Fager, Jeffrey. 1993. *Land Tenure and the Biblical Jubilee: Uncovering Hebrew Ethics Through the Sociology of Knowledge*. Journal for the Study of the Old Testament Supplement Series No. 155. Sheffield: JSOT Press.

Featherstone, Liza and United Students Against Sweatshops. 2002. *Students Against Sweatshops*. London and New York: Verso.

Fei, John and Gustav Ranis. 1964. *Development of the Labor Surplus Economy: Theory and Policy*. Homewood, IL: Richard Irwin.

Fei, John, Gustav Ranis, and Shirley Kuo. 1979. *Growth with Equity: The Taiwan Case*. New York: Oxford University Press for the World Bank.

Feinberg, Joel. 1973. *Social Philosophy*. Englewood Cliffs, NJ: Prentice-Hall.

1986. *Harm to Self*. New York: Oxford University Press.

Feldman, Leon (ed.). 1972. *Ancient and Medieval Jewish History*. New Brunswick, NJ: Rutgers.

Finn, Daniel. 1996. *Just Trading: On the Ethics and Economics of International Trade*. Nashville, TN: Abingdon Press; Washington, DC: Churches' Center for Theology and Public Policy.

Finnis, John. 1980. *Natural Law and Natural Rights*. Oxford: Clarendon Press.

Foster, George. 1967. "Peasant Society and the Image of Limited Good," in Jack Potter, May Diaz, and George Foster (eds.), *Peasant Society: A Reader*. Boston, MA: Little, Brown.

Frank, Robert and Philip Cook. 1996. *The Winner-Take-All Society: Why the Few at the Top Get So Much More Than the Rest of Us*. New York: Penguin Books.

Fraser, Nancy. 1989. "Talking about Needs: Interpretive Contests as Political Conflicts in Welfare-State Societies," *Ethics* 99:291–313.

Friedman, Milton. 1962. *Capitalism and Freedom*. With the assistance of Rose Friedman. Chicago: Chicago University Press.

Galiani, Sebastian, Paul Gertler, and Ernesto Schargrodsky. 2003. "Water for Life: The Impact of the Privatisation of Water Services on Child Mortality." Unpublished working paper. http://faculty.haas.berkeley.edu/gertler/

Gamoran, Hillel. 1971. "The Biblical Law Against Loans on Interest," *Journal of Near Eastern Studies*, 30:127–34.

Gauthier, David. 1986. *Morals by Agreement*. New York: Oxford University Press.

Gemser, B. 1953. "The Importance of the Motive Clause in Old Testament Law," in *Congress Volume, Copenhagen*. Vetus Testamentum Supplements, Vol. I. Leiden: E. J. Brill.

Gewirth, Alan. 1981a. "The Basis and Content of Human Rights," in J. Roland Pennock and John Chapman (eds.), *Human Rights*. Nomos XXIII series. New York: New York University Press.

1981b. "Are There Any Absolute Rights?" *Philosophical Quarterly* 31:1–16. Reprinted in Jeremy Waldron (ed.), *Theories of Rights*. Oxford: Oxford University Press, 1984.

1982. *Human Rights: Essays on Justification and Applications*. Chicago: University of Chicago Press.

1985. "Economic Justice: Concepts and Criteria," in K. Kipnis and D. Meyers (eds.), *Economic Justice: Private Rights and Public Responsibilities*. Totowa, NJ: Rowman & Allanheld.

Ginzberg, Eli. 1932. *Studies in the Economics of the Bible*. Philadelphia: Jewish Publication Society of America.

Giordani, Igino. 1944. *The Social Message of the Early Church Fathers*. Paterson, NJ: St. Anthony Guild Press.

Glaeser, Edward, David Laibson, and Bruce Sacerdote. 2002. "An Economic Approach to Social Capital," *Economic Journal*, 122:F437–F458.

Gnuse, Robert. 1985. *You Shall Not Steal: Community and Property in the Biblical Tradition*. Maryknoll, NY: Orbis.

Goldin, Ian and Odin Knudsen 1990. "The Implications of Agricultural Trade Liberalization for Developing Countries," in Ian Goldin and Odin Knudsen (eds.), *Agricultural Trade Liberalization: Implications for Developing Countries*. Paris: OECD.

Gordon, Barry. 1989a. *The Economic Problem in Biblical and Patristic Thought*. Leiden: E. J. Brill.

1989b. "The Problem of Scarcity and the Christian Fathers: John Chrysostom and Some Contemporaries," *Studia Patristica*, 22:108–20.

1994. "Rich, Poor and Slave in the Socioeconomic Thought of the Later Church Fathers," in Thomas Nitsch, Joseph Phillips, Jr., and Edward Fitzsimmons (eds.), *On the Condition of Labor and the Social Question: One Hundred Years Later*. Toronto Studies in Theology, Vol. 69. Lewiston: Edwin Mellon Press.

Gottwald, Norman. 1979. *The Tribes of Yahweh: A Sociology of the Religion of Liberated Israel, 1250–1050 B.C.E.* Maryknoll, NY: Orbis.

Greenberg, M. 1972. "Sabbatical Year and Jubilee," *Encyclopedia Judaica*, XIV:577–78. Jerusalem: Encyclopaedia Judaica.

Gundersen, C., M. Morehart, L. Whitener, L. Ghelfi, J. Johnson, K. Kassel, B. Kuhn, A. Mishra, S. Offutt, and L. Tiehen. 2000. "A Safety Net for Farm

Households. U.S. Department of Agriculture," *Economic Research Service, U.S. Department of Agriculture, Agricultural Economic Report 788.* Washington, DC: USDA.

Gundersen, C. and S. Offutt. 2003. "Farm Poverty and Safety Nets." Working Paper. Iowa: Iowa State University.

Gunderson, Martin. 1979. "Threats and Coercion," *Canadian Journal of Philosophy,* 9:247–59.

Hagstrom, Jerry. 2003. "Argentina Seeks Agriculture 'Compensation' in FTAA Talks," *Congress Daily,* November 25.

Hausman, Daniel. 1992. "When Jack and Jill Make a Deal," in Ellen Frankel Paul, Fred Miller, Jr., and Jeffrey Paul (eds.), *Economic Rights.* New York: Cambridge University Press; Bowling Green, OH: Social Philosophy and Policy Foundation.

Hausman, Daniel and Michael McPherson. 1996. *Economic Analysis and Moral Philosophy.* Cambridge: Cambridge University Press.

Hays, Richard. 1996. *The Moral Vision of the New Testament: Community, Cross, New Creation: A Contemporary Introduction to New Testament Ethics.* San Francisco: HarperCollins.

Heap, Shaun Hargreaves. 1989. *Rationality in Economics.* New York: Basil Blackwell.

Hehir, J. Bryan. 1998. "Catholic Social Teaching and the Challenge of the Future," in *Woodstock Report (June) 54.* Washington, DC: Woodstock Theological Center.

Hengel, M. 1974. *Property and Riches in the Early Church:* London: S.C.M.

Henle, R. J. 1980. "A Catholic View of Human Rights: A Thomistic Reflection," in Alan S. Rosenbaum (ed.), *The Philosophy of Human Rights. International Perspectives.* Westport, CT: Greenwood Press.

Heritage Foundation. 2002. *Index of Economic Freedom.* Washington, DC: Heritage Foundation.

Hirsch, Fred. 1976. *Social Limits to Growth.* Cambridge, MA: Harvard University Press.

Hirschman, Albert. 1970. *Exit, Voice, and Loyalty: Responses to Decline in Firms, Organizations, and States.* Cambridge, MA: Harvard University Press.

Hirst, Paul and Grahame Thompson. 1999. *Globalization in Question.* Second edition. Cambridge: Polity Press.

Hockman, Elaine and Charles Morris. 1998. "Progress Towards Environmental Justice: A Five-Year Perspective of Toxicity, Race and Poverty in Michigan, 1990–1995," *Journal of Environmental Planning and Management,* 41:157–76.

Hollenbach, David. 1979. *Claims in Conflict.* New York: Paulist Press.

   1994. "A Communitarian Reconstruction of Human Rights: Contributions from Catholic Tradition," in R. Bruce Douglass and David Hollenbach (eds.), *Catholicism and Liberalism.* Cambridge: Cambridge University Press.

   2002. *Common Good and Christian Ethics.* Cambridge: Cambridge University Press.

Holmes, Steven. 2003. "For Job and Country: Is this Really an All-Volunteer Army?" *New York Times*, April 6.

Hossain, Mahabub. 1988. *Credit for Alleviation of Rural Poverty: The Grameen Bank in Bangladesh*. Research Report Series No. 65. Washington, DC: International Food Policy Research Institute in collaboration with the Bangladesh Institute of Development Studies.

Huber, Wolfgang. 1979. "Human Rights – A Concept and its History," in Alois Muller and Norbert Greinacher (eds.), *The Church and the Rights of Man*. Concilium Religion in the Seventies Series No. 124. New York: Seabury Press.

Hutchins, B. L. and A. Harrison. 1903. *A History of Factory Legislation*. Westminster: P. S. King & Son.

John XXIII. 1961. *Mater et Magistra*. Boston, MA: Daughters of St. Paul.
1963. *Pacem in Terris*. Boston, MA: Daughters of St. Paul.

John Paul II. 1981. *Laborem Exercens*. Boston, MA: Daughters of St. Paul.
1987. *Sollicitudo Rei Socialis*. Boston, MA: Daughters of St. Paul.
1991. *Centesimus Annus*. Boston, MA: Daughters of St. Paul.

Kahan, A. 1972. "Economic History," in *Encyclopaedia Judaica*, XVI:1266–1324. Jerusalem: Encyclopaedia Judaica.

Kasper, Walter. 1990. "The Theological Foundations of Human Rights." *The Jurist*, 50:148–66.

Kenwood, A. and A. Lougheed. 1992. *The Growth of the International Economy: 1820–1990*. Third edition. New York: Routledge.

Kershnar, Stephen. 1999. "Uncertain Damages to Racial Minorities and Strong Affirmative Action," *Public Affairs Quarterly*, 13:83–98.

Keynes, John Maynard. 1936. *The General Theory of Employment, Interest, and Money*. New York: Harcourt Brace.

Kirby, Peter. 2003. *Child Labour in Britain, 1750–1870*. New York: Palgrave Macmillan.

Kirzner, Israel. 1990. "The Meaning of Market Process," in Alfred Bosch, Peter Kowlowski, and Reinhold Veit (eds.), *General Equilibrium or Market Process: Neoclassical and Austrian Theories of Economics*. Tubingen: J. C. B. Mohr. Reprinted in Boettke and Prychitko (1998, II).

Klay, Robin and John Lunn. 2003. "'Just Remuneration' Over a Worker's Lifetime," *Markets and Morality*, 6:177–200.

Kuttner, Robert. 1997. *Everything for Sale: The Virtues and Limits of Markets*. New York: Alfred A. Knopf.

Kuznets, Simon. 1966. *Modern Economic Growth: Rate, Structure and Spread*. New Haven: Yale University Press.

Lacy, Robert and John Walter. 2002. "What Can Price Theory Say about the Community Reinvestment Act?" *Federal Reserve Bank of Richmond Economic Quarterly*, 88:1–27.

Lancaster, Kelvin. 1966. "A New Approach to Consumer Theory," *Journal of Political Economy*, 74:132–57.

Landreth, Harry and David Colander. 1994. *History of Economic Thought.* Third edition. Boston, MA: Houghton Mifflin.

Lang, Bernhard. 1985. "The Social Organization of Peasant Poverty in Biblical Israel," in *Anthropological Approaches to the Old Testament.* Philadelphia, PA: Fortress Press; London: SPCK.

Langholm, Odd. 1998. *The Legacy of Scholasticism in Economic Thought: Antecedents of Choice and Power.* Cambridge, UK and New York: Cambridge University Press.

Lankes, Hans Peter. 2002. "Market Access for Developing Countries," *Finance and Development,* 39:8–13.

Lebacqz, Karen. 1983. "Justice, Economics and the Uncomfortable Kingdom," *Annual of the Society of Christian Ethics,* 27–53.

Leo XIII. 1891. *Rerum Novarum.* Boston, MA: Daughters of St. Paul.

Lewis, W. Arthur. 1954. "Economic Development with Unlimited Supplies of Labor," *Manchester School,* 22 (May):139–91.

Lim, Joseph. 1993. "Rural Finance in the Philippines: Lessons from the Past and Prospects for the Future," *Philippine Review of Economics and Business,* 30:51–90.

Lind, Michael. 2003. "The Cancun Delusion," *New York Times,* September 12.

Lipton, Michael. 1988. *The Poor and the Poorest: Some Interim Findings.* World Bank Discussion Papers No. 25. Washington, DC: World Bank.

Lohfink, Norbert. 1986. "The Kingdom of God and the Economy in the Bible," *Communio: International Catholic Review,* 13:216–31.

　1987. *Option for the Poor: the Basic Principle of Liberation Theology in Light of the Bible.* Berkeley, CA: Bibal Press.

　1991. "Poverty in the Laws of the Ancient Near East and of the Bible," *Theological Studies,* 52:34–50.

　1994. "'Subdue the Earth?' (Genesis 1:28)," in *Theology of the Pentateuch: Themes of the Priestly Narrative and Deuteronomy.* Translated by Linda Maloney. Minneapolis, MN: Fortress Press.

Lowery, Richard. 2000. *Sabbath and Jubilee.* St. Louis, MO: Chalice Press.

Mack, Eric. 1978. "Liberty and Justice," in *Justice and Economic Distribution.* Englewood Cliffs, NJ: Prentice-Hall.

MacPherson, C. B. 1973. "Elegant Tombstones: A Note on Friedman's Freedom," in *Democratic Theory: Essays in Retrieval.* Oxford: Clarendon Press.

Mallampally, Padma and Karl Sauvant. 1999. "Foreign Direct Investment in Developing Countries," *Finance and Development,* 36:34–37.

Maloney, Robert. 1974. "Usury and Restrictions on Interest-Taking in the Ancient Near East," *Catholic Biblical Quarterly,* 36:1–20.

Malthus, Thomas Robert. 1798 [1960]. *On Population (An Essay on the Principle of Population, as It affects the Future Improvement of Society. With Remarks on the speculations of Mr. Godwin, M. Condorcet, and other writers).* Edited and introduced by Gertrude Himmelfarb. New York: Modern Library.

Maritain, Jacques. 1947. *Person and the Common Good.* Translated by John J. Fitzgerald. New York: Charles Scribner's Sons.

Martin, Rex. 1989. "Human Rights and Civil Rights," in Morton Winston (ed.), *The Philosophy of Human Rights.* Belmont, CA: Wadsworth.

Matera, Frank. 1996. *New Testament Ethics: The Legacies of Jesus and Paul.* Louisville, KY: Westminster John Knox Press.

Mays, James. 1987. "Justice: Perspectives from the Prophetic Tradition," in David L. Petersen (ed.), *Prophecy in Israel: Search for an Identity.* Philadelphia: Fortress Press; London: SPCK.

McGregor, Joan. 1988–89. "Bargaining Advantages and Coercion in the Market," *Philosophy Research Archives,* 14:23–50.

McLaughlin, Katy. 2004. "Is Your Grocery List Politically Correct?" *Wall Street Journal,* February 17.

McMillan, John. 2002. *Reinventing the Bazaar: A Natural History of Markets.* New York: W. W. Norton.

McNeil, Donald. 2004. "Malaria Vaccine Proves Effective," *New York Times,* October 15.

Meislin, Bernard and Morris Cohen. 1964. "Backgrounds of the Biblical Law Against Usury," *Comparative Studies in Society and History,* 6:250–67.

Miller, Patrick. 1985. "The Human Sabbath: A Study in Deuteronomic Theology," *Princeton Seminary Bulletin,* 6:81–97.

Mills, Nicholaus (ed.). 1994. *Debating Affirmative Action: Race, Gender, Ethnicity, and the Politics of Inclusion.* New York: Delta.

Mirowski, Philip. 1989. *More Heat than Light: Economics as Social Physics, Physics as Nature's Economics.* Cambridge: Cambridge University Press.

Mott, Stephen Charles. 1982. *Biblical Ethics and Social Change.* New York: Oxford University Press.

Moxnes, Halvor. 1988. *The Economy of the Kingdom: Social Conflict and Economic Relations in Luke's Gospel.* Philadelphia, PA: Fortress Press.

National Conference of Catholic Bishops. 1986. *Economic Justice for All: Pastoral Letter on Catholic Social Teaching and the U.S. Economy.* Washington, DC: United States Catholic Conference.

Neufeld, Edward. 1953–54. "The Rate of Interest and the Text of Nehemiah 5:11," *Jewish Quarterly Review,* 44:194–204.

⸻ 1955. "The Prohibitions Against Loans at Interest in Ancient Hebrew Laws," *Hebrew Union College Annual,* 26:355–412.

New York Times. 2003. "Airline's Close Call To Skirt Bankruptcy," *New York Times,* April 27.

North, Douglass and Robert Paul Thomas. 1973. *The Rise of the Western World: A New Economic History.* Cambridge: Cambridge University Press.

North, Robert. 1954. *Sociology of the Biblical Jubilee.* Rome: Pontifical Biblical Institute.

Noth, Martin. 1960. *The History of Israel.* Second edition. New York: Harper & Row.

Nozick, Robert. 1974. *Anarchy, State, and Utopia.* New York: Basic Books.

Nurkse, Ragnar. 1953. *Problems of Capital Formation in Underdeveloped Countries.* New York: Oxford University Press.

O'Brien, David and Thomas Shannon (eds.). 1977. *Renewing the Earth: Catholic Documents on Peace, Justice, and Liberation.* Garden City, NY: Image Books.

Ogletree, Thomas. 1983. *The Use of the Bible in Christian Ethics: A Constructive Essay.* Philadelphia, PA: Fortress Press.

Olson, Mancur. 2000. *Power and Prosperity: Outgrowing Communist and Capitalist Dictatorships.* New York: Basic Books.

Organisation for Economic Development Co-operation and Development (OECD). 2001. *Market Effects of Crop Support.* Paris: OECD.

2003a. *Agricultural Policies in OECD Countries: Monitoring and Evaluation 2003.* Paris: OECD.

2003b. *OECD in Figures 2003.* OECD Observer, 2003 Supplement 1. Paris: OECD.

O'Rourke, Kevin and Jeffrey Williamson. 1999. *Globalization and History: the Evolution of a Nineteenth-Century Atlantic Economy.* Cambridge, MA: MIT Press.

Paley, William. 1802 [1972]. *Natural Theology.* Reprint. Houston, TX: St. Thomas Press.

Paul VI. 1967. *Populorum Progressio.* Boston, MA: Daughters of St. Paul.

1971. *Octogesima Adveniens.* Boston, MA: Daughters of St. Paul.

Paul, Ellen Frankel, Fred Miller, and Jeffrey Paul (eds.). 1992. *Economic Rights.* Cambridge: Cambridge University Press.

Pennock, J. Roland. 1981. "Rights, Natural Rights, and Human Rights – A General View," in J. Roland Pennock and John Chapman (eds.), *Human Rights.* Nomos XXIII series. New York: New York University Press.

Phan, Peter. 1984. *Social Thought. Message of the Fathers of the Church.* Wilmington, DE: Michael Glazier.

Piccinini, Antonio and Margaret Loseby. 2001. *Agricultural Policies in Europe and the USA: Farmers Between Subsidies and the Market.* New York: Palgrave.

Pius XI. 1931. *Quadragesimo Anno.* Boston, MA: Daughters of St. Paul.

Pleins, J. David. 2001. *The Social Visions of the Hebrew Bible.* Louisville, KY: Westminster John Knox Press.

Polanyi, Karl. 1944. *The Great Transformation.* New York: Farrar and Rhinehart.

Porter, J. R. 1990. "Wealth and Poverty in the Bible," in Michael Alison and David L. Edwards (eds.), *Christianity and Conservatism.* London: Hodder & Stoughton.

Prasad, Eswar, Kenneth Rogoff, Shang-Jin Wei, and M. Ayhan Kose. 2003. *Effects of Financial Globalization on Developing Countries: Some Empirical Evidence.* IMF Occasional Paper No. 220. Washington, DC: International Monetary Fund.

Ramsey, Boniface. 1982. "Alsmgiving in the Latin Church: The Late Fourth and Early Fifth Centuries," *Theological Studies*, 43:226–59.

Ranieri, Cristina. 2004. "Italian Banks Reassess Smaller Firms," *Wall Street Journal*, March 11.

Raphael, D. D. 1967. "Human Rights, Old and New," in *Political Theory and the Rights of Man*. London: Macmillan.

Raz, Joseph. 1982. "Liberalism, Autonomy, and the Politics of Neutral Concern," in Peter French, Theodore Uehling, Jr., and Howard Wettstein (eds.), *Social and Political Philosophy*. Midwest Studies in Philosophy, Vol. 7. Minneapolis, MN: University of Minnesota Press.

Remick, Helen (ed.). 1984. *Comparable Worth and Wage Discrimination: Technical Possibilities and Political Realities*. Philadelphia, PA: Temple University Press.

Rescher, N. 1966. *Distributive Justice: A Constructive Critique of the Utilitarian Theory of Distribution*. Indianapolis, IN: Bobbs-Merrill.

Rosenberg, Nathan and L. E. Birdzell, Jr. 1986. *How the West Grew Rich: The Economic Transformation of the Industrial World*. New York: Basic Books.

Rosenstein-Rodan, P. 1943. "Problems of Industrialization of Eastern and Southeastern Europe," *Economic Journal*, 53:204–7.

Schenker, Adrian. 1998. "The Biblical Legislation on the Release of Slaves: The Road from Exodus to Leviticus," *Journal for the Study of the Old Testament*, 78:23–41.

Schnackenburg, Rudolf. 1965. *The Moral Teaching of the New Testament*. Translated by J. Holland-Smith and W. J. O'Hara. Freiburg: Herder.

Schoepfle, Gregory. 2000. "U.S. Trade Adjustment Assistance Policies for Workers," in Alan Deardorff and Robert Stern (eds.), *Social Dimensions of U.S. Trade Policies*. Ann Arbor, MI: University of Michigan Press.

Schrage, Wolfgang. 1988. *The Ethics of the New Testament*. Translated by David E. Green. Philadelphia, PA: Fortress Press.

Schultz, Theodore W. 1964. *Transforming Traditional Agriculture*. New Haven, CT: Yale University Press.

1975. "The Value of the Ability to Deal with Disequilibria," *Journal of Economic Literature*, 13:827–46. Reprinted in Boettke and Prychitko (1998, I).

Scitovsky, Tibor. 1954. "Two Concepts of External Economies," *Journal of Political Economy*, 62:70–82.

Sen, Amartya. 1981a. "Rights and Agency," *Philosophy and Public Affairs*, 11 (1): 3–39.

1984. "Rights and Capabilities," in *Resources, Values and Development*. Cambridge, MA: Harvard University Press.

1985. "The Moral Standing of the Market," in *Ethics and Economics*. Oxford and New York: Blackwell for the Bowling Green State University, Social Philosophy and Policy Center.

1999. *Development as Freedom*. New York: Random House.

Sethi, S. Prakash. 1994. *Multinational Corporations and the Impact of Public Advocacy on Corporate Strategy: Nestlé and the Infant Formula Controversy.* Issues in Business Ethics, Vol. 6. Boston, MA: Kluwer Academic.

Shipman, Alan. 2002. *Transcending Transaction: The Search for Self-generating Markets.* London and New York: Routledge.

Shubik, Martin. 1971. "Pecuniary Externalities: A Game Theoretic Analysis," *American Economic Review,* 61:713–18.

Shue, Henry. 1980. *Basic Rights: Subsistence, Affluence, and U.S. Foreign Policy.* Princeton, NJ: Princeton University Press.

Simon, Herbert. 1959. "Theories of Decision Making on Economics." *American Economic Review,* 49 (4): 253–83.

1976. "From Substantive to Procedural Rationality," in S. Latsis (ed.), *Method and Appraisal in Economics.* Cambridge: Cambridge University Press. Reprinted in Frank Hahn and Martin Hollis (eds.), *Philosophy and Economic Theory.* New York: Oxford University Press, 1979.

Singer, Hans, D. Sapsford, and P. Sarkar. 1998. " The Prebisch-Singer Terms of Trade Controversy Revisited," in *Growth, Development and Trade: Selected Essays of Hans W. Singer.* Economists of the Twentieth Century Series. Cheltenham, UK and Northampton, MA: Elgar.

Smith, Adam. 1776 [1937]. *The Wealth of Nations.* Edited by Edwin Canaan. New York: Modern Library.

Smith, Dustin. 2002. "The Truth about Industrial Country Tariffs," *Finance and Development,* 39 (September): 14–15. Based on Edward Gresser. 2002. "America's Hidden Tax on the Poor: The Case for Reforming US Tariff Policy." Progressive Policy Institute Policy Report (Washington, DC).

Snaith, Norman H. 1964. *The Distinctive Ideas of the Old Testament.* New York: Schocken Books.

Soss, Neal. 1973. "Old Testament Law and Economic Society," *Journal of the History of Ideas,* 34:323–44.

Speak, David. 1988. "Rights, Rhetoric, and Adam Smith," in Yeager Hudson and Creighton Peden (eds.), *Philosophical Essays on the Ideas of a Good Society: Studies in Social and Political Theory.* Lewiston, ME: Edwin Mellen Press.

Spengler, Josef J. 1968. "Hierarchy vs. Equality: Persisting Conflict," *Kyklos,* 21:217–38.

Starnes, Richard. 2002. "Coffee Companies Roasted for Squeezing Farmers: Oxfam Hopes to Shame Buyers Into Providing Consistently Fair Price," *The Ottawa Citizen,* September 18.

Sumner, John Bird. 1816 [1850]. *A Treatise on the Records of the Creation and on the Moral Attributes of the Creator.* Sixth edition. London: J. Hatchard.

Tarditi, Secondo, Kenneth Thomson, Pierpaolo Pierani, and Elisabetta Croci-Angelini (eds.). 1989. *Agricultural Trade Liberalization and the European Community.* Oxford: Clarendon Press; New York: Oxford University Press.

Thomas, Paulette. 1999. "Selling Big Insurers on Inner-City Policies," *Wall Street Journal,* May 6.

Thurow, Roger and Geoff Winestock. 2002. "How An Addiction to Sugar Subsidies Hurts Development," *Wall Street Journal*, September 16.

Treaster, Joseph. 1996. "Writing Policies in Cities Once Written Off," *New York Times*, October 30.

Trebilcock, Michael, Marsha Chandler, and Robert Howse. 1990. *Trade and Transitions: A Comparative Analysis of Adjustment Policies.* London and New York: Routledge.

Trimiew, Darryl. 1997. *God Bless the Child That Got Its Own: The Economic Rights Debate.* Atlanta, GA: Scholars Press.

Trouiller, Patrice and Piero Olliaro. 1998. "Drug Development Output from 1975 to 1996: What Proportion for Tropical Diseases?" *International Journal of Infectious Diseases* 3:61–3.

Trouiller, Patrice, Piero Olliaro, Els Torreele, James Orbinski, Richard Laing, and Nathan Ford. 2002. "Drug Development for Neglected Diseases: A Deficient Market and a Public-Health Policy Failure," *Lancet*, 359 (9324):2188–94.

Tyers, Rod and Kym Anderson. 1992. *Disarray in World Food Markets: A Quantitative Assessment.* Cambridge, UK and New York: Cambridge University Press.

United Nations Conference on Trade and Development (UNCTAD). 1998. *World Investment Report: Trends and Determinants.* Geneva: UNCTAD.

United Nations Development Programme (UNDP). 2001. *Human Development Report 2001.* New York: Oxford University Press.

United States Government. 1987. *Economic Report of the President, 1987.* Washington, DC: Government of the United States.

Vatican Council II. 1965a. "Dignitatis Humanae," in *The Documents of Vatican II.* Edited by Walter Abbott. New York: Guild Press.

1965b. *Gaudium et Spes.* Boston, MA: Daughters of St. Paul.

Vaux, Roland de. 1965. *Ancient Israel.* Two volumes. New York: McGraw Hill.

Verhey, Allen. 1984. *The Great Reversal: Ethics and the New Testament.* Grand Rapids, MI: Eerdmans.

Viner, Jacob. 1978. *Religious Thought and Economic Society.* Edited by Jacques Melitz and Donald Winch. Durham, NC: Duke University Press.

Wahid, A. N. (ed). 1993. *Grameen Bank: Poverty Relief in Bangladesh*, Boulder, CO: Westview.

Waldow, H. Eberhard von. 1970. "Social Responsibility and Social Structure in Early Israel," *Catholic Biblical Quarterly*, 32:182–204.

1974. "Israel and Her Land: Some Theological Considerations," in Howard N. Bream, Ralph D. Heim and Carey A. Moore (eds.), *A Light Unto My Path; Old Testament Studies in Honor of Jacob M. Myers.* Philadelphia, PA: Temple University Press.

Walsh, William and John Langan. 1977. "Patristic Social Consciousness – The Church and the Poor," in John Haughey (ed.), *The Faith That Does Justice.* Woodstock Theological Studies 2. New York: Paulist Press.

Walzer, Michael. 1983. *Spheres of Justice: A Defense of Pluralism and Equality.* New York: Basic Books.

Warfel, William. 1996. "Market Failure in Urban Property Insurance Markets: An Assessment of Potential Solutions," *CPCU Journal,* 49:83–86.

Waterman, A. M. C. 1991. *Revolution, Economics, and Religion: Christian Political Economy, 1798–1833.* Cambridge, UK and New York: Cambridge University Press.

Wee, Herman van der. 1986. *Prosperity and Upheaval: the World Economy, 1945–1980.* Translated by Robin Hogg and Max Hall. Berkeley, CA: University of California Press.

Weisbrot, Mark and Dean Baer. 2002. *The Relative Impact of Trade Liberalization on Developing Countries.* Washington, DC: Center for Economic and Policy Research.

Wertheimer, Alan. 1987. *Coercion.* Princeton, NJ: Princeton University Press.

1996. *Exploitation.* Princeton, NJ: Princeton University Press.

Winston, Morton. 1989. "Understanding Human Rights," in Morton Winston (ed.), *The Philosophy of Human Rights.* Belmont, CA: Wadsworth.

World Bank. 1990. *World Development Report.* New York: Oxford University Press.

2000. *World Development Report 2000/2001: Attacking Poverty.* New York: Oxford University Press.

2001. *Global Economic Prospects 2002: Making Trade Work for the World's Poor.* New York: Oxford University Press.

2003. *Sustainable Development in a Dynamic World: Transforming Institutions, Growth, and Quality of Life.* New York: Oxford University Press.

Wray, L. Randall. 1995. "If Free Markets Cannot 'Efficiently Allocate Credit', What Monetary Policy Could Move Us Closer to Full Employment?" *Review of Political Economy,* 7:186–211.

Wright, Christopher. 1990. *God's People in God's Land: Family, Land, and Property in the Old Testament.* Grand Rapids, MI: W. B. Eerdmans.

Yale Task Force on Population Ethics. 1974. "Moral Claims, Human Rights and Population Policies," *Theological Studies,* 35:83–113.

Yergin, Daniel and Joseph Stanislaw, 1998. *The Commanding Heights: The Battle Between Government and the Marketplace That Is Remaking the Modern World.* New York: Simon and Schuster.

Zimmerman, David. 1981a. "Coercive Wage Offers," *Philosophy and Public Affairs,* 10:121–45.

1981b. "More on Coercive Wage Offers: A Reply to Alexander," *Philosophy and Public Affairs,* 10:166–71.

Index

access pricing (entry cost to market
  participation) 57, 198, 220
access to basic needs
  constitutive elements of economic security as
    divine gift 77
  modern Catholic social documents 104–106
  New Testament 87–88
  patristic literature 92–94
  restoration, biblical principle of 126–27
agricultural protectionism 178, 209–12
  ameliorative action 204–209
    LDC farmers 207–209
    OECD farmers 204–207
    restitution 209
    restoration 204, 209
  arguments against 183–85
  arguments in favor of 179–83
  collective duties to all community members
    191–95
  common good as due order 186–96
  common good as due proportion 196–203
  commutative and legal justice 186–89, 206
  competing claims, ordering (lexical rules)
    185–86, 202–203
  distributive justice 189–96
  environmental responsibility 195–96
  geographic or specialty labeling restrictions as
    alternative to 205
  historical background 179, 180
  LDC farmers see less developed country
    (LDC) farmers and agricultural
    protectionism
  marginalized persons, communal duty
    regarding 190–91
  moral evaluation of 185–203
  OECD see Organization for Economic
    Co-operation and Development
    (OECD) and agricultural protectionism
  regressive distribution of public benefits and
    burdens 196–202
  restoration, biblical principle of 204, 209

rights-based framework, use of 185–86
  statistics regarding current practices 181
Alt, Albrecht 135
Ambrose of Milan (St.) 95, 98
ameliorative action
  agricultural protectionism case study see
    agricultural protectionism
  communal responsibility for 36–41, 218, 219
  rights-based model used to design and execute
    175, 204–209
Anderson, Kym 184, 185, 188, 197, 199,
    207, 211
Apostolic Constitutions 98
Aquinas (St. Thomas) 65–66, 93, 101, 106
Argentina, effects of agricultural protectionism
  on 185
Aristotle
  Aquinas, influence on 101
  mixed action account of economic
    compulsion 4–5, 17, 214
Augustine of Hippo (St.) 95, 99

Baer, Dean 207
bargaining position approach to economic
  compulsion (McGregor) 8–12
Basil the Great (St.) 92, 96, 97
Becker, Gary 46, 220
Berlin, Isaiah 130
Bible see entries at Hebrew scriptures; New
  Testament; individual books
Birch, Bruce 128
bounded rationality of economic agents 25
  corporate or communal agency 25, 36
  nonmoral account of economic compulsion
    (Zimmerman) 35–36
  remote cause of economic
    compulsion 31–33
  social valuation based on 52
Bowles, Samuel 52
Brueggemann, Walter 127
Buchanan, James 50

Cahill, Lisa Sowle 150, 169, 176
capitalism, moral foundations of 224–26
charity, social obligation of *see* community and
  sociality
Chrysostom (St. John) 95, 96, 97, 98
Clark, J. B. 53
Clarke, Thomas 93
Clement of Alexandria 93, 95, 97, 98
Clement of Rome 98
Coase, Ronald 217
coercion, economic, compulsion *vs.* 12–16, 142;
  see also economic compulsion
Coleman, John 144, 151, 176
common good as due order 152–58, 186–96
common good as due proportion 170, 196–203
community and sociality 218, 219
  ameliorative action, responsibility for 36–41,
    218, 219
  capitalism, moral foundations of 224–26
  corporate or communal economic agency
    36–41
  economic security as divine gift, constitutive
    elements of 77
  Hebrew scriptures 83–84
  modern Catholic social documents 106–107
  New Testament 88–89
  patristic literature 95–97
  relationships central to rights-based model for
    assessing economic compulsion 153–58
  restoration, biblical principle of
    personal and collective responsibility
      for 129
    social safeguards institutionalized parallel
      to marketplace 122–23
community members
  agricultural protectionism and collective
    duties to 191–95
  social and instrumental rights for 163–65
commutative justice 152, 186–89, 206
compensatory disproportionalities 55–57
competing rights-claims, lexical rules for
  ordering *see* lexical rules for ordering
  competing rights-claims
compulsion *see* economic compulsion
consumption tax 206
consumption-distress loans 113
Corn Laws (Great Britain) 179
corporate effort *see* community and sociality
Covenant Code (Exodus) and principle of
  restoration 112, 137
  rights-based model for assessing economic
    compulsion 167
  slave manumission 116, 118
Cranston, Maurice 161
creation narratives (Genesis) 77, 93, 109

credit markets, access to 57–63
Cyprian 97, 100

Dahlman, Carl 217
Day, Dorothy 71
debt and biblical principle of restoration 113–16;
  see also restoration, Biblical principle of
Deuteronomic Code and principle of restoration
  112, 137
  rehabilitation rather than just relief 127
  rights-based model for assessing economic
    compulsion 167
  sabbatical principle, as appropriation of 133
  slave manumission 116, 118
Didache 98
Didascalia apostolorum 98
dignity and human rights 144, 176, 217
disproportionate effects of pecuniary
  externalities *see* regressive effects of
  pecuniary externalities
distributive justice 152, 189–96, 204
divine gift, economic security as *see* economic
  security as divine gift
due order, common good as 152–58, 186–96
due proportion, common good as 170, 196–203
Dutch markets' role in early modern
  commercial revolution 37

ecological responsibility 157, 195–96
economic agents
  atomization of 23–25, 31–33
  corporate or communal agency 36–41
  see also bounded rationality of economic
    agents
economic argument for amelioration of
  economic distress 220
economic coercion, compulsion *vs.* 12–16, 142
economic compulsion 3, 41–42
  bargaining position approach (McGregor)
    8–12
  capitalism, moral foundations of 224–26
  coercion *vs.* compulsion 12–16, 142
  communal responsibility for ameliorating
    36–41
  consequential *vs.* trivial 16–17, 150, 175, 221
  defining 17–19, 214
  expectations regarding what is and is not
    acceptable 221–24
  mainstream economic thought's denial of 3
  marketplace elements contributing to 19–31
    (*see also* marketplace elements
      contributing to economic compulsion)
  mixed action account (Aristotle) 4–5, 17, 214
  moral baseline account (Wertheimer) 5–7
  nonmoral account (Zimmerman) 5–7, 35–36

normalcy criterion approach, criticism of 8–12
proximate causes 33–35
reasons for concern regarding 217–21
remote causes 31–33
theories of 4–12
unintended effects *see* externalities; pecuniary
    externalities
economic security as divine gift 77, 109–10, 219;
    see also access to basic needs; community
    and sociality; personal responsibilities
constitutive elements of 77
Hebrew scriptures 77; *see also* Hebrew
    scriptures, economic security as divine
    gift in
modern Catholic social documents 103–109
New Testament 87–92
    access to basic needs 87–88
    community and sociality 88–89
    personal responsibilities 89
patristic literature 92–100
    access to basic needs 92–94
    community and sociality 95–97
    personal responsibilities 97–99
rights-based model for assessing economic
    compulsion adapting vision of 144–46,
    167–69, 175
scholastic just price theory 100–103
Engel's Law 206
entry cost to market participation (access
    pricing) 57, 198, 220
environmental responsibility 157, 195–96
Epiphanius 98
Epistle to Diognetus 99
Erhlich, Paul 30
eschatological aspects of biblical principle of
    restoration 133, 135
European Union (EU), agricultural
    protectionism in 181, 184, 185, 196–99, 200,
    201
Exodus, Covenant Code and principle of
    restoration 112, 137
    rights-based model for assessing economic
        compulsion 167
    slave manumission 116, 118
expectations regarding what is and is not
    acceptable 221–24
externalities
    participation in market generating
        nonpecuniary network externalities
        37, 38
    regressive effects *see* regressive effects of
        pecuniary externalities
    technological *vs.* pecuniary externalities 27–31,
        213
    see also pecuniary externalities

FDIs (foreign direct investments) 63–65
Feinberg, Joel 168–69
Fièvez, Dominique 200
foreign direct investments (FDIs) 63–65
France, effects of agricultural protectionism
    in 200
Fraser, Nancy 222
freedom of association, constraints on 19–22,
    31–33
freedom of market participants 38
Friedman, Milton 19
full transaction costs 48, 58, 68–70, 73, 74, 220

Gaudium et Spes (Vatican Council II) 107, 129
gender-based social valuation 54–55
Genesis and creation narratives 77, 93, 109
gentrification 72
Gewirth, Alan 144, 151
Gintis, Herbert 52
global trade, effects of 66, 72, 212, 215–17
Goldin, Ian, and Knudsen, Odin 188, 208
goods of the earth
    responsibility of caring for 157, 195–96
    universal destination of 104
Gordon, Barry 88, 91, 92, 96, 99
Gregory of Nyssa (St.) 92

Hebrew scriptures
    belonging, significance of Hebrew sense
        of 141
    economic security as divine gift in 77
        community and sociality 83–84
        conditional nature of God's promise on
            human response 81–83
        Genesis narratives 77, 93
        historicity 78–81
        land, centrality of 78
        personal responsibilities 84–86
        rights-based model for assessing economic
            compulsion 144–46, 167–69, 175
        Sabbath legislation 81
    restoration in *see* restoration, biblical
        principle of
    Sabbath legislation
        economic security as divine gift 81
        restoration, biblical principle of 133–35, 138
Hehir, Bryan 107
Hekscher-Ohlin model 215
Hirschman, Albert 32
Holiness Code (Leviticus) and principle of
    restoration 112, 137
    rights-based model for assessing economic
        compulsion 168
    sabbatical principle, as appropriation of 133
    slave manumission 118

Hollenbach, David 148–50, 151, 158, 160, 171, 176, 202–203
household production model 46, 63, 220
human development index 190
human dignity as justification for human rights 144, 176, 217
human rights *see* rights-based model for assessing economic compulsion

IMF (International Monetary Fund) 194
income constraint 47
incomplete markets 66–68
individual rights and responsibilities. *see* entries at personal
instrumental rationality 25
interest and biblical principle of restoration
  ancient Near Eastern interest rates 114
  ban on charging interest on fellow Hebrews in law codes 114, 116
International Monetary Fund (IMF) 194
international trade, effects of 66, 72, 212, 215–17

Japan, agricultural protectionism in 181, 196–99, 200
John Chrysostom (St.) 95, 96, 97, 98
John XXIII
  Mater et Magistra 106–107
  Pacem in Terris 143, 148–50, 151, 153, 171, 176
John Paul II *see Laborem Exercens*
Jubilee Law and principle of restoration
  debt legislation 115
  land return 118–20
  messianic typology of 135
  progressive *vs.* regressive structure 124
  rights-based model for assessing economic compulsion 167
  slave manumission 116, 117
just price, scholastic doctrine of
  custom, law, and usage determining just price 141
  economic security as divine gift 100–103
  restoration, biblical principle of 136
justice
  distributive justice 152, 189–96, 204
  legal and commutative justice 152, 186–89, 206
  threefold division of 152

Keynes, Maynard 123
Kuttner, Robert 71, 136, 225

labor markets
  compensatory disproportionalities in 55–57
  unrestricted 68–70

Laborem Exercens (John Paul II)
  access to basic needs 105
  community and sociality 107
  personal effort and striving 108
  restoration, biblical principle of 123
Lancaster, Kelvin 46, 220
land
  centrality in Hebrew scriptures 78
  return of land under Jubilee Law 118–20
  rights-based model for assessing economic compulsion 145
Langan, John 94, 100
Langholm, Odd 19, 102
Lankes, Hans Peter 197, 208
LDC *see* less developed country (LDC) farmers and agricultural protectionism
legal and commutative justice 152, 186–89, 206
Leo XIII, *Rerum Novarum*
  access to basic needs 104–105
  community and sociality 106
  rights-based model for assessing economic compulsion 151
less developed country (LDC) farmers and agricultural protectionism 209–12
  ameliorative action 207–209
  arguments against protectionism 183–85
  competing claims with OECD farmers 185–86
  distributive justice 189–96
  legal and commutative justice 185–86
  regressive distribution of public benefits and burdens 199–202
Leviticus, Holiness Code and principle of restoration 112, 137
  rights-based model for assessing economic compulsion 168
  sabbatical principle, as appropriation of 133
  slave manumission 118
lexical rules for ordering competing rights-claims 151, 170–74
  agricultural protectionism case study 185–86, 202–203
  Barrera's degrees of unmet needs 171–73, 203
  Hollenbach's strategic moral priorities 171, 202–203
  personal rights 173
  social rights 173–74
liberalization of capital markets 65–66
Lind, Michael 207, 208
Lipton, Michael 71
Lohfink, Norbert
  economic security as divine gift 80, 86, 88, 92, 97–99

restoration, biblical principle of 122, 133
rights-based model for assessing economic
    compulsion 145

MacPherson, C. B. 22
Malthus, Thomas 94, 219
marginalized and poor, preferential
    option for
    agricultural protectionism and communal
        duty regarding marginalized persons
        190–91
    biblical principle of restoration 123–26,
        124
    rights-based model for *see* rights-based
        model for assessing economic
        compulsion
    see also preferential option for poor and
        marginalized
Maritain, Jacques 150
marketplace elements contributing to economic
    compulsion 19–31
    atomization of individual economic agents
        23–25, 31–33
    freedom of association, constraints on 19–22,
        31–33
    liberalization of markets 65–66
    missing or incomplete markets 66–68
    price discrimination 43
    technological externalities 27–31
    volatility, dealing with 70–71
    see also bounded rationality of economic
        agents; pecuniary externalities
Martin, Rex 161
Mater et Magistra (John XXIII) 106–107
McGregor, Joan 8–12, 13, 14, 18, 32, 40, 69
McMillan, John 14, 32, 41
Miller, Patrick 81, 133, 138
missing markets 66–68
mixed action account of economic compulsion
    (Aristotle) 4–5, 17, 214
moral baseline account of economic compulsion
    (Wertheimer) 5–7
moral foundations of capitalism 224–26
Mott, Stephen 133

network externalities 37, 38
New Testament
    economic security as divine gift in 87–92
        access to basic needs 87–88
        community and sociality 88–89
        personal effort and striving 89
    restoration, biblical principle of 132, 133
nonmoral account of economic compulsion
    (Zimmerman) 5–7, 35–36
North, Robert 81

obligations and rights-based model for assessing
    economic compulsion
    common good as due order 152–58
    personal rights and 160
    roots of Catholic rights discourse in 150
    social and instrumental rights embedded
        in 162
Ogletree, Thomas 78, 83–84
Old Testament *see* Hebrew scriptures
Organization for Economic Co-operation and
    Development (OECD) and agricultural
    protectionism 209–12
    ameliorative action 204–207
    arguments against protectionism 185
    competing claims with LDC farmers 185–86
    constituent nations 181
    distributive justice 189–96
    LCD farmers, effect on 199–202
    legal and commutative justice 185–86
    regressive distribution of public benefits and
        burdens 196–99
    statistics regarding current practices 181
    use of term 185

Pacem in Terris (John XXIII) 143, 148–50, 151,
    153, 171, 176
Paley, William 94, 219
pareto optimality 69, 74, 217
patristic literature
    economic security as divine gift in 92–100
        access to basic needs 92–94
        community and sociality 95–97
        personal effort and striving 97–99
    restoration, biblical principle of 136
patron–client dependencies lacking in Hebrew
    scriptures 125, 131
Pauline emphasis on personal effort and
    striving 89
pecuniary externalities 27–31
    consequential *vs.* trivial effects 16–17, 150,
        175, 221
    proximate causes of economic compulsion
        33–35
    reasons for caring about effect of 217–21
    regressive effects *see* regressive effects of
        pecuniary externalities
    technological externalities *vs.* 27–31, 213
person-specific transaction costs 46, 48
personal aptitudes and regressive effects of
    pecuniary externalities 49–51
personal responsibilities
    economic security as divine gift
        constitutive elements of 77
        Hebrew scriptures 84–86
        modern Catholic social documents 108

personal responsibilities (*cont.*)
  New Testament 89
  patristic literature 97–99
  restoration, biblical principle of 129
  social rights entailing 206
personal rights as part of model for assessing
    economic compulsion 148, 158–61,
    167–68, 173
Pius XI, *Quadragesimo Anno* 108, 151
poor and ultrapoor, regressive effects of
    pecuniary externalities on 71–72
Populorum Progressio 107
preferential option for poor and marginalized
  agricultural protectionism and communal
      duty regarding marginalized persons
      190–91
  biblical principle of restoration 123–26, 124
  rights-based model for assessing economic
      compulsion
    Barrera's degrees of unmet needs 171–73
    hierarchical ordering of social rights 174
    relationships central to 154
    social and instrumental rights 165–66
price discrimination 43
procedural rationality 26
prosbul 124

Quadragesimo Anno (Pius XI) 108, 151

race-based social valuation 54–55
rational choice 57
rationality of economic agents, bounded nature
    of *see* bounded rationality of economic
    agents
Raz, Joseph 16, 22, 33, 34
regressive effects of pecuniary externalities 43,
    73–74
  access pricing 57
  agricultural protectionism as case
      study 196–202
  compensatory disproportionalities 55–57
  consumption tax 206
  credit markets 57–63
  foreign direct investments (FDIs) 63–65
  gentrification 72
  international trade/globalization 66, 72, 212,
      215–17
  liberalization of capital markets 65–66
  missing or incomplete markets 66–68
  personal aptitudes or capabilities 49–51
  poor and ultrapoor, examples taken
      from 71–72
  price discrimination as theoretical framework
      for 43
  restoration principle counteracting 123–26

social valuation *see* social valuation, regressive
    effects of
  unrestricted labor markets 68–70
  volatility, dealing with 70–71
Rerum Novarum (Leo XIII)
  access to basic needs 104–105
  community and sociality 106
  rights-based model for assessing economic
      compulsion 151
restitution and agricultural protectionism
    reforms 209
restoration, biblical principle of 111, 136–38
  agricultural protectionism case study 204,
      209
  centrality of economic law to
      Covenant 121–22
  collateral, restrictions on 115
  Covenant Code (Exodus) 112, 137
    rights-based model for assessing economic
        compulsion 167
    slave manumission 116, 118
  debt legislation 113–16
  demanding nature of 123–26, 130–31, 133
  Deuteronomic Code *see* Deuteronomic Code
      and principle of restoration
  eschatological aspects 133, 135
  formal characteristics 121–31
  Holiness Code (Leviticus) 112, 137
    rights-based model for assessing economic
        compulsion 168
    sabbatical principle, as appropriation of 133
    slave manumission 118
  hope as central theme of 121
  interest on fellow Hebrews, ban on charging
      114, 116
  interest rates in ancient Near East 114
  Jubilee Law *see* Jubilee Law and principle of
      restoration
  land return 118–20
  law codes 111–12
  New Testament 132, 133
  patron–client dependencies, lack of 125, 131
  positive nature of obligation 130–31
  progressive *vs.* regressive structure of law
      123–26, 124
  prophetic writings 131
  rehabilitation rather than just relief 126–27
  relationships central to rights-based model for
      assessing economic compulsion 156
  responsibility for, personal and collective 129
  Sabbath legislation 133–35, 138
  sacrificial nature of 133
  slave manumission 116–18
  social safeguards institutionalized parallel to
      marketplace 122–23

systemic and institutionalized nature of
128–29
theological precedents and warrants for
131–36
rights-based model for assessing economic
compulsion 141–43, 222–23
agricultural protectionism as case study of
185–86; *see also* agricultural
protectionism
ameliorative action, use of model to design
and execute 175, 204–209
bodily rights 158, 167
common good as due order 152–58
common good as due proportion 170
community members, social and instrumental
rights for 163–65
competing claims *see* lexical rules for ordering
competing rights-claims
conceptual structure 158–69
consequential and trivial claims,
distinguishing 150, 175, 221
developmental economic rights 160, 168
diagram of 149
disadvantages and drawbacks 150–52
economic security as divine gift, adaptation of
biblical vision of 144–46, 167–69, 175
human dignity as justification for human
rights 144, 176, 217
instrumental rights 149, 161–67, 168–69, 206
justice, threefold division of 152
lexical rules *see* lexical rules for ordering
competing rights-claims
livelihood rights 158, 167
obligations *see* obligations and rights-based
model for assessing economic
compulsion
Pacem in Terris, rights model based on 143,
148–50, 151, 153, 171, 176
participatory economic rights 160, 167
personal rights 148, 158–61, 167–68, 173
poor and marginalized, preferential option for
see preferential option for poor and
marginalized
purpose of model 174–76
relationships central to 153–58
agricultural protectionism as case study
186–96
personal rights 159, 160
social and instrumental rights 161–67
tabular display of 155
Shue's formulation 143, 146–48, 151
social rights 148, 149
competing claims, ordering 173–74
conceptual structure, place in 161–67,
168–69

personal as well as governmental
obligations, entailing 206
tabular display of 155

Sabbath legislation in Hebrew scriptures
economic security as divine gift 81
restoration, biblical principle of 133–35, 138
Schenker, Adrian 81, 134
scholastic just price theory
custom, law, and usage determining just
price 141
economic security as divine gift 100–103
restoration, biblical principle of 136
Schultz, Theodore 50, 70
security, economic *see* economic security as
divine gift
Sen, Amartya 46, 51, 52
Shandu, Monica 200
Shipman, Alan 26
Shue, Henry 143, 146–48, 151
Simon, Herbert 25
Simon, Julian 30
slave manumission in Hebrew scriptures 116–18
Smith, Adam 41
social responsibility *see* community and sociality
social rights 148, 149
competing claims, ordering 173–74
conceptual structure of rights-based model,
place in 161–67, 168–69
personal as well as governmental obligations,
entailing 206
social status theory of the just price 101
social valuation, regressive effects of 52–57
access pricing 57
compensatory disproportionalities 55–57
gender-based 54–55
objective 52–54
race-based 54–55
subjective 54–57
solidarity, principle of 206
Soss, Neal 124
South Africa, effects of agricultural
protectionism in 200
Speak, David 222
stewardship of the earth, responsibility for 157,
195–96
Stolper-Samuelson theorem 215
subsidiarity, principle of 85, 108
Summers, Larry 55
Sumner, John 94, 219

technological *vs.* pecuniary externalities 27–31, 213
Tertullian 98
Thomas Aquinas (St.) 65–66, 93, 101, 106
Thurow, Roger 185, 200

transaction costs 45, 48, 58, 68–70, 73, 74, 220
Trimiew, Darryl 144, 151, 222, 224
Tyers, Rod 184, 185, 188, 197, 199, 207, 211

unintended effects *see* externalities; pecuniary
    externalities
United States, agricultural protectionism in 181,
    196–99, 200, 201, 202, 204
universal destination of the goods of the earth,
    principle of 104
utilitarianism 217

Vanberg, Viktor 50
Vatican Council II, *Gaudium et spes* 107, 129
volatility of market, dealing with 70–71

Waldow, H. Eberhard von 78, 135
Walsh, William 94, 100
Weisbrot, Mark 207
Wertheimer, Alan 5–7, 14, 18, 34, 40, 141, 218,
    219, 222
Winestock, Geoff 185, 200
World Bank 184, 194
World Trade Organization (WTO) 70, 194,
    210
Wright, Christopher 78, 119, 127, 168

Yale Task Force on Population Ethics 148–50,
    151, 158

Zimmerman, David 7–8, 12, 22, 35–36